Other Titles by *Langaa* RPCIG

Francis B. Nyamnjoh
Stories from Abakwa
Mind Searching
The Disillusioned African
The Convert
Souls Forgotten
Married But Available

Dibussi Tande
No Turning Back. Poems of Freedom 1990-1993
Scribbles from the Den: Essays on Politics and Collective Memory in
Cameroon

Kangsen Feka Wakai
Fragmented Melodies

Ntemfac Ofege
Namondo. Child of the Water Spirits
Hot Water for the Famous Seven

Emmanuel Fru Doh
Not Yet Damascus
The Fire Within
Africa's Political Wastelands: The Bastardization of Cameroon
Oriki'badan
Wading the Tide

Thomas Jing
Tale of an African Woman

Peter Wuteh Vakunta
Grassfields Stories from Cameroon
Green Rape: Poetry for the Environment
Majunga Tok: Poems in Pidgin English
Cry, My Beloved Africa
No Love Lost
Straddling The Mungo: A Book of Poems in English & French

Ba'bila Mutia
Coils of Mortal Flesh

Kehbuma Langmia
Titabet and the Takumbeng
An Evil Meal of Evil

Victor Elame Musinga
The Barn
The Tragedy of Mr. No Balance

Ngessimo Mathe Mutaka
Building Capacity: Using TEFL and African Languages as Development-
oriented Literacy Tools

Milton Krieger
Cameroon's Social Democratic Front: Its History and Prospects as an
Opposition Political Party, 1990-2011

Sammy Oke Akombi
The Raped Amulet
The Woman Who Ate Python
Beware the Drives: Book of Verse

Susan Nkwentie Nde
Precipice
Second Engagement

**Francis B. Nyamnjoh &
Richard Fonteh Akum**
The Cameroon GCE Crisis: A Test of Anglophone Solidarity

Joyce Ashuntantang & Dibussi Tande
Their Champagne Party Will End! Poems in Honor of Bate Besong

Emmanuel Achu
Disturbing the Peace

Rosemary Ekosso
The House of Falling Women

Peterkins Manyong
God the Politician

George Ngwane
The Power in the Writer: Collected Essays on Culture, Democracy &
Development in Africa

John Percival
The 1961 Cameroon Plebiscite: Choice or Betrayal

Albert Azeyeh
Réussite scolaire, faillite sociale : généalogie mentale de la crise de
l'Afrique noire francophone

Aloysius Ajab Amin & Jean-Luc Dubois
Croissance et développement au Cameroun :
d'une croissance équilibrée à un développement équitable

Carlson Anyangwe
Imperialistic Politics in Cameroon:
Resistance & the Inception of the Restoration of the Statehood of
Southern Cameroons

Bill F. Ndi
K'Cracy, Trees in the Storm and Other Poems
Map: Musings On Ars Poetica
Thomas Lurting: The Fighting Sailor Turn'd Peaceable /Le marin
combattant devenu paisible

**Kathryn Toure, Therese Mungah
Shalo Tchombe & Thierry Karsenti**
ICT and Changing Mindsets in Education

Charles Alobwed'Epie
The Day God Blinked

G.D. Nyamndi
Babi Yar Symphony
Whether losing, Whether winning
Tussles: Collected Plays

Samuel Ebelle Kingue
Si Dieu était tout un chacun de nous?

Ignasio Malizani Jimu
Urban Appropriation and Transformation : bicycle, taxi and handcart
operators in Mzuzu, Malawi

Justice Nyo' Wakai
Under the Broken Scale of Justice: The Law and My Times

John Eyong Mengot
A Pact of Ages

Ignasio Malizani Jimu
Urban Appropriation and Transformation: Bicycle Taxi and Handcart
Operators

Joyce B. Ashuntantang
Landscaping and Coloniality: The Dissemination of Cameroon
Anglophone Literature

Jude Fokwang
Mediating Legitimacy: Chieftaincy and Democratisation in Two African
Chiefdoms

Michael A. Yanou
Dispossession and Access to Land in South Africa: an African
Perspevctive

Tikum Mbah Azonga
Cup Man and Other Stories

John Nkemngong Nkengasong
Letters to Marions (And the Coming Generations)

Amady Aly Dieng
Les étudiants africains et la littérature négro-africaine d'expression française

Tah Asongwed
Born to Rule: Autobiography of a life President

Frida Menkan Mbunda
Shadows From The Abyss

Bongasu Tanla Kishani
A Basket of Kola Nuts

Fo Angwafo III S.A.N of Mankon
Royalty and Politics: The Story of My Life

Basil Diki
The Lord of Anomy

Churchill Ewumbue-Monono
Youth and Nation-Building in Cameroon: A Study of National Youth Day
Messages and Leadership Discourse (1949-2009)

Youth and Nation-Building in Cameroon

A Study of National Youth Day Messages and Leadership Discourse (1949-2009)

By

Churchill Ewumbue-Monono

Langaa Research & Publishing CIG
Mankon, Bamenda

Publisher:
Langaa RPCIG
Langaa Research & Publishing Common Initiative Group
P.O. Box 902 Mankon
Bamenda
North West Region
Cameroon
Langaagrp@gmail.com
www.langaa-rpcig.net

Distributed outside N. America by African Books Collective
orders@africanbookscollective.com
www.africanbookscollective.com

Distributed in N. America by Michigan State University Press
msupress@msu.edu
www.msupress.msu.edu

ISBN: 9956-558-32-X

DISCLAIMER

All views expressed in this publication are those of the author and do not necessarily reflect the views of Langaa RPCIG.

Content

Annexes

African Youth Charter Anthem

A new era has come to the cradle of the human being

The Great Land of our Ancestors has gotten a new blessing

Wonderful Africa, here is your New Generation

Your future lies in your youthful population

War, tyranny and poverty must come to their end

African Youth make up your mind and let us join our hands

If we dare to share a Culture of Excellence

We'll really offer to Africa a new chance

Chorus: *African Youth you're the New Hope for your continent*

African Youth you'll make things different and have to be different

African Youth, Optimism, Unity are within the African Youth Charter

So it's time to work, decide and succeed together!

Preface

"Remember also your creator in the days of your Youth, before the evil days come, and the years draw nigh, when you will say 'I have no pleasure in them' (Eccl.12:1)".

Churchill Ewumbue-Monono has done a brilliant job in his captivating piece "The Youth and Nation-Building in Cameroon". He uses Cameroon's Youth Day (11th February) as a case study. But his analysis of the different youth day themes in Cameroon is of great significance not only to Cameroon but also to the entire African continent, where over 60% are below the ages of 20.

His idea to launch on this important work was conceived and refined while he was serving as a Senior Diplomat in Addis Ababa. This is the centre and hub of African Unity. His painstaking research which led him to delve into original resources is laudable. The centre piece of Ewumbue-Monono's argument is that the Youth Days in Africa serve no purpose if they are utilized only for festivity and beautiful parades. These days, should provide a great opportunity for reflection by the youth, their participation in nation building and their future role as leaders. Considering the mess we are in now, how can the youth make a difference?

Cameroon is a good example to treat this important issue of the place and role of the African Youth because of the bi-cultural nature of the Cameroon nation. Following the UN sponsored Plebiscite of 11th February 1961, in which the overwhelming majority of Anglophone Cameroonians voluntarily voted to become independent by joining their kith and kin of the French-speaking Republic of Cameroon, some very serious questions are now being asked. And they are the same questions facing all of Africa today; issues of governance, justice, equitable distribution of national resources, ethnicity, marginalization of minority groups etc.

How we deal with these issues today, will to a large extent determine what kind of Africa we will have tomorrow. Like Edmund Burke, the distinguished Member of the Parliament of Massachusetts of the 19th Century said *"Tell me the sentiments that prevail in the minds of your youth, and I will tell you what character the next generation will take"*.

Now looking at the Cameroon situation, the youth, especially those of English extraction seem to be wondering whether they have not been served with a raw deal. And this stretches through the whole continent, where people of the world are concerned that Africans are not regarded as pawn on the chess board of private prejudices and jaundiced politics and tribal jingoism.

Many years ago, His Excellency Ahmadou Ahidjo, whom some hold as the founding father of modern Cameroon said "We shall build with enthusiasm a nation of which our youth will be proud". Ewumbue-Monono's work seeks to investigate whether this dream is being pursued and what are its consequences for the rest of the continent.

Rt. Rev. Dr. Nyansako-ni-Nku
President of the All African Council of Churches (AACC)
Buea – February 2009

Prologue

The Youth and Nation-Building in Cameroon highlights the efforts of the leadership of a typical African country like Cameroon in mobilizing the youths through the National Youth Day to participate in the country's development initiatives.

It examines youth governance as an international problem as well as the role of the Youth Day as an international policy advocacy tool. It also describes the development of a national youth policy in Cameroon as well as the origin and development of the National Youth Day as a vehicle for ideology, the creation of domain consensus by the masses, and the articulation of government policy.

The study not only compiles the various messages to the youths, but also documents and analyses their themes and their relevance to the country's leadership. Finally, it reflects on the relevance of the Cameroon National Youth Day and its messages to the wider issue of leadership as the foundation for African Renaissance.

The Youth and Nation-Building in Cameroon, however , does not address the reactions, perceptions, and actions of the youth to these messages and government policies towards them, which could be the subject of another study. It nevertheless lays the foundation for such a study which might be an important indicator in assessing youth governance in the continent.

The book's significance comes from the observation that Cameroon, «Africa in Miniature», is one of the few countries in the continent where the celebration of a National Youth Day has been institutionalized for the past 45 years. With the adoption in 2008 of 1st November as the African Youth Day to be celebrated every year, barely eight years after the celebration of 12 August as the International Youth Day in 2000, there is no doubt that experiences like those from Cameroon could help in a meaningful celebration of the African Youth Day in the continent.

With a Prologue and an Epilogue, the study itself is divided into two parts. The first part, with two chapters, provides the global policy framework for youth governance and the celebration of the Youth Day, as well as provides an understanding of the policy environment and context in which the Youth Day is celebrated in Cameroon.

The second part, with five chapters, presents the youth messages across different stages of the country's political history: the Colonial Period (1949-1960), the West Cameroon Period (1960-1967), the Federal Youth Day Period (1968-1972), the Ahidjo Unitary State Period (1972-1982), the One-Party Democracy New Deal Period (1982-1992), and the period of the New Democratic Order (1992-2009).

The study ends with a description of efforts by the ECA, OAU, and AU in developing a continental youth agenda between 1963 and 2008. It also provides the basis for a deeper reflection of the critical role of the youths in forging an African renaissance.

The Youth and National-Building in Cameroon is however the personal reflections of someone whose heart beats with the Cameroon nation. The reflections of a man who was born in Great Soppo, Buea, during the "Re-unification Week" of February 1961 when Cameroon gained international attention as "an experiment in nation-building" because of the re-unification through the UN Plebiscite of 11 February 1961, of the French and English parts into a Federal republic.

Like any other child of that generation attending Primary School in Buea, Tombel, or Tiko between 1966 and 1973, the National Youth Day, 11 February, was just a youth festival. It was a day of festivities, fanfare and spectacles, a day of leisure, sports and cultural distractions, and a day of friendly reunions in youth organizations like the Boys Scout and the Junior Red Cross. We never knew it was a day for any serious reflection by the leadership, and we had no time for thinking.

It was only in my last years in St. Joseph's College Sasse and during my High School days in CCAS Kumba (1978-1980) as a late adolescent that debates were introduced as part of the youth day activities, and most of the debate topics had nothing to do with the official Youth Day themes selected by the leadership. In fact, in CCAS Kumba, such debates were even organized by the Debate and UNESCO Clubs which and merely brought in the lecturers as mediators.

Even at this stage, the National Youth Day still remained a Festival Day, and though during march past there was a CCAS Kumba YCNU Cell, instituted probably to lend support to our Geography Lecturer, Caven Nnoko Mbele, who had been elected YCNU Section President for Meme, most of the students dressed in party uniforms more for the fanfare than out of any serious political convictions.

What interested us were the Torch Processions on the eve of the Youth Day at the Town Green, and the festivities that followed the day after. There was no time for reflections on national issues, and we never knew there were any. In fact, students were not even allowed to have radio sets in the dormitories to know whether there were addresses to the youth by the Head of State.

The Youth Day started having a different significance to me as a student in the International Higher School of Journalism (1980-83) as it became a major beat for us because our proximity to the youth public. In March 1983, as Editor-in-Chief of the School's practicing Magazine, *ESSTI-FORUM*, we produced a special edition on the Youth Problem in Cameroon entitled « La Jeunesse en Question ». The magazine had six sections: Youth and the State (Churchill Ewumbue-Monono), Youth Education (Jean-Barthelemy Amougou), Youth and Leisure (Armah Tetteh), Youth and Love (Koffi Moglo), Youth and the Family (Georgewill Fombe), Youth and Employment (Nzinga Amougou), and the Youth and Politics (Mvoto Obounou).

The publication came at a time when ASMAC under the ebullient Director, Professor Jacques Fame Ndongo, had become a Think Tank for President Biya's New Deal policy. The significance of this publication is that it came against the backdrop of the 17th Youth Day and the first New Deal Youth Day celebrated under the auspices of President Paul Biya who had just taken the realms of power in November 1982, and was bent on rejuvenating the nation's political class.[1]

---

1. Apart from appointing youths as General Managers of Parastatals and Members of Government, the new President used the municipal elections to catapult a number of YCNU Section Presidents like Nnoko Mbele, PRL Ikundi, Manasseh Ngembane as Mayors.

In my editorial entitled "Beyond Ages and Stages", I therefore intimated that:

> It is high time our government took a permanent stand towards the youths. Cameroon is too young to sacrifice her youths. Our country cannot continue to invest on people who will only ruin her future. Should we stand and see our nation collapse in our hands?[2]

The magazine also had a 12-page supplement on the Youth Day celebrations in Yaoundé, Mbalmayo, Soa, and Obala as well as an analysis of *Cameroon Tribune*'s coverage of the celebrations since the 9th edition in 1975.

Coordinating the coverage of the 17th Youth Day marked my own *prise de conscience* of the role of this day, not only as one of festivities but also that of reflection, and which motivated me to conduct research on the youth day messages and their themes. For the first time I realized that in the secondary towns of Francophone Cameroon, a serious propaganda element was given to the National Youth Day celebrations. In Mbalmayo for instance where the celebrations were presided over by the SDO Mr. Nanvou Benoit, I realized that prior to the celebrations, President Biya's message to the Youth was re-played through a cassette recorder.

In Anglophone Cameroon, there was never a re-broadcast of the President Message to the Youth before the festivities, or perhaps I was overtaken by the festive mood that I never realized it. Things have however changed considerably in recent years as the re-broadcast of the President's messages has become an important feature of Youth Day celebrations in former West Cameroon, introduced mostly by either Francophone Administrators appointed in the Anglophone Cameroon, or Anglophone Administrators who have served in the Francophone Cameroon.

Whatever the case, the success of our special edition on the youth made the school to send us out again later in 1983, this time I was sent to Sangmelima, but since then my ears have been to the ground with respect to the Youth Day message and theme.[3]

Even after my journalism studies, I embarked on studies in Public Diplomacy, between 1986 and 1989, which enabled me to understand the potentials of youth exchange programmes in promoting international understanding. In fact, I had a first-hand appraisal when I participated in the design of some Sports and Youth-at-Risk initiatives for Africa by the State Department as a 1991-92 Hubert Humphrey Fellow.

Since 1991, my interests in the Youth Day increased as they became some of the rare occasions the President of the Republic used to address the burning national

---

2. See Ewumbue-Monono Churchill: "Beyond Ages and Stages", Editorial, *ESSTI-FORUM*, March 1983, No 2, p. 4

3. In fact I personally remember my trip in Sangmelima, which was facilitated by a dynamic student in the Lycée, Alphonse Mbe. I met him again in 1996 when we were trying to set up the Movement for the Support of Paul Biya (MSPB), and then later learnt he was elected MP from Dja et Lobo in 1997 as part of the CPDM package of allocating 30% of elective positions to the youths and women.

issues of the time especially during the entire period of democratic transition between 1991 and 1996, marked by youth activism and a conscious attempt by the leadership to appeal for their participation in the transition in a more responsible manner.[4]

I was therefore not interested in the folkloric and festive significance of this Day, but on the messages and themes adopted by the leadership. As a young father, I also started paying attention to giving my children the necessary resources to enable them have fun during this Youth Festival, while I concentrated more on the true meaning of the themes and messages. And I know, that as part of a circle, their own turn too will come when they will understand the Day is not just a festival, but also a day set aside for a deeper reflection on the very essence of our nationhood.

Like most young men at the time, I also participated in the debates on the country's democratization and was a proponent of enhancing the role and potentials of the youths as catalysts for democratic change in the country. In fact, either as a Civil Society actor within SWELA or a political operative within the CPDM, my focus was on youth empowerment.

Within the CPDM for instance, where I was a Provincial Charge de Mission for the Southwest Province, I benefitted from the rare guidance of eminent statesmen like Chief E.T Egbe, Chief Ephraim Inoni, N.N Mbile, and Hon. John Ebong Ngole in laying out a strategy to mobilize the youths of the province to participate more actively and meaningfully in the national political process.

The result was a massive recruitment of youth leaders as YCPDM party leaders and *Chargé de Missions* during party missions at all levels, their involvement in pro-democracy youth movements, as well as their recruitment into the School of Youth and Sports. The outcome was apparent as with a high level of youth political mobilization, the Southwest province grabbed the national Presidency of the YCPDM in 1996, and between 1997 and 2007, most of these young men emerged as some of the nation's most resourceful politicians serving as MPs, Mayors, and CPDM Leaders, and taking over from the first generation of youth leaders like P.R.L Ikundi and Caven Nnoko Mbele who also graduated to these positions in the early 1980s.

It is with this background that I arrived in Addis Ababa in 1997, when issues related to youth governance started simmering into the agenda of the continental organizations like the OAU and ECA. I remember how following the 1998 GENIVAR Reforms of the OAU Secretariat, a full-fledged Youth Section was created and placed under the Rwandese, Charles Mironko, recruited straight from America, and charged with the responsibility of charting a continental youth programme and policy for the Organization. And by the time I left in 2006, the ECA had adopted the theme of "Youth and the Leadership Problem in Africa" for its fifth Africa Development Forum (ADF-V).

---

4. The themes selected during this period of democratic transition for the National Youth Day celebration were Freedom, Democracy and Discipline (1991), Patriotism, Responsibility and Commitment (1992), Youth, Peace, Unity and Future of Cameroon (1993), Youth and the Mastery of the Democratic Process (1995), Youth, National Unity, African Unity (1996), Youth and Solidarity (1997)

In April 2006, I was transferred to Moscow, where I worked under the guidance of one of Cameroon's most successful Ministers of Youth and Sports, Ambassador Dr. Andre Ngongang Ouandji. In his idle moments, Ambassador Ouandji intimated me on his experiences, especially the glory and fame he brought to Cameroonian football during his Administration between 1980 and 1983, when he also served as the "transition minister" in the Ahidjo and Biya youth governance policies.

In September 2007, I was elected President of the Union of African Diplomats in the Russian Federation (UADRF), a position which put me in contact with the problems of the African Youths in the Diaspora, and I had to support the activities of a number of African Youth and Student Associations in Moscow. Of interest was the fact that I discovered that for a very long time, the Cameroon Student Association in Moscow had preserved a long tradition of celebrating the National Youth Day annually at the former Patrice Lumumba Friendship University with the support of the Embassy. It was one of the Student Unions with that tradition and I was proud of it. However, I also realized that most of these students did not understand the significance of the Day, and in most cases were not interested in the theme and the message of the year as delivered by the President of the Republic. To them, it was an opportunity for festivities to beat off the stress and cold in Moscow.

As part of our work programme, the UADRF also decided to celebrate the African Youth Day in Moscow every November. These new responsibilities sent me back to the drawing board to research on Cameroon's National Youth Day messages as I imagined such messages could also serve as a platform for the African Union Commission in designing its own continental messages and programmes.

But my greatest gratification has been the preface of the Rt. Rev. Dr. Nyansako-ni-Ku, who at the inception of the Youth Day in 1964 made an optimistic reflection entitled "The Significance of the Youth Day". The dreams and hopes, fears and suspicions of unity that this Day symbolized, are still there 45 years later, but this time not just for Cameroon alone, but for the entire African continent.

Churchill Ewumbue-Monono
Moscow, February 2009

Part One

The International and National Policy Framework for Youth Governance

1

The Global Concern for Youth Governance and the Youth Day

The management of Youth Affairs has become one of the most challenging global issues today. It is estimated that 50% of the world's population, representing 1.5 billion people, are between the ages of 10 and 25, which cover the categories of early adolescent (10-14), late adolescent (15-19), and Youth (15-24).

The 2006 African Youth Charter however defines youth as any individual aged 15-35 years, thereby providing sufficient compromise for all African countries, most of whom have defined youth as individuals between 29 and 40 years in their National Youth Policies.[1]

The importance of youth matters as a global concern as stated by the UN in 2000 has been based on the fact that:

> Young people are a source of creativity, energy, and initiative, of dynamism and social renewal. They learn quickly and adapt readily. Given the chance to go to school and find work, they will contribute hugely to economic development and social progress.[2]

In spite of these potentials, there has been a growing youth crisis because of the absence of role models, breakdown of social and cultural systems, as well as exposure to violence and chaos. Moreover, globalization has produced a "Global Youth Culture", where young people share ideas, values, music, symbols, through the mass media and electronic technology.

International concern for the proper management of youth affairs started as early as 1965 when the UN General Assembly adopted a "Declaration on the Promotion among Youth of the Ideal of Peace, Mutual Respect, and Understanding between People". In December 1979, the UN General Assembly revived interest in global youth governance when it initiated the idea of an International Youth Year as part of its package to mobilize the international community towards the implementation of the International Development Strategy of the Third UN Development Decade.

This concern led to the adoption of Resolution 35/126 of 11 December 1980, designating 1985 as the International Youth Year with the theme "Participation, Development, and Peace". Among other things, the objective of the International Youth Year was to generate interest in the specific aspirations of the youths, increase cooperation in youth development at all levels, mobilize efforts to promote educational, professional, and living conditions of young people, as well as ensure their active participation in the overall development of their societies.

---

1. See the African Youth Charter, African Union Commission, Addis Ababa, 2006

2. See "We the People: The Role of the UN in the 21st Century".

To set the ball rolling, an Advisory Committee for the International Youth Year was created which held its first session in Vienna in March-April 1981 to adopt a Programme of Action. The Committee adopted the "Guidelines for Further Planning and Sustainable Follow up on Youth Issues", which was endorsed by the UN General Assembly as Resolution 40/41.

The next milestone on global cooperation in youth governance came in 1994 when the NGO Forum of the Cairo Conference on Population and Development adopted the "Cairo Youth Declaration", which was endorsed in 1995 by the UN General Assembly as Resolution 50/81 with focus on the "World Programme of Action for the Youth to the Year 2000 and Beyond" (WPAY). The 1995 WPAY adopted 10 priority areas for youth development, which were increased to 15 in 2003 to include: education, employment, Hunger and Poverty, Health, Environment, Drug Abuse, Juvenile Delinquency, Leisure, Girls and Young Women, Participation, Globalization, ICT, HIV-AIDS, Armed Conflicts, and Inter-generational relations.

Apart from the WPAY, the 1995 World Summit on Social Development in Copenhagen, Denmark adopted the "Copenhagen Youth Declaration", which focused on Youth Rights, Youth Policy, Young Women, Education, Racism, Xenophobia, Health, Population, Economy, Environment, Sustainable Development, and Global Governance.

Since 1995, the international community had created a number of mechanisms to cooperate on the global youth governance, which include the World Youth Forum, the World Youth Festivals, the Global Conferences on National Youth Services, and the World Conference of Ministers of Youth Matters.

The idea of a World Youth Forum (WYF) started in 1960 in Moscow, leading to two meetings in 1961 and 1964, though but the first World Youth Forum took place in 1991. This was followed by that of November 1996 in Vienna (Austria), and Praga (Portugal) in 1998, which adopted the "Praga Plan of Action" on youth participation in the political process and the strengthening of civil society participation in youth governance. The next WYF took place in Dakar in August 2001 and adopted the "Dakar Youth Empowerment Strategy".

The World Youth Festivals organized by the World Federation of Democratic Youth (WFDY) have also been opportunities to reflect on youth governance. Created in November 1945 in London, the WFDY launched the first Festival of Youth and Students in Prague in 1947. Since then, it has held 15 of such festivals including those in Budapest (1949), Berlin (1951), Bucharest (1953), Warsaw (1955), Moscow (1957), Vienna (1959), Helsinki (1962), Sofia (1968), Berlin (1973), Havana (1978), Moscow (1985), Pyongyang (1997), Algiers (2001), and the 16th edition in Caracas (2005).

The Global Conferences on National Youth Service has been another mechanism for global youth governance and cooperation. The first took place in 1992 in the US, and was followed by others in Nigeria (1994), Papau New Guinea (1996), UK (1998), Israel (2000), etc.

Other global youth governance mechanisms have included the International Youth Conferences like that in Prague in 2009, or those by global institutions like the Commonwealth, the Francophonie, and the G-8. The Commonwealth, for instance, initiated a Youth Programme in 1974 (CYP) and has a bi-annual conference of Commonwealth Youth Ministers to coordinate youth programmes among its Member States. At present, there is a "Commonwealth Plan of Action for Youth Empowerment, 2007-2015", whose implementation in Africa is usually discussed at the regional youth caucus, and monitored by the Regional Commonwealth Youth Centre for Africa in Lusaka, Zambia. In fact, the 2009 edition of the Commonwealth Day was centred on the theme "Commonwealth at 60: Serving a New Generation", illustrating the organization's attachment to youth governance.

The G-8 and EU have instituted the Youth Forum as important components of their policy dialogues with African countries. On 27-30 June 2008, the G-8 held a Youth Forum as part of its Summit.

Youth governance has become an important issue within the Francophonie movement and in contemporary Franco-African relations. In effect, the first Africa Youth Forum was held on 8-9 November 2005 in Bamako, Mali against the backdrop of the 23rd France-Africa Summit in the city in December 2005, whose theme was "The Youth Problem in Africa". Moreover, the various regional organizations in Africa, Europe, Americas, and Asia have adopted their own mechanisms to promote youth governance and cooperation.

Global Youth Governance and Cooperation have also been carried out under a number of mechanisms by International NGOs and religious bodies such as the IFSW, which organized an International Youth Conference in Prague in 2008, the Baptist Youth World Conference, and the Youth Festivals of the Catholic Church. In 1985 for instance, Pope John Paul II launched the World Youth Day in Barcelona, Spain. Since then, it has been celebrated in Buenos Aires, Argentina (April 1987), Santiago de Compostela, Spain (August 1989), Czestochowa, Poland (August 1991), Denver, USA (August 1993), Manila, Philippines (January 1995), Paris, France (August 1997), Rome, Italy (August 2000), Toronto, Canada (July 2002), Cologne, Germany (August 2005), and Sydney, Australia (August 2008).

In addition, global youth governance has been pursued through sectoral conferences such as the Global Forum on Youth and the Information and Communication Technology launched in September 2007 under the theme "Youth as Agents of Change", as well as the Global Youth Coalition.

Finally, global youth governance and cooperation made an important stride with the organization of the First World Conference of Ministers of Youth in Lisbon in August 1999. To immortalize this new dynamism, the conference adopted 12 August as the International Youth Day, which was endorsed by the UN General Assembly Resolution 54/120 of 17 December 1999.

1.1: The Youth Day as a Policy Advocacy Tool

The celebration of Youth Days by countries, regional and international organizations, has become one of the ways of raising awareness on youth governance worldwide. At present, there are over 50 of such Youth Days celebrated the year round in various countries and by various organizations which include: 12 January (India), 8 February (Congo Republic), 11 February (Cameroon), 12 February (Venezuela), 28 February (USA), 10 March (Commonwealth), 15 March (Zambia), 18 March (Portugal), 20 March (Oklahoma, USA), 21 March (Tunisia), 29 March (Taiwan), 1 April (Benin), 14 April (Angola and British Virgin Island), 21 April (Global Youth Service Day), 14 May (China), 19 May (Turkey), 25 May (Former Yugoslavia), 2 June (Tunisia), 16 June (South Africa), 9 July (Morocco), 12 August (United Nations), 21 September (Bolivia), 26 September (Turks and Caicos Island), 14 October (Congo DR), 1 November (African Union), etc.

The Youth Days are usually celebrated around certain themes aimed at generating awareness or promoting popular understanding of national, regional, and global policy issues. For instance, since 2000 that the international community has been celebrating the International Youth Day (IYD), the following have been retained as themes:

- IYD 2001: Addressing Health and Unemployment;
- IYD 2002: Now and for the Future: Youth Action for Sustainable Development;
- IYD 2003: Finding Decent and Productive Work for Young People Everywhere;
- IYD 2004: Youth in an Inter-generational Society;
- IYD 2005: MPAY + 10: Making Commitments Matter;
- IYD 2006: Tackling Poverty Together;
- IYD 2007: Be Seen, Be Heard: Youth Participation for Development; and
- IYD 2008: Youth and Climate Change: Time for Action.

Like the UN which uses the IYD to promote policy dialogue and advocacy on global issues, other organizations such as the Commonwealth, AU, as well as national governments, have also been using this tool to promote their own agenda. For instance, the theme for the first African Youth Day in 2008 was "Positive African Values, Peace, and Solidarity".

It is within this context that one can understand the origins and development of the Cameroon National Youth Day as a policy dialogue and advocacy tool.

2

Youth Policy and the Youth Day in Cameroon: 1949-2009

The development of a policy and institutional foundations for youth governance in Cameroon have closely followed the various stages of the country's political history: the colonial period (1949-1960), the federation period (1961-1972), the Ahidjo Unitary State period (1972-1982), the One-Party Democracy New Deal period (1982-1992), and the period of the New Democratic Order (1992-2009).

2.1: The Colonial Period: 1960-1960

Prior to independence, the management of youth affairs depended on the colonial policies of the various administering authorities to which the Anglophone and Francophone sections of the country were subjected to.

In Anglophone Cameroon, which was administered by the British between 1922 and 1960 as an integral part of Nigeria, the management of youth affairs was attached to the Ministry of Education. As part of its responsibility to prepare the people for nationhood, the British colonial administration created a Youth Training Centre at Man'O War Bay, near Victoria, to train young men from all over Nigeria on the ideals of citizenship, leadership and community development. The success of the Man'O War Youth Training Centre in preparing the youth in the entire Nigeria was spelt out by the Nigerian Federal Minister for Education Hon. Jaja Nwanchukwu during his visit to the Centre between April 18 and 20 1958, in which he revealed that the Man'O War Training Centre had trained 2,000 students since its creation. Most of the graduates of this Centre became the first-generation prominent local and national leaders in the Nigerian Federation.[3]

With the emergence of some form of self-government in Southern Cameroons in 1954, youth governance was still maintained under the Ministry of Education, headed by F.N. Ajebe-Sone (1954-1957), and later, by the Ministry of Social Services headed by V. Lainjo (1958-1959), and A.N Jua (1959-1961).

In Francophone Cameroon, the management of youth affairs was under the Service for Youth and Sports, in the Ministry of Education, which between 1954 and 1960 was regulated by Order N°3959 of 27 July 1954 on the general organization, attribution and functioning of the Service for Youth and Sports, in the Ministry of Education. With independence in 1960, and the creation of the presidential system, the administration of youth matters was transferred to Presidency by Decree 60/70 of 1960, under a Secretariat for Youth, Sports and Information headed variously by Simon Songue (1959), Gabriel Ndibo Mbarsola (1960), and William Eteki Mboumoua.

---

3. One of the outstanding trainees of the Man'O War Training Centre is the Hon. W.N.O Effiom who has exercised considerable political leadership in post-independent Cameroon, serving as an MP, Cabinet Member, Speaker, and Grand Chancellor.

The pre-independence period was also marked by the growth of a number of politically-motivated youth movements, many of which were clamouring for independence and the reunification of the country. In Francophone Cameroon, such movements included the *Jeunesse Camerounaise Française* (JEUCAFRA) created in 1938, followed by others like the *Jeunesse Democrates du Cameroun* (JDC), *the Jeunesse des Populations du Kamerun* (JUPOKAM), the Jeunesse Ouvriere du Cameroun (JOC) created in 1954, and the *Jeunesse Rurale du Cameroun* (JEURUCA) created in 1959.

In Anglophone Cameroon, youth organizations started with the introduction of the Boys Scouts in the territory in 1924, in which school masters like P.M. Kale militated. In effect, it was during a Scouts jamboree in Lagos that Kale came across most of the Nigerian politicians and activists who influenced the creation of the *Cameroon Youth League* (CYL) in 1939 as the first real nationalist movement in the territory. Apart from the CYL, a number of politically-motivated youth organizations sprouted in Anglophone Cameroon like the *Bakweri Youth Association* (BYA) led by Fred Mbwaye, the *Bamenda Youth Association* (BYA) led by J.A. Fominyen, and the *National Union of Kamerun Students* (NUKS), which served as the basis for aggregation into political parties.

2.2: The Federation Period: 1961-1972

In 1961, the Anglophone and Francophone sections of Cameroon were reunified and consolidated in a two-state federation which lasted until 1972. During this period, youth governance evolved into a federal subject. This evolution occurred in two phases. The first phase, "the General Commissariat Phase" lasted between 1962 and 1965 and was devoted to institutional development.

During this first phase, a number of efforts were made to put in place institutions for managing youth affairs. In March 1962, for instance, a General Commissariat for Youth, Sports, and Popular Education was erected within the Presidency by Decree N°62/DF/106 of March 1962 and modified in 1963 by Decree No 63/DF/324 of July 1963. To launch a post-independence national youth policy, the Secretary of State issued Circular Letter No 377/LG/JS/EP of 19 June 1962 ordering a census of all youth associations in the country.

The 1963 youth administration reforms also provided the General Commissariat with a number of structures to manage youth matters such as the *National Youth Movement* targeting youths of 12 to 18 years, the Pioneer *Cameroonian Youth Movement* targeting youths between the ages of 18 and 30 years, and the *National Committee for Youth and Popular Education* (CONAJEP). Earlier, Decision No 02/CG/JS/EP of 15 February 1963 spelt out the organization of Holiday Camps. During the General Commissariat regime, youth administration was headed by Dr. Vroumsia Tchinaye (1963-1964), and later, Ibrahim Mbombo Njoya (1964-1965) as General Commissioners.

This first phase also corresponded to a period of multi-party politics in the country, at least in Anglophone Cameroon. Apart from government institutions, youth mobilization and governance was therefore also carried out between 1960 and 1965 through the main political parties. The KNDP for instance had an impressive

Youth Vanguard headed by John Tatah, "King of Youths"; the CUC created a Youth Brigade in 1965 under Thomas Enoko of Ekona, while the UC had also developed a youth wing, the JUC from its Second Congress in 1961-1962 coordinated by a Youth Secretariat which by 1965 was headed by Jean Batayene, assisted by Sadou Daoudou. In June 1964 for instance, the UC party organized a seminar on youth employment in which the Youth Commissioner, Vroumsia Tchinaye made a report.

Moreover, the General Commisariat phase was also marked by the aggregation of youth movements such as the Boys Scouts and the Red Cross into national organizations. It is in this light that Mr. J.G. Ngale, the Regional Commissioner for the West Cameroon Boys Scouts, and Mr. Agbabiakar, the Secretary to the Scouts Council, attended the National Scouts Rally in Yaoundé on 26-30 March 1964 for the creation of a national movement.

The second phase of youth administration during the Federation period, the "National Education Phase", lasted between 1965 and 1970. It started with the promulgation of Decree No 65/DF/374 of 28 August 1965 and Decree No 65/DF/350 of 5 August 1965 reorganizing the Ministry of National Education, Youth and Culture, in which youth governance was attached to the Ministry of National Education as a Directorate of Education, Youth, and Culture. During this period, the main architect of the Federal Government's youth agenda was Zachee Mongo So'o, who had served as President Ahidjo's Director of Civil Cabinet.

Under the Ministry of National Education, a number of reforms were made in 1967 which gave youth administration greater harmony and dynamism as a federal subject. First, was the adoption of 11 February in 1967 as a National Youth Day, and not just a West Cameroon Youth Day. Then in May 1967, the Ministry was reorganized by Decree No 67/DF/222 of 22 May 1967, providing greater autonomy and new directorates for the Education, Youth and Culture portfolios. These reforms continued in November 1967 when youth movements were further regulated by Decree N°67/DF/503 of 21 November 1967, and later by Decree N°69/DF/302 of 8 August 1969.

The 1967 youth policy reforms were also reflected in the country's June 1967 Defence Law, which provided for the creation of a civilian reserve force as part of the nation's "popular defence" strategy. Pre-military training was therefore organized for youths between 18 and 40, and between 1967 and 1990, over 10,000 young Cameroonians had undergone pre-military training.[4]

The third phase in youth governance during the Federation period, "the Youth and Sports Phase", started in 1970 with the creation of a Federal Ministry of Youth and Sports by Decree N°70/DF/273 of 12 June 1970 with a distinct Department of Youth Affairs, and a distinct Department of Sports. Michel Njensi was appointed the first Federal Minister of Youth and Sports, serving between June 1970 and March 1971 before he was replaced by Francois Xavier Ngoubeyou, who carried the mantle until the federal system was dissolved in May 1972.

---

4. See Ewumbue-Monono, C: The Youth and Political Empowerment in Cameroon. P. 24 Unpublished.

Apart from these governmental structures, the "National Education" and "Youth and Sports" phases of the Federation period between 1966 and 1972 were marked by the increasing role of the unified party, the *Cameroon National Unio*n (CNU), in the management of youth affairs. Created in September 1966 through the merger of the UC, KNDP, CUC, CPNC, and UC, the new party made youth governance a major focus of its mass mobilization strategy. At its inception in 1966 and until its first Congress in March 1969 in Garoua, the Secretary for Youth Affairs in the CNU Central Committee was Chief E.T Egbe from the CUC who was assisted by Sadou Daoudou from the UC. They were re-elected during the March 1969 Garoua Congress, together with Michel Njiensunti to manage youth affairs until the Douala Congress of 1975.

The period between 1967 and 1970 was equally marked by increased international cooperation for youth policy development as manifested in the relations with Israel, which led to the creation of the *National Civic Centre for Participation in Development* (NCCPD) in 1973, the visit to Cameroon of the Youth Adviser in the US State Department, Robert D. Gross, and the participation of YCNU officials in the 25th anniversary of the United Nations in New York in 1970.[5]

Another important development during this period however was the clamour for the management of youth affairs as a federated state subject in West Cameroon, to enable the youth play a greater role in the state's socio-economic development. These sentiments were strongly expressed in Sammy Kum Buo's "A Proposal for a West Cameroon Youth Corps" in February 1972 in the *Journal of Cameroon Affairs* published by the Association of Cameroon Students in America. The idea of a West Cameroon Youth Corps built around the American Peace Corps could have provided the youths in West Cameroon a framework to participate more effectively in the region's much prized community development programmes. Such ideas however were buried with the proclamation of the unitary state barely three months later.

2.3: The Ahidjo Unitary State Period: 1972-1982

With the proclamation of the unitary state in May 1972 and the formation of a unitary government, the Youth and Sports portfolio was retained, though modified by Decree N°72/470 of 15 September 1972. In the next ten years that President Ahidjo headed the unitary government, the Ministry of Youth and Sports was managed respectively by Felix Tonye Mbog (1972-1979), Rene Ze Nguele (1979-1980), and Andre Ngongang Ouandji (1980-1983).

During this period, the focus of government's policy was the mobilization of the rural youths for economic development and the fight against rural exodus. The period was therefore marked by a number of government initiatives aimed at animating the youth in the rural world. First, was the National Civic Centre for Participation in Development, created in July 1973 to train youths between the ages of 17-35 in self-reliant development projects. Between 1974 and 1984, the

---

5. Ewumbue-Monono, ibid, p. 36.

NCCPD trained over 4,230 young farmers and spent over 700 million francs CFA to settle them. Its greatest operations was the "Operation Green Sahel" in the North, and the "Operation Bafang-Yabassi".[6]

The second important mechanism to animate the rural youths was FONADER's "Young Farmers' Schemes" initiated in the 1980s, which helped to train and settle thousands of young farmers. Finally, the government created a number of Youth and Animation Centres to enhance popular education in integrated development programmes. On 18 January 1979, a Ministerial Order further created the Mobile Animation Units in every Division for mass education, group animation, initiation of youths to integrated development, and functional literacy. Another Ministerial Order of 27 April 1988 stipulated that these Youth and Animation Centres should be used for economic integration and training of the youth.[7]

Youth matters were also given a higher premium by the CNU party during this period. In effect, during its Extraordinary Congress of June 1972, the party instituted a National Youth Conference as a policy forum to discuss youth matters. The first National Youth Conference however took place only in December 1979. In addition, the party created the CNU Party School, *Ecole des Cadres*, for the ideological training of the YCNU officials.

The party also tried to dynamise the Youth Secretariat in the Central Committee. Following the 1975 Douala Congress of Maturity, Toumou Etienne, a Youth Counsellor, was elected Youth Secretary and was assisted by Bahanoui, a Senior Customs Officer and erstwhile President of the Wouri YCNU, as well as Professor Anomah Ngu. The team served until the 1980 Bafoussam Congress when it was also replaced with an all-academic one comprising Professor Bwele Guillauime as Secretary, assisted by Professor Anomah Ngu and Dr. Bol Alima.

2.4: The One-Party Democracy New Deal Period: 1982-1992

With the emergence of Paul Biya as the second President in November 1982, the development of youth governance passed through two phases. First, was the period between 1982 and 1992, marked by a one-party political system during which the portfolio was administered by four ministers: Andre Ngongang Ouandji (November 1982- June1983), Dr. Fofie Tapydji (1986-1990), Ibrahim Mbombo Njoya (1990-1992), and Theordore Lando (April-November 1992).

During this period, the President first enunciated his youth policy in a press interview in 1984 with the *Club de la Press du Tiers Monde*, in which he iterated that:

> I see Cameroon, proud of its youth, ardent youth born in effort and rigour, educated and mastering youth, thanks to apprenticeship, to school, the sciences and techniques capable of inspecting themselves in a social fabric where there shall be equal opportunities and careers open to all levels of competence.[8]

---

6. See Ewumbue-Monono, C: "Training the Rejected. The Story of the National Civic Service". *ESSTI-FORUM*, March 1983, pp7-10.

7. See Ministerial Order No 001/M/MJS/IG/DJ of 18 January 1979 and Ministerial Order No 001/M/MJS/DJA/52 of 27 April 1988.

8. See Patrick Sam Kumbam (ed): Paul Biya and the Quest for Democracy in Cameroon, 1985, p. 47.

In his policy statement during the March 1985 Bamenda Congress, the President insisted that:

> The youths within the context of the New Deal must be given the greatest attention-more attention than in the past. This concern which must become pre-eminent in the party, undoubtedly calls for the rationalization of the activities and organization of the YCNU so as to give it the means of performing its task efficiently. This means the setting up on a real national party youth movement with a national Bureau like that of the WCNU. In the final analysis, Cameroonian youths should be made increasingly responsible by giving them greater autonomy within the party.

At the operational level, the New Deal's first emphasis was on improving its animation techniques for social, political, and economic mobilization. Consequently, the Ministry of Youth and Sports organized a workshop on "Youth and Animation Under the New Deal" in Yaoundé in 1984, followed in September 1985 by a National Colloquium on Youth and Animation in Dshang, and another one in Yaoundé in March 1987.

With the advent of the economic crisis in the late 1980s, the New Deal's Youth policy changed from just animation to that of addressing socio-economic problems like youth employment. In 1988 for instance, the *Fund for Small and Medium Size Industries* (FOGAPE) launched the "Young Entrepreneur" programme aimed at granting loans to Cameroonians with promising projects who lacked the finances. After screening some 1400 files, 139 were retained as suitable for loans. Moreover, in April 1990 the President created the *National Employment Fund* (NEF) to help prepare youths for employment.

At the party level, the CNU Central Committee was reshuffled on 24 May, 1984 and the position of Youth Secretary conferred to Hon. Thomas Ebong Ngalame who organized the Second National Youth Conference of November 1984 under the theme "The Responsibility of the Youth in the Implementation of the New Deal Policy." Moreover, the YCNU National Bureau was constituted under Ebai Namme, an economics graduate and Fako YCNU Section President. He held the position until he was swept away by the tides of democratization in the early 1990s.

2.5: Youth Governance and the New Democratic Order (1992-2009)

The second phase of President Biya's youth governance was highly influenced by the political compromise that came with the transformation of the political system to a pluralistic, multiparty one. With the liberalization of the political order in Cameroon in 1990, youth governance virtually went out of control as a plethora of youth associations sprouted to fill the vacuum. Within the political community, most of the political parties developed youth wings, while even within the ruling CPDM, a distinct youth civil society emerged outside the YCPDM. Within the civil society, there were over 200 new youth organizations, some of which were regrouped under the Cameroon Council on Youth and Population created in 1994.

Between 1992 and 1997, youth governance therefore became part of wider political governance as the Ministry of Youth and Sports was one of those ministries "sub-contracted" to the opposition UPC party in the coalition Government that emerged after the 1992 Presidential election. During President Paul Biya's first multiparty mandate of 1992-1997, the Ministry of Youth and Sports was managed by Bernard Massoua II of the UPC (1992-1994), Professor Joseph-Marie Bipoum Woum of the CPDM (1994-1996), and Samuel Makon Wehiong of the UPC (1996-1997).

After the 1997 Presidential election, which gave the President a mandate to govern until 2002, the portfolio became more stabilized, especially with Decree N° 96/049 of 12 March 1996 reorganizing the Ministry and the growth of more meaningful youth organizations such as the *Presse Jeune*, created in 1997 to popularize youth issues in the country through publications such as *Rebondir Magazine, Le Journal des Enfants*, and *Agir Magazine.*[9]

In December 1997, Professor Joseph Owona, the former Secretary-General of the Presidency of the Republic was appointed the Minister for Youth and Sports, giving the portfolio an additional stature as a "Core CPDM Ministry". He was replaced in March 2000 by Dr. Bidoung Mkpatt, a professional Youth Counsellor and Director of the Higher National Institute of Youth and Sports (INJS), who served as Minister between 2000 and 2004, during which he clamoured for the upgrading of the youth portfolio. Consequently in April 2004, a Secretariat for Youth Affairs was created under Denis Oumarou, while the Ministry was headed by Siegfried Etame Massoma.

In December 2004, the New Deal youth governance in Cameroon came a full cycle with the creation of a separate Ministry of Youth Affairs by Decree N°2004/320 of 8 December 2004, which among other things, had new structures such as the Department of Youth Economic Promotion, and the Department of Citizen Education, Social Integration, and Youth Participation. The new Ministry was given a professional orientation with the appointment of a seasoned Professional Youth and Sports lecturer, Adoum Garoua, who in four years has given the Ministry the necessary vision, and made it one of the most dynamic apparels of the New Deal.

In 2006, the Minister embarked on the development of a new youth policy with assistance from international organizations like the UNFPA, and youth organizations like CAPECAM, which in February 2006 had organized a National Youth Forum in Yaoundé on the WPAY+10 that brought together 150 leaders. The Forum focused on six main issues: Youth Entrepreneur/Empowerment, Environmental Sustainability, Employment Creation, Information and Communication Technology for Development, Education For all, and Peace and Non-Violence.

In July 2006, a national workshop was organized to adopt a number of policy initiatives like the Support Programme to Rural Youths for the Fight against Poverty (SPRY-FP), the Support Programme to Urban Youths for the Fight against Poverty

---

9. The Youth Press has always remained an important feature of Cameroon's media landscape. Prior to the country's democratic transition, the following youth-related had ornamented this landscape: *Jeune Fille est tu Responsible* (1957), *Junior* (1960), *Essor de Jeunes* (1961-1974), *La Voix des Jeunes* (1955-67), *Belle Jeunes* (1959-66), *Jeune Cameroun* (1962), *Jeunesse Rurale* (1962-72), *Servir* (1967), etc

(SPUY-FP), the National Youth Integration Fund (NYIF), and the Multifunctional Centres for the Promotion of Youths (MCPY). Moreover, in 2007, the creation of the National Youth Council (NYC) was finalized.

The institutional evolution of youth governance in Cameroon however cannot present a true picture of the policy dynamics, which is usually expressed by the themes of the National Youth Day messages.

2.6: The National Youth Day and Policy Articulation in Cameroon

A policy advocacy initiative, the origins of the National Youth Day in Cameroon can be traced to the special days celebrated by youth organizations in the Southern Cameroons such as 22 February, the "Thinking Day", celebrated by the Girl Guides and Brownies in commemoration of Lady Banden Powell. There was also the Commonwealth Youth Sunday marked by the reading of a Message from the Queen, Church services and a march-past by youth groups such as the Boys Scouts, Girl Guides, Boy's Brigades, Red Cross and other youth organizations. It was presided by His Honour the Commissioner for Southern Cameroons, or his Deputy who took the salute and read the speech to the parades. In outlining the importance of the Commonwealth Youth Sunday on 18 May 1958, the Commissioner for Southern Cameroons, iterated that:

> "It is desirable that the youth of this country should be encouraged to embrace a concept of dedication not only to the welfare of the territory to which they belong, but also to the service of God and their fellow-men in other countries which are linked together by similar aspirations and the common causes of humanity. To this end, Commonwealth Youth Sunday has been organized as a day on which young people in all parts of the Commonwealth may join in a common act of worship and dedication".[10]

The Commonwealth Youth Sunday was celebrated in Southern Cameroons for the first time on 2 June 1957. Between 1957 and 1961when Cameroon left the Commonwealth, five Commonwealth Youth Sundays were celebrated in the territory, viz: 2 June 1957 (1st Edition), 18 May 1958 (2nd Edition), May 1959 (3rd Edition), 29 May 1960 (4th Edition), and 14 May 1961 (5th Edition).

The "Thinking Day" and the "Commonwealth Youth Sundays" were however limited to members of youth movements, most of who were in the Victoria and Kumba Divisions. It did not have a very important territorial impact like the "National Days" which were celebrated throughout the territory. In colonial Southern Cameroons, there were two of such important national days. First was the "Empire Day", which was celebrated in the territory for the first time in 1949 and featured sporting and cultural events, as well as by a march past. Then was the Southern Cameroons Day, celebrated every 26 October to commemorate the creation of a quasi-region for Southern Cameroons in 1954.

---

10. See Southern Cameroons Newsletter, NAB, May 1958

The West Cameroon leadership therefore opted to transform a "National Day" into a "Youth Day" as a tool for nation-building and consolidation, and greater mobilization of the population, most of whom were youths.

With the desire to keep 1st October as a national day to commemorate the reunification, the choice for a Youth Day was between either 26 October, the Southern Cameroons Day, or 11 February, the Plebiscite Day. Following the 11 February 1961 and the formal reunification of Southern Cameroons and the French Cameroons on 1st October 1961, Southern Cameroons was replaced by the federated state of West Cameroon, which made its continuous celebration irrelevant, especially as the KNDP propagandists saw in 26 October a stamp of Dr. Endeley's success. In acknowledging both the importance and irrelevance of the day, the Prime Minister, Dr. John Ngu Foncha argued that:

> The 26th of October which marked the separation of Cameroon from Eastern Nigeria region was celebrated as a partial national day because we were still under Trusteeship rule. However, its observance gave us the impetus to regain a wider nationhood, for separation from Eastern Nigeria was the beginning of our independence.[11]

In 1962 therefore, less than a year after reunification, Dr. Foncha recommended that it was befitting to dedicate West Cameroon's National Day to its youth on whom the future of the nation depended. Consequently, on 26 October 1962, the first "Youth and Sports Day" was organized in West Cameroon in a manner different from the usual national day celebrations. As stipulated in a circular by the SDO Bamenda George Kisob to organizers in his administrative jurisdiction:

> The 26th of October will no longer be known as National Day but Youth Day. Since it is no longer a National Day, there will be no Guard of Honour. The March-past will be done by the school children only. There would be only one speech to be read and this would be the Prime Minister's Speech.[12]

A number of reasons could be advanced for the choice of 11 February as the West Cameroon Youth Day over the other national days. First, it was a matter of practical convenience for organization of festivities and examinations for school children. As stated in August 1963 by the Secretary of State for Education and Social Welfare, the Hon. L.M Ndamukong:

> Youth Day is February 11th each year. This means that the school sports normally held on October 26th, will now be on February 11th. The new date has two advantages over the old one – it enables sports to take place in

---

11. See West Cameroon press Release No 22059 26 October, 1963. Cited in Ejede Ejede F. Importance of Youth week activities in Buea Town. INJS, June 1984

12. See Fokwang, Jude: "Origins of the National Youth Day in Cameroon" *The Post*, February 2009

the dry season and it enables children studying for examination in November to devote their time to their studies. Teachers and pupils should, therefore, note that February 11th 1964, is the date on which youth sports will take place. On October 1st, Reunification Day, which is a public holiday, school children will, as usual, participate in the march past.[13]

Second was its political significance in the process of nation-building. As justified by the Prime Minister for West Cameroon J.N Foncha on 14 January 1964, "the idea of the Youth Day springs from the desire that Cameroonian Children should inherit and continue to implement what has been achieved".[14] He continued on 7th February 1964 by stressing that the day should be one of festivities for children, but also one of stocktaking and reflection for adults, arguing that :

> To children, February 11th might just mean a well spent day for sports and feasting and to the grown-ups that day should mean something more, for it was on that day 3 years ago that by an overwhelming number of 233.571 to 97.741 a majority of 135.830, the people of West Cameroon made history by their almost unanimous, honest, and voluntary decision to achieve independence and re-unification with the former Cameroon Republic …[15]

The date of 11 February's political significance was equally highlighted in 1964 when the young Journalist-Pastor Rev. Nyansako-ni-Nku argued that:

> By dedicating this day to the youth, they are offered a challenge to serve their nation. By this, the Cameroonian youth are called upon to be aware of their contribution to national reconstruction. But above all, they are being reminded of the onerous task of leadership which lies before them because the future is theirs.[16]

Third, the day was perceived in professional terms as an opportunity to improve on the level of competiveness and sports culture in West Cameroon. On 20 January 1964, the Regional Inspector of Youths, Sports and Popular Education argued that:

> The West Cameroon Government has decided to celebrate the first anniversary of the Youth Day celebrations by providing the youths an opportunity to demonstrate, all the physical activities practiced as a source of entertainment for the general public, as well as to encourage a healthy spirit of fellowship, enjoyment and competition, which will improve the general standards of youth activities throughout the country…

---

13. See "Eleventh February to be observed as Youth Day and School Sports". Press Release No 2628 of 22 August 1963 issued by the Ministry of Education and Social Welfare.
14. Ibid
15. See "The Memorable Day". Press Release No 2990 of 7th February 1964
16. See Nyansako-ni-Nku: "The Significance of the Youth Day", Press Release, February 1964

If the Youths of this Region, who fall within the age range of 12 to 25 years or so, are to prove their mettle in competitions with their counterparts in East Cameroon and with other nations, as we hope it is necessary now to make take active part in the Youth Day Celebrations...[17]

Moreover, the day was designed as a Youth Festival, comprising "athletic contests, football matches, netball, basketball and volleyball tournaments, folklore dances, canoe races, a Durbar and various artistic performances such as choral singing competitions", which will "fittingly portray the potential of the young people of West Cameroon."[18]

To improve on the Commonwealth Youth Sunday formula which was limited in scope, the Secretary of State for Education and Social Welfare, Hon. L.M Ndamukong embarked on a tour between 29 January and 5 February of Kumba, Bamenda, Wum, and Nkambe Divisions to oversee preparations for the celebrations.[19]

The 11th of February was therefore celebrated as a Youth Day in West Cameroon exclusively in 1964 and 1965. In 1964, celebrations marking the inaugural ceremony started on Sunday 9th with a Thanks-giving Service offered by the Bishop of West Cameroon, His Lordship Julius Peteers, followed by football and volley ball matches between East and West Cameroon Colleges, and an open-air dance with music from the Police Band.

On Tuesday 10th February, celebrations took place in Victoria where the Prime Minister and his East Cameroonian hosts: the Prime Minister Charles Assale, Hon. Marigoh Mboua, and the Sultan of Foumban watched a Canoe race won by Bota over Bimbia.

The final phase of the celebrations on 11th February took place in Buea and marked by athletic competitions, traditional dances, a reception offered by the Prime Minister and his wife at his Lodge for 500 guests, as well as choral competitions and a film show at the Buea Motor Park.

In 1965, the Youth Day celebration centres were Buea and Bamenda. In Buea, celebrations were presided over by the Prime Minister and were marked by sporting competitions, traditional dances by 15 groups, choral singing and folklore by youth clubs, an open air cinema show at the Motor Park, and decoration of meritorious Cameroonians.[20]

In Bamenda, celebrations were presided over by the Vice-Prime Minister in Charge of Finance Hon. A.N Jua and lasted until 12 February when the Prime Minister and Mrs. Foncha arrived to watch the display of traditional dances at the Mankon Stadium.

President Ahidjo sent special messages to the Youths of West Cameroon during these events, and following a positive technical evaluation by the General Commissariat for Youth and Popular Education in 1965, the event was celebrated in East and West Cameroon in 1966 for the first time.

---

17. See "Youth Day Inaugural Celebrations". Press Release, 20th January 1964
18. See "Prime Minister Announces Broad Outline of Youth Day Celebration in West Cameroon". Press Release 2924, 14 January 1964
19. See "West Cameroon Youth Day Celebrations, 1964". Press Release, 1960 and 2961 28 January 1964
20. See "Youth Day Celebrations in Buea". Press Release No 3760 15 February 1965

Consequently, in 1967, the Youth Day which was initially celebrated on in the English speaking part of the country became a national event during which the President of the Republic made nation-wide broadcasts not only on youth policy, but also on the leadership's expectations of the youth's contribution towards national development.

2.7: Youth Day Themes and Leadership Ideology

Every Youth Day, the theme chosen by the leadership of the country underlies all the activities organized during the youth week. Between 1967 and 2009, there have been 43 editions of the National Youth Day, centred on specific themes which translate critical issues in the country's leadership ideology.

A word content analysis of the themes of the 43 editions of the National Youth Day into 12 categories shows that the most dominant themes in both the Ahidjo and Biya regime have been National Unity and Solidarity (9); Participation and Commitment (8); Responsibility and Mastery (8); Development (7); Rigour, Moralization and Discipline (7); Peace and Dialogue (6); Support for Ruling Political Party and Ideology (5); Green Revolution and Manual Work (4); Economic Crisis and Recovery (4); Patriotism and Citizenship (4); Culture (2); and Sports (2). These categories could be grouped into three: political mobilization, development and economic mobilization, participation and social mobilization. The following table further shows the different values attached by the two national leaders t o youth issues as manifested in the choice of themes.

Table 1: Thematic Analysis of Youth Day Messages and Comparative Leadership Discourse

Youth Day Theme	Total Frequency	Percentage	Frequency under Ahidjo	Frequency under Biya
National Unity and Solidarity	9	13.2	4	5
Participation and Commitment	8	11.7	4	4
Responsibility and Mastery	8	11.7	4	4
Development	7	10.2	3	4
Rigour Moralization, Discipline	7	10.2	1	6

Peace and Dialogue	6	8.82	1	5
Support for Party and Ideology	5	7.35	3	2
Green Revolution and Manual Work	4	5.8	4	0
Economic Crisis	4	5.8	0	4
Patriotism and Citizenship	4	5.8	0	4
Fight Against Aids and Social Ills	2	2.9	0	2
Sports Promotion	2	2.9	0	2
Cultural Promotion	1	1.4	0	1
African Unity	1	1.4	0	1
Total	**68**	**100**		

Source: Compiled by the author from the Youth Day Themes: 1967-2009

From the table above, it is clear that the Cameroonian leadership has given a high premium to the use of the Youth Days to articulate its social policies. The role of the Youth as an agent of social mobilization dominated leadership themes like Participation and Commitment, Responsibility and Mastery, Rigour, Moralization, and Discipline, as well other social issues. These themes make up a total word count of 28 representing 41.1% of the use of the Youth Days in articulating government policies.

Participation and Commitment have also been dominant themes used by the Cameroonian leadership in their messages to the youths. Under Ahidjo, it was used four times (1970, 1978, 1979, and 1980), and the same importance was given to President Biya who equally used them four times in 1985, 1992, 2004, and 2008.

The appeal for responsibility and mastery of issues has been an important theme in the leadership's Youth Day messages. Under President Ahidjo, these words appeared four times in the theme (1968, 1970, 1981, and 1982), while under President Biya, they were equally used four times in 1988, 1992, 1995, and 2005. Closely associated with this theme of responsibility and mastery has been that of Rigour, Moralization, and Discipline, which was used once by Ahidjo in 1981, but which

19

became the cornerstone of the Biya Leadership Ideology as they have been used six times in 1983, 1984, 2000, 2006, 1991, and 2007.

Finally, the role of the Youth Day as an advocacy tool for social mobilization has dominated some of the themes in the Biya Administration such as cultural promotion (2003), sports promotion (1990 and 1994), the fight against AIDS and social ills (2001 and 2007).

The use of Youth Days by the Cameroonian leadership for political mobilization is articulated in the themes of national unity and solidarity, peace and dialogue, as well as support for the ruling party and its ideology. In all they make up 25 of the word count and represent 36.7% of the total efforts by the leadership to articulate government policies to the youth.

Under Ahidjo, National Unity and Solidarity were used four times as themes of the Youth Day (1969, 1970, 1975,and 1977), while under Biya they have been used five times (1989, 1993, 1994, 1996, and 1997). In the 1996 theme, this concept of unity embraced not only national but also African unity. Moreover, President Biya also used the theme of patriotism and citizenship four times in 1992, 2007, 2008 and 2009 to create a national consciousness among the youths.

Although the theme of Peace and Dialogue was used only once in 1972 under President Ahidjo, it became a dominant issue during the Biya Administration as it has been used five times in 1985, 1986, 1993, 2003, and 2004.

The political mobilization function of the youths in promoting the ruling party and its ideology was more dominant during the Ahidjo regime, where it was used three times as a Youth Day theme in 1975, 1979, and 1980 as opposed to the Biya regime where it has been used only twice in 1987 and 1995.

Finally, the use of the Youth Days to articulate government messages for economic development and emancipation has been expressed in such themes as the Youth and Development, Green Revolution and manual work, as well the economic crisis. There are 15 word counts under this category representing 22% of the government effort in articulating its policies to the youth.

The theme of Youth and Development was used three times during the Ahidjo regime (1971, 1973, and 1982), as opposed to four times during the Biya regime (1985, 1986, 2006, and 2008). However, during the Ahidjo era, the role of the rural youth in agricultural development and as an agent of the Green Revolution dominated the Leadership's Messages, and appeared four times in the themes of the National Youth Day in 1973, 1974, 1976, and 1978.

During the Biya regime, development issues were dominated by the economic crisis and the need for recovery, to which he devoted four of the Youth Day themes in 1998, 1999, 2002, and 2004.

2.8: Influences on Choice of Youth Day Themes

Although the Cameroonian leadership used the National Youth Day celebration to pass certain messages, their themes have been determined mostly by specific national and international events.

Between 1967 and 1972, when the country was still under a federal system, the main focus was on national unity and nation-building as exemplified by the creation of the CNU Party in 1966, and its first congress in Garoua in 1969. The launching of the second five-year development plan in 1971 was also reflected in the year's theme of "Youth and Development".

Between 1972 and 1982, President Ahidjo paid a lot of attention to two issues: promoting the Green Revolution, which was launched during the 1973 Buea Agro-Pastoral Show; and mobilizing support for the CNU party. The theme of human investment, manual work, and Green Revolution therefore dominated Ahidjo's discourse in 1973, 1974, 1976, and 1978.

The Youth Day messages between 1972 and 1982 also had a direct bearing on Ahidjo's promotion of the CNU party. Against the backdrop of the 1975 Douala Congress, the year's theme was "Unity Among the Youths of the CNU", while in 1979 and 1980, the themes "Commitment of the Youths to National Life" reflected the resolutions of 1979 YCNU Conference and the 1980 Bafoussam Congress, whose theme "Mastery of Development" was echoed in the 1982 Youth Day theme.

The emergence of Paul Biya in November 1982 as Cameroon's second President and his pledge to adopt "Rigour and Moralization" as his governing principles, marked a departure from Ahidjo's leadership ideology, which was reflected in the Youth Day themes. To mobilize the Cameroonian youths around his new ideology, the 1983 and 1984 themes for the National Youth Day were devoted to "Rigour and Moralization". If the early appeals were those of political mobilization, the choice of the theme on "moralization" in 2000, and later in 2006 was probably to address an image problem as since 1999, Cameroon had been rated among the most corrupt countries by Transparency International. Moreover, to rally the youths around the New Deal's doctrine of "Communal Liberalism", launched in 1986, the 1987 National Youth Day theme was based on President Biya's rhetorical question of "What Youth for the New Deal?"

The period of democratic transition in Cameroon between 1991 and 1996 was marked by an active participation of the Youths in most cases as water-bearers for political violence. This state of affairs motivated the leadership's appeal for moderation in the democratization process in its themes "Freedom, Democracy, and Discipline" (1991), "Patriotism, Responsibility, Commitment" (1992), "Youth, Peace, Unity, and Future of Cameroon" (1993), and "Youth and the Mastery of the Democratic Process" (1995). The relevance of this theme of youth violence and democratic transition in Africa was also reflected in the 2001-2002 themes of the African Youth and Globalization Programme which focused on "Youth Violence, Activism, and Citizenship". The re-emergence of political violence in 2007-2008 further motivated leadership appeals for responsible citizenship and patriotism.

International events also influenced the choice of the National Youth Day themes. The 1985 theme for instance was a domestication of the theme of the UN's International Youth Year of "Participation, Development, and Peace", while the 1986 theme of "Youth, Peace, and Development" was further aligned to the proclamation of that year as the International Year of Peace by the UN.

The 1990 Youth Day theme on "Sport, Faith, and Hope", was influenced by the country's brilliant participation in international sporting events, notably the 1990 World Cup in Italy, while that of 1994 on "Sport, Youth, and National Integration" was also a proclamation by the UN of the year as the International Year of Sports and Olympic Ideal.

The choice of the theme "Youth, National Unity, African Unity" in 1996 was also to translate the leadership's attachment to Pan-Africanism at a time when Yaoundé was preparing to host the 36th Summit of the OAU in July 1996 and President Biya was ready to take the command as the Organization's new Chairman-in-Office.

Similarly, the organization of the International Conference on AIDS in Yaoundé in 2001 also influenced the theme on "Youth and the Fight against AIDS", whose relevance was captured in the Pan-African Youth Forum on AIDS in Dakar in March 2004. The 2002 theme on Youth and Entrepreneurship also captured the preoccupation of the African Ministers who organized an International Conference on Youth Employment in Egypt in September 2002. The theme on Youth and Culture for Peace adopted in 2003 for instance was also influenced by the need to generate interest in the UN's International Year for the Culture of Peace in 2000 as well as the International Decade on Culture and Peace in 2001-2010.

In spite of its potentials as an advocacy tool for government's policy, international agenda, and leadership ideology, the National Youth Day has failed to choose themes that could address critical issues related to youth governance such as leadership, ICT, drug abuse, corruption, globalization, youth rights, and environment.

Part Two

Youth Day Messages and Leadership Discourse: 1949-2009

3

The Empire Day and Commonwealth Youth Day Messages:
1949-1961

3.1: Commissioner's Address to the Youth on Empire Day, 1949

Boys and Girls,

I am very happy to meet you all here today and to greet you with a message from His Excellency the Governor. The Governor is at present at home on leave but he has remembered how school children all over Nigeria will be gathering on this day and has sent a personal message which he has said should be given to you. These are His Excellency's words to you.

"Empire Day last year fell on a day while I was in the middle of a long tour of Nigeria. I was actually at Onitsha and shall never forget the early morning parade of 18,000 school children, and how before they began their sports they marched past six abreast, while I stood at the salute for nearly an hour. I was very happy to be there.

This year, several gatherings will be taking place in many parts of the country, and although I am away on leave, I will like to send from the United Kingdom a message to Nigeria, and especially to the boys and girls. I hope that you will enjoy your holiday and your sports on this Empire Day and about Nigeria's place in it.

Your first thought should be to learn about your own country of Nigeria – about its history and its geography, how it is governed, and how local government works. What plans there are for development and to create better conditions of life for the people. All this is an important part of your education as good citizens and good Nigerians.

It is also good to think of how Nigeria fits into the British Commonwealth and about its place in the world. The British Commonwealth is often described – rightly – as a family of nations. We all know that a big united family, the members of which are loyal to each other and well disposed towards other people, can be a powerful influence for good in a community. So it is with the British Family of nations. There are these who criticize the British Empire but all honest people know that it is an influence for good in the world community.

Nigeria is one of the younger members of the family, but it is big and vigorous and is growing in strength and wisdom. And the rest of the family is watching its growth with friendly interest and pride. You boys and girls have a big part to play in your country's progress. Work hard. Play hard, be kind to others, be respectful to your parents and elders, and make up your minds to be good citizens."

That is the message which His Excellency has sent to you and to all this other gatherings of school children today all over this country. If His Excellency were here today speaking especially to you children of Cameroons schools. I am nations which you belong which is interested in your welfare. In the case of you Cameroons children the still bigger company of the world's United Nations, which the British family loyalty supports, has a constant interest in your welfare.

Before I watch you march past, I should like to give you my very best wishes and the very best wishes of all Government Officers here for your enjoyment of this Day.

3.2: Address to the Youths by Commissioner of the Cameroons on Empire Day, Buea, 1951

Another Empire Day comes round, and once more I send an Empire Day Message, addressed particularly – though not exclusively – to the boys and girls. I hope that you will all have enjoyment and fun this holiday. (Incidentally, I also hope that your parents have not felt obliged to spend a lot of money on new clothes or school uniforms for you on this occasion; your march-past can be smart and impressive if you are all neat and tidy and if you step out with pride and with cheerful faces).

As I have done in the past, I ask you on this day, in addition to having fun, to think seriously about your own country, Nigeria, and about its place as a member of the great, friendly, freedom-loving family of nations that is the British Commonwealth.

The pace of progress in Nigeria has greatly quickened in recent times; exciting things are happening; and the country is growing in importance and self-confidence. The other members of the Commonwealth family are watching our progress with friendly interest.

This progress brings with it obligations and responsibilities, as well as privileges, and I ask you all today to make up your minds that you will always try to conduct yourselves in a way that will help to make this country strong and united and justly admired. In the classroom, work hard. On the playing field, play hard and with good sportsmanship.

In your homes, be respectful and helpful to your parents and elders. And all the time be kind to others. As you grow up, try to be God-fearing and upright and tolerant. If you of the coming generation follow this advice, Nigeria will be strong and united and justly admired.

Good luck to you all.

3.3: Address by the Acting Commissioner of the Cameroons, Mr. J.S Dudding, on the Occasion of the First Commonwealth Youth Day, Buea, 2 June 1957

The first thing that I must do is to congratulate you all on your excellent appearance and turnout. I know what hard work always goes into the preparation of clothes and uniforms for ceremonies such as this, and I also know that many of you travelled long distances, perhaps on foot, to assemble here today. You can be proud of the effort that you have made, but it is important that you should realize with due humility the deep significance of the occasion which brings you all together.

This is the first time that Commonwealth Youth Sunday has been celebrated in the Southern Cameroons, and no doubt some of you are wondering exactly what its purpose is, and what it means. I will tell you.

26

Observance of the day started 20 years ago at the coronation of the late King George VI. When a King is crowned in Great Britain it is the practice for him to dedicate himself to the service of God and of the Commonwealth. When King George VI was crowned, the young people of Great Britain decided in the same way to dedicate themselves to the service of God and of their fellows.

The first dedication ceremony was held at a service at Westminster Abbey in London which was attended by Youth organizations from all over the United Kingdom. The effect of this service was profound, and in subsequent years its celebration rapidly spread to the other countries of the Commonwealth, until today it is being celebrated by young people of more than 50 countries throughout the world. These young people now for the first time include you yourselves, the young people of the Cameroons.

It is a very moving thought that today in places so far apart as Malaya and the West Indies, Hong Kong and Gibraltar, Nigeria and the Islands of the South Seas, young people are bound together by the same spirit of unselfish endeavour. After this parade you will go the Church, and while you are there, I ask you to think about this time there thousands of other young people of different races, colours, and creeds throughout the world who are worshipping at the same service as you yourselves. They, like you, will be dedicating themselves to the services of one another and by so doing, you and they will be making an important spiritual contribution to goodwill between peoples and nations on which the future of the world must depend. And remember – it is you young people who by your beliefs and by your actions will decide what the future of the world will be.

It is fitting that the patron of Commonwealth Youth Sunday should be Her Majesty the Queen. Not only is Her Majesty the great abiding symbol of the unity of the Commonwealth family of nations, but she is also the mother of a family of children of her own who one day, when they reach the same age as yourselves, will be dedicating themselves to the same ideals. You will, I know, be glad to learn that Her Majesty today has sent a special message to the young people of the Commonwealth, and I will close my address by reading it to you. It is addressed from Buckingham Palace in London and is signed "Elisabeth Regina", that is to say, "Queen".

"I am happy to send my greetings to all of you who will be observing Commonwealth Youth Sunday, 1957. In doing so you will form a vast congregation girding the earth; a congregation differing in colour, race, and creed yet united as members of our British family of nations. It is sometimes said that what the world now needs most is a solid bridge between East and West. The British Commonwealth, the Commonwealth Youth Sunday too, since it is built to the same pattern, is surely such a bridge, not between East and West, but between East, West, North, and South. In celebrating this Day therefore you are in a very real sense reminding the world of a lesson which is still surely needs to learn.

You are engaged in the great adventure of growing up. And you are growing up in a world which is itself as full of the possibilities of adventures as it was in the age of my predecessor, Queen Elisabeth the First. Indeed, in the world of tomorrow, the opportunities of adventurous service will be far more widespread than they were three or four centuries ago. For modern science has both entrusted us with vastly greater material power and has brought the most distant parts of the world into far closer contact and far greater interdependence upon each other. For these reasons you are likely to need greater knowledge, and perhaps even greater wisdom, than did the men of the seventeenth century. But you will certainly need the enterprise, the courage and the trust in God which they so conspicuously displayed.

It is my earnest prayer that, whether you are still at school or college or already at work in the world, you may be seeking to fit yourselves for the tasks which lie ahead by looking upon your daily duties as a training ground for character as well as mind.

May God bless you all".

4

The West Cameroon Youth Day Messages: 1964-1966

4.1: Address by the Prime Minister for West Cameroon, Hon. J.N Foncha, on the Inauguration of Youth Day in West Cameroon, Buea, 11 February, 1964

Dear Cameroonians and friends of the Federal Republic of Cameroon, we are assembled here today to institute a SPORTS DAY for the youths of West Cameroon. We have chosen 11th February because of the special significance in the history of the Federal Republic of Cameroon, for on Saturday, 11th February, 1961, the people of the then British Cameroons won their independence by voting for it. The plebiscite was an event which occupied the energies and taxed the rights our people. The landslide victory is therefore an achievement for which Cameroonians should be remembered and congratulated. By this vote, the people of the then Southern Cameroons decided to reunite with their brothers in the then Republic of Cameroon, which had earlier achieved independence on 1st January, 1960, while Southern British Cameroons which was forcibly separated from the southern sector by the British Administering Authority was manoeuvred by the Federation of Nigerian. The inauguration of annual sports this day will enable the growing generation to remember this spectacular attainment which brought about our independence.

February is important in some other happenings. It was during this month in 1955 that the Kamerun National Democratic Party (KNDP) was launched. Today makes the KNDP five years and eighteen days when the people of Southern Cameroons voted solidly for it on January 24, 1959, and enabled it to form the Government. The month February therefore has been marked by important events during our reign as the governing party. It is therefore justifiable that February 11th should be a public holiday for the commemoration of these important events, and to think out ways and means of overcoming the problems that face our youths.

The idea of Youth Day springs from our desire that our children should inherit and continue to implement what we have achieved. We know that we shall not always be the ones to direct the affairs of the nation, and hence it is our desire to work for the proper upbringing and preparation of the youths so that they may truly take with the right motives. To do this, they should understand our stand and policy so as to avoid future misinterpretation. A study of the formation of the KNDP will reveal what we have in mind.

In founding the KNDP, we were careful to avoid the very things detested in other parties. We made up our minds to have no malice against anyone, even our political opponents. Hence the talk of "Friendly disposition towards all men, no matter their political aims" was laid.

The word "DEMOCRACY" is the moving spirit in our party. By living up to its true meaning, we were able to give to our following confidence and courage they needed in their progressive man and difficulties and to win the confidence of the majority of the people. We have thus proved that democracy in practice is a major force and accounts for our success.

Falsehood was sternly discouraged among our followers. Our party's persistency to truth has shown that we have lived up to our motto, "THAT TRUTH SHALL PREVAIL". In the KNDP everyone is given the opportunity to criticize and suggest amendments. Any grievance may be expressed without fear. The sound principles and carefully considered policies of the KNDP are clear and easily understood. If they are right, why not let us follow them? Why not join the KNDP so that we all working unitedly can contribute to the determined the efforts of the Government to better the lot of our suffering people.

We do not believe in the multiplicity of political parties within one country. We believe in a set up of one-party system in which freedom of speech can be practiced without fear of victimization. We believe in criticizing and correction from within.

It is however not our intention to force those who not wish to associate with us freely to come into our fold. We will never condone dishonesty and will continue to match and reject those we cover to have inimical interests for declaring to the KNDP. We do not intend to force others by law to join our party. We only appeal in the interest of progress and the elimination of poverty to all good citizens to join us. But as "birds of a feather flock together", we will leave those of contrary views to go their way.

Our five years in the government has been a period of continuous progress, even during the dark and uncertain days before the plebiscite. A casual look into West Cameroon as it was in 1959 will reveal the truth we are telling. Progress is a continuous act of a people. Having thus brought the nation out of the difficulties we are determined to continue to work to bring about happiness and prosperity. We must now see what to do in order to attain to it.

God has provided the means of happiness and prosperity wherever human beings live. The earth is our source of wealth. The land which we all see on it and in it, and the sea with all that it contains are treasuries from which human beings can draw in order to obtain the means on which to live. To obtain this, we must work. Our ability at work combined with our intelligence determines the amount of wealth we should have. Hard work properly directed will provide more wealth than just mere work without proper arrangement.

Having convinced ourselves that work is necessary in order to live, we should now see what we have around us in Cameroon on which to apply ourselves to obtain our needs. Our land is rich and grows all kinds of food and cash crops. We have the plantations which serve as practical schools from where we can learn.

It is not necessary to talk of minerals as those are not the responsibilities of everybody. Minerals can only be exploited with advantage by rich man who form themselves into companies or by the government. We should be interested in those things which we can do by ourselves without the necessity of obtaining huge capital investments from outside the Federal Republic of Cameroon.

I wish to stress the importance of articles of Cameroon origin. Our crafts are exquisite, complicated to foreigners, yet easy to the indigenous craftsmen. They are rare to find even in the Cameroon, not to mention other countries. All varieties of carving, weaving and moulding can provide employment for a large part of the population.

Properly made, all those articles will find places among the exports of the Federation. Strangers who visit the country would like to take home some of these locally made crafts as souvenirs. It all depends on the interest we take in producing them. The development of crafts cannot therefore be limited to the uneducated. The more educated a person is, the greater his appreciation of articles of quality becomes, and the more will he devise specialized tools for their production.

We must now think of what our boys and girls should do in order to prepare themselves for a brighter future. Sports provide a wide opportunity for young Cameroonians to become national and even international figures. Such opportunities are opened to all but can only be got from hard work and persistent efforts. I am sure many of you are quite fit to take the challenge now.

Ambition to win must not get you out of honesty with yourself and your friend. Remember that a good sportsman is one who avoids injuring others for the purpose of winning. A clean game gives satisfaction and more praise then a foul one, which points are disputed and whose sportsmen are blood for being rude and rough. Dexterity and other artful manoeuvres give more chances of success than brutal kicking and knocking your opponents from behind. Therefore feel for the wellbeing of your friends and opponents when on the field. Play to win, but when you lose, take it easy, learn from your mistakes and make up for them next time.

Akin to sports are all sorts of traditional entertainments. A well-orderly nation must have its musicians and dancers. These must be carefully studied. They should form a branch of our education programme. Without it, life in our communities would be dull and uninteresting.

In a country where tourism promises to be a rich source of national income, the means of entertainment must be available in every tribe. Visitors into the country will like to spend their evenings usefully by attending entertaining activities that are a part of the community's life. We have heard and sometimes witnessed entertaining groups from Europe and America. We rushed and bought tickets to see their performances. We left the hall praising them. We are unable to imitate them, but we should always bring home a new idea. This should be to perfect our own folklores in order to be in a position to show them round our country and other countries in the world. A team of Cameroon musicians will attract just as much crowd in other countries. Therefore, you can earn a good and honest income for yourselves and for the country by merely practicing to sing and dance.

I must not be understood to mean that young Cameroonians should not pursue the higher academic studies. Instead, I have always encouraged those who the gift in any branch of studies to pursue it until they realize the end.

Our studies should lead us to one noble end – the service of our country. Patriotism is manifested in the service of one's country. Therefore we should also aim at fitting ourselves profitably in the Civil Service where we can utilize our knowledge to the benefit of the greatest number.

The Civil Service is a complex organ of the Government. To make it as successful as we desire, we must employ those who are trained in the departments in which they will make use of the knowledge they have acquired. Careful posting in this way means the maintenance of efficiency, speed, progress and stability in administration.

As a rule, those who seek admission into the Civil Service must be prepared to begin at the bottom. They should learn the simple office routine and procedure and gain the experience that will enable them to excel in the special duties assigned to them. To begin at the bottom does not mean to remain there. They should work and study to earn promotion by competitive examinations or by efficiency. Fair promotion is that which is earned by producing results which make us fit to occupy the next post higher up.

Graduates enter the Civil Service at special points reserved for them. The higher their degrees the higher up the scale they go. This is an incentive to all graduates who should strive to specialize in one thing before they seek admission into the Civil Service.

Although graduates enter the Civil Service at special points prepared for them, they are nevertheless considered as beginners. They have to undergo a probation period before they will be confirmed in their posts. This is necessary because knowledge must be transformed into practical possibility. The years of probation enable them to acquire practical experience in the actual performance of their duties. They are watched as any other junior civil servants, and their confirmation of appointment can be refused unless they show interest, ability, obedience, and cooperation.

It should be appreciated that that the Civil Service is highly selective and competitive. It is so because the Government must be sure that all the complicated organs that keep up the Administration of the country are functioning effectively. They at the head are answerable for any inefficiency in their departments must be sure that those subordinate to them do not neglect any part of their duties, thereby bringing the department to disrepute. The Government itself is answerable to the people as a whole, for it is they who make up the sovereign authority in the country. Speed and efficiency must be kept up. All citizens who have found places in the service of the country should endeavour to keep them and should do their best for stability and progress in the country. All should be prepared to accept due disciplinary measures should they go against any of the rules.

Above all, no heads of departments should impose on their subordinates. They impose when they do not know their duties, they brag and shout on others, and in the end, do not even mind whether they work under their supervision has been properly done. But at the same time, if it is necessary to institute disciplinary measures against any of their subordinate officers, they should be those concerned the fruits for which they must be punished.

A lot has been said about crimes in the Civil Service. The worse of these go under the name of bribery and corruption. Akin to it is favouritism. Those who find themselves on top or who have been privileged to have better positions demand

and receive money and gifts just for merely recommending someone for employment or promotion. These crimes are grave because they cut through the rock of efficiency in the Civil Service, as well as unjust because in this way, the qualified ones are sometimes left out and the unqualified occupied or promoted.

However, it should be underscored that heavier punishment will continue to be meted to those criminals until others learn to quench their appetites and the unnecessary desire to be rich without labour. I appeal to all good citizens to disclose anyone who may be caught guilty of such practices. It is only by the cooperation of the general public that those in authority can successfully suppress and eradicate bribery, corruption, and favouritism in the Civil Service.

All citizens should interest themselves in the affairs of their villages by taking part in planning and participating in the community work of the town. God wants and is pleased to see us rendering the free services to our neighbours. All girls and boys should learn to be kind and helpful first to their parents and then to one another including strangers in our country. To strangers, we all should learn to do more because they need comfort, for their parents or families and friends are not here to associate with them. Our boys and girls are also in their countries and need the same comfort. Those little courteous services go to build the character of a nation.

While most Cameroonians are hard working, some are lazy. The lazy ones do not keep their jobs for long. They go about speaking all sorts of ills against their employers and soon resign. They go about in the country, visiting Government offices one after the other and the commercial firms. It should be underscored that no jobs no jobs which have the means of subsistence are mean.

Standard Six School leavers are among the Cameroonians I have described above. Ten years ago all those who passed Standard Six examinations had clerical jobs or became Time Keepers and later on Headmen in plantations. This is not possible nowadays because in addition to the increased number of First School Certificate holders, students who have undergone five or six years in the secondary schools are competing for the same jobs. It is easily seen that the Secondary School Leavers will be preferred for the same jobs than other literate people with lower qualifications.

I have spoken of employment in general. I should now emphasize the need for girls and women taking part in employing themselves usefully in those jobs which befit them. Of course, they are already competing successfully with the men folk in various branches of the Civil Service. This is all right. They have however not thought they could be employed as domestic servants to which they are equally competent. Some illiterate girls have already been successful in making good stewards, why not the literate ones. Cooking and serving at table, sweeping and tidying the houses, the care of babies, etc are all jobs in which literate girls can seek employment.

There is also the opponent in that farming as done by our mothers is mean job for literate girls and women. This is not true. Anything that a person does to earn a living, as I have said before, is not mean. I am convinced that everyone can find something to do in a country gifted with natural resources as ours. The mean work any healthy person can do is to beg. Begging is indeed the only mean job I can think of, for then they have made themselves useless and are pests to others. Let begging be restricted to cripples, as this is not their fault.

I should be a happier person if the youths of the Federal Republic of Cameroon will strive to be self-reliant. Independence must begin with every citizen. Satisfaction comes only after one has done a useful piece of job for oneself or for another. Happiness and prosperity is the result of careful planning and hard work. The government is planning and the people should bend down to production.

But who should be responsible for the training and guidance of our children in order to attain to the lofty ideals we are at. Of course parents, teachers, and the Government should share the responsibilities and cooperate to have good results. Teachers should concentrate with the teaching of children to read and write, but would not for the sake of shortness of time neglect character and physical training which are both best taught from infancy.

Parents should see to it that their children practice good habits. They should insist on their children being obedient, honest, truthful and helpful. Unless they begin those good habits at home, they will never be used to them when they are adults. We are worried when our children misbehave. When they hurt their friends badly, when they are lazy, disobedient, and finally when they are driven from attending classes because they are very bad. Unless we take part in keeping them upright while they are young, the worse will happen when they are adults. They may be sacked from their jobs or imprisoned for any crime.

In order to avoid those misfortunes from befalling our children, let us be alert to our responsibilities. Let us insist that they do the right things. Let us cooperate with teachers in order to know the faults or good habits of our children and be able to correct or encourage them.

These are some of the ways to make our children what we want them to be in life.

Cooperation with the Government as I have described will help to solve some of the problems that daily face our youths.

Whatever plan we make, let us always remember to ask God to lead us through, otherwise we labour in vain. On Youth Day therefore, let us devote part of the preparation in praying that God will give strength, knowledge and wisdom to overcome the difficulties that lies ahead of them.

Long Live the Youths of the Federal Republic
Long Live the President of the Federal Republic
Long Live the Federal Republic of Cameroon.

4.2: Addressed by the President of the Republic to the Youths of West Cameroon on the Occasion of the Youth Day Inaugural Celebration, Yaounde, 11 February 1964

It is a special pleasure for me to address to you on the occasion of the celebration of your traditional Youth Day my warm message of hope and encouragement.

I know that, through the West Cameroon Youth who are celebrating, I am speaking to all the Youth of the Cameroon Federation: this Youth who are the hope of our people mobilized for the building of a happy country. The young are the natural heirs of a Nation: one of these days, which are close at hand for some, they will assume its burdens and responsibilities.

It is therefore a message of encouragement for it is with their own destiny that the young are now faced and it is essential that they have awareness of the truth: it will without question incite you to work at a time when you may be thinking of relaxing your efforts, it will arouse in you the desire to know the efforts of the generations who preceded you to achieve a civilization and culture of which you are today the products before becoming tomorrow the masters.

After strengthening the vertical threads of that social fabric which will lead you from the past into the future, you must also think of weaving horizontal threads, in other words, bonds between yourselves, the youth of our same country, coming from different social environments, between Federated State and Federated State.

Indeed in the huge and magnificent task which lies before you, you must all be courageous together, clear-minded together and happy together. Solidarity must be your creed.

The intellectual elite of our youth must in particular shed its reserve and light the way. For it is called upon, without distinction of political, tribal or religious considerations, to bring its total and sincere collaboration to the Government and place itself in the service of all the peoples in the interest of harmonious development of all social strata of the nation.

You must realize that the Cameroon youth in general, and more particularly the Youth of West Cameroon belong to a "pilot generation" which has been called upon to conclude and destined to make a success on the African continent of one of the most daring experiments in history, that of achieving a harmonious symbiosis starting from a duality of cultures, motivations and influences.

Tomorrow, before the bar of history, our undaunted Cameroon Youth will be able to pride itself upon having assimilated two cultures that are not easily reconcilable having integrated the positive contributions of these foreign cultures into its own cultural heritage and having made of it an original synthesis of knowledge adapted to the collective needs of the times and of Africa. This Youth will carry the torch of African Unity through culture.

I am happy to note that the Youth of West Cameroon are enthusiastically participating in the effort to harmonize our cultural and educational institutions, a harmonization which is intended to efficiently exploit our bicultural situation, which is intended to make our bilingualism a precious arm rather than a handicap, and finally which is intended to achieve unity of thought in the interests of our common aspirations and our common destiny.

As regards the Federal Government – and this is my message of hope - I can assure you that you can count on it. All our solicitude goes out to you to help you to become integrated, under the best possible conditions, into the life of the nation. Within the limits of our financial ability, all facilities will be given to those who deserve it to acquire a solid education preparing them to adult life, to help them to find their place, that is to say to teach them "the nature of the general evolution in which they are involved and toward which they must not remain passive".

In other words, facilities will be made available to you, without tribal or religious discrimination, in order to acquire an education either in the University institutions of the Federal Republic, of which I pledge the Federal character, or in specialized foreign establishments, not just for your own sake but also to increase the efficiency of the community.

Young people of West Cameroon, if I have succeeded by this message in inspiring you with additional energy to face confidently up to the tasks awaiting you and to give you new reasons for believing in yourselves and your country, our beloved Cameroon, I shall deem myself fully satisfied.

Long Live the Republic!
Long Live Cameroon!

4.3: Address by the Prime Minister of West Cameroon, Hon. J.N Foncha on the Occasion of the Youth Day in West Cameroon, Buea, 11 February, 1965

My dear Cameroonians, it is with joy I address you on the occasion of the celebration of the first anniversary of the West Cameroon Youth Day. It is a pleasure to see so many of you turn up to watch and cheer the children in their sports competition.

I take this opportunity to wish the Youth of the Federation sincere greetings both to those at home and abroad. To those abroad, I call on them to be at heart and soul with us on this great day, which commemorates freedom for West Cameroon. I also wish to remind those at home, sweet home, for nothing is better than sweet fatherland. I wish them success in their studies and invite them to seek employment at home when they have qualified.

Before I turn to the activities of the day, I should like to avail myself of your presence here to say a few words about some government activities. In these days a greater part of the activities of all governments of the world is centred on development. In our case, the old saying that "man was born free" is remembered, and that spirit has animated many statesmen to fight and win freedom for themselves and their peoples. Freedom gives the opportunity to develop. The fortunate countries of the world, who have long been independent and who are better off economically, socially, and otherwise have seen the need to assist the newly independent countries order to bring them up to appreciable standards. Assistance from within or without can best be utilized according to the inclinations and abilities of each developing country. Our inclination and ability has much to do with development.

We in Cameroon stand equal opportunity to develop all that God has provided for us. It is only by development that we can achieve our desired goal, which is peace, happiness, and prosperity. This disposition of mind and our action, individually or collectively makes all the difference.

Our disposition should be that of peace within ourselves and in the nation. In peace, we think and plan and progress. In order to be at peace within ourselves, we must learn to live at peace with our neighbours. The consideration of the wellbeing of our neighbours makes us give them the respect they deserve and in the end they return the same to us. In other words, we should be loving and helpful to our neighbours, and in consideration they should be helpful to us. We should extend this to all foreigners who associate with us in one way or the other.

I congratulate all those who have by so behaving themselves made peace and order to exist in the Federated State of West Cameroon. It is by self-restraint that this has been possible. There is no doubt that there have been quarrels among families, neighbours and tribes, but by self-restraint all have been satisfied at the appropriate time and place. No quarrels are impossible to be settled by this Government. Following the right procedures, quarrels over inheritance, property or land have ended well because of self-restraint in consideration of the wellbeing of our neighbours. I therefore wish to assure you that Government is looking into the quickest means of disposing Chieftaincy disputes, land disputes, and the dispensation of Justice in general. No report is overlooked if it takes the right channel to the authority concerned. Cooperating with those in authority is all we ask, as without it Government is placed in a difficult position and the dispensation of Justice is complicated.

Having put ourselves in the right position namely peace and order, we can make big strides in development. We have a lot to do and are still far from our goal which must be achieved in stages, with patience and hard work.

In the course of the past five years the constructions of many roads have been started. Those which existed before need improvement in widening and strengthening or rebuilding of the bridges. All these require a lot of money. Many of the new roads are either in progress or completed. Some are short and some are long, and it will take years to complete them. One completed main road calls for many more feeder ones into the villages and later on into the compounds and so on. Development has no end.

In a matter of roads, I have to congratulate those of you who have applied themselves to communal work in order to achieve their completion. There should be no slackness in this matter. You should take pride in going out for communal work when called upon to do so. Many hands make light work, we say. The heavy road equipment we have are very few in comparison to their need. They will be employed mainly to cut down steep hill sides and fill deep valleys. The people themselves should continue to do the digging where there it is fairly easy to do so. It has become so necessary to speed up the completion of these roads so that Government will have to find new sources of income within West Cameroon to finance them. I should here express with appreciation and thanks on behalf of the people of West Cameroon the move by the European Economic Community and the United States Government to finance the construction of some of the major roads. These when completed will form the transport link between East and West Cameroon as well as speedy movement within West Cameroon.

While roads will continue to figure prominently is our Community Development projects, I must emphasize the increasing need for maternity clinics with attached dispensaries. These will become our principal first aid centres. They will be enlarged from time to time according to need and use. I assure you that Government will do its share by increasing the yearly vote for it.

The development plans are being completed. But plans by themselves do not bring progress. We have got to execute them to the best of our ability. This again calls for cooperation in all things we have in hand, otherwise we do not get ahead speedily. Otherwise too, we spend our time on individual projects which do not carry us far. Obedience to the authority is necessary. We request you to obey the authorities that exist in your villages centred around your chiefs and village councils, you should plan for the development of your villages and then tribe and in this way, we in West Cameroon will be contributing our share in the overall development of the Federal Republic of Cameroon.

In many of my talks I have stressed the importance of honesty as one of the means to lay the foundation of happiness and prosperity of the nation. Cameroonians in the majority are honest people. There are however a few dishonest ones. These have lived by exploiting the masses in many cunning ways. They have lived discovered that the people are cooperating with the Government in detecting their crimes in exposing them. In this way, they will meet difficulties in continuing further exploitation. They therefore have started to change their tactics, for dishonesty can be carried out in many ways. One of these is the attempt to hide behind the Government's policy of freedom of thought and expression. Some of them started to talk about tribal hatred, political domination, discrimination in employment and so on. The attempt is to distract the people from their business and from love to hatred. They hope to bring about tribal hatred and violence through which they will be in a position to push on their exploitation without being noticed.

It should be understood that Government will not retract from a policy of freedom of thought and expression. We believe this to be the right of free men in an independent country. But it will be understood that freedom of thought and expression and is within the law of the land. Democracy is the rule of law. Citizens who think, speak, and act within the law are free. Those against the law are against democracy itself and thereby forfeit the freedom for themselves. They are the bad elements in the community the law must hold them bound.

I must state emphatically that the authority vested in the Government must be recognized, respected, and obeyed. Any attempt to bypass it will be halted and the culprits brought to book. Justice will pursue them until they have their due retribution. In this way, the law will protect honest citizens from undue exploitation. I call on all citizens worthy of their place to resist false propaganda, subversive movements, and give full support to government's actions for honesty and hard work in business so that we can lay the happiness and prosperity of the nation on a solid foundation. I cannot over-emphasize the necessity for same thoughts and expressions which are the contributory factors to peace and stability of the nation.

The Government is making great efforts to provide for the need of the youths. Better opportunities exist now for learning than ever before. Greater effort is being made to increase facilities for employment in spite of the fewness of vacancies in the government departments. Education syllabuses are being adjusted to train boys and girls to be self-employed if after leaving school they cannot have employment elsewhere. A truly educated person is one who makes use of the facilities within his surroundings to begin a noble and honest business, and there to improve. Such are the citizens who may request for government's assistance. Government wants the cooperation of all youths in order that its efforts may be good fruits in future. Cooperation can best be given by doing some things which meant to be done and by doing them properly. Good habits are best learnt at school when we are young. It is my hope that you may use the opportunities offered you to prepare yourselves as good citizens of the Federation of Cameroon for the purpose of education is to train the citizens to be happy and useful.

One of the interesting items of the day's activities is folk-dances. You are aware that Government wishes folklores to be learnt and practiced in schools. This is to emphasize the importance we attach to good tradition. We want these to be demonstrated in an original fashion by any villagers who are prepared to do so. The aim is to afford school children the opportunity to learn and if possible to improve and excel upon the present practice. It is our wish that folklores should live and grow, for by so doing, can we continue the social activities of our nation.

As regards sports, all should appreciate that Government is taking more and more interest to see that they are properly taught. The Federal Government is making it possible for sportsmen to earn a living by becoming professionals in sports. Special teachers have been trained to teach sports in schools, and all children should take interest in them. Unfortunately, the results of athletic competitions are still poor. Not enough practice has been taken in the past. We are keenly watching to see the improvements made during the past twelve months to be demonstrated today.

I have stressed the importance of good habits because they count for the better future of boys and girls. Sports activities provide proper opportunity to cultivate good habits. During sports practice we learn to respect our neighbours or opponents and to accord them their rights and their safety. A good sportsman must be fair to his opponent. He should aim to win by his thorough practice, skill and dexterity. When victory is the result of skill and dexterity, the winners deserve the admiration of the spectacle. A brutal sportsman is an uncultured person and brings a bad name to his team or school.

You are on the stage of life's drama. Play well your part while you are young, so that you may leave a good name behind, and achievement for others to copy.

My presence among you is a pleasure for me. I shall return home relaxed and refreshed, and I hope all spectators present for the way I do.

I thank you and your teachers for the preparations you made towards this day.

God be with you.

4.4: Address by the Prime Minister of West Cameroon, Hon. A.N Jua on the Occasion of the 1st National Youth Day, Buea, 11 February 1966

Secretaries of State,
Members of the Diplomatic Corps,
My Fellow Cameroonians,

It is with humility mingled with joy that I thank this concourse of patriots and friends of West Cameroon today, on the occasion of our fifth anniversary of our Youth Day, which is also Plebiscite Day. It gives me great pride and pleasure to extend my warm greetings to Cameroonians and all in my capacity as Prime Minister since I took over office some eight months ago from my predecessor, Dr. J.N Foncha, Vice President of the Federal Republic. His tasks as the Prime Minister of West Cameroon was an up-hill one but with determined efforts he laid for one State a foundation that will endure throughout the years. I have taken up from there and hope that you will give the same cooperation and loyalty which you gave him during his tenure of office.

As I stand before this great concourse, I see Cameroonians of all ages, of all sexes, dressed in poetic beauty and dead anxious to play their part in making this day a complete success. I cannot but ask you why at all we are here? I am thrilled by your great enthusiasm and anxiety to make this day, this Youth Day, a Red Letter Day. February 11 1961 brought into being a new Republic, a Federal idea, indeed new dimensions of freedom. This day, February 11th 1961 or Plebiscite Day was the day we realized our conscience for the State in its deepest conception. This implies a full realization of the people's ideas. We did not vote for re-unification out of fear; we had a free choice and the choice we made was what our consciences felt right.

My Fellow Cameroonians, this is a unique opportunity for us to rekindle our faith in our youths as the only hope of our people. They are the natural heirs of our nation; they are the defenders and responsible rulers of tomorrow who must hear the nation's burdens and responsibilities which will fall to their lot and we have therefore a bounden duty to prepare them for the takeover. My Government sees Education as a vehicle of ideas, as a potent instrument of social change, and as a vital weapon with which our youths will prepare themselves in assuming these responsibilities of tomorrow. Accordingly, an ambitious and enthusiastic educational programme aimed at developing the mental, spiritual, and physical capabilities of these youths had been launched and results are most encouraging. In this field, development has been rapid, especially as this sound, solid foundation had been laid. The most spectacular increase in total enrolment was seen in the Secondary Schools where the 1965 figure of 2,300 students represented 56% increase over the 1964 figure of 1,500. This was due to the courageous decision to open many new Secondary Schools in 1963. As the annual intake of over 900 pupils filters through the upper classes of secondary schools, so the total increases in enrolment will continue to be spectacular in the coming years.

In the primary schools, development has been steady due to the policy of controlled expansion. In spite of this, primary school enrolment rose from 116,000 to 124,000 pupils. A significant and highly desirable trend is the levelling process, in numerical terms, between the number of boys and girls. In 1965 the proportion of boys to girls was less than two to one respectively.

In the field of primary education, the boldest decision taken over the past year was the introduction of education rating throughout West Cameroon. This Scheme, which enables parents to send their children to Primary schools without paying tuition fees, for the first four years, relieves them of much anxiety and strain. For the first time in our history parents have been enabled to avoid, through the introduction of this education rating, the agonizing choice of whether or not to send their sons or their daughters to school.

The number of teacher training colleges, responsible for our ever-growing primary school population, has been increased and expanded in size. During the past year, the number of teachers under training rose from 1.374 to 1.698, an increase of nearly 24%. Government has approved the introduction of a four-year's continuous course, with a new and more relevant syllabus, Cameroonian in taste and in content, in order to increase the production of trained teachers without lowering standards. My Government is alive to the needs of our surging population that will forge ahead with this programme in spite of the difficulties which may come its way.

My fellow countrymen, the task before us has many components. Education is only one of them. I firmly believe and I have no doubt that you will share with me that a sound education is like a house on a solid foundation. Our independence and sovereignty would be meaningless unless these attributes of our freedom are built on a system of economic self-sufficiency. In the light of these convictions, I have not hesitated to create in my Government, a Ministry of Development and Internal Economic Planning. The creation of this Ministry, you no doubt know, was to ensure the coordination and control of internal economic activities for which the State of West Cameroon is fully responsible, and thus able to put to full use our limited manpower resources.

Since Economic progress is the continuous act of a people, I have watched with intense pride the gradual growth of our national economy. In the sphere of Communication, the Public Works Department and the Department of Community Development have played and are still playing a major role in the provision of a network of roads which connect most parts of the country. In the field of plantation planning, Cooperative Societies, Marketing and Inspection, and self-help (Community Development), my Government has provided loans for the improvement of cocoa, palm oil, coffee, rubber, and the supply of electricity. In the field of cooperatives alone, a total of 27,250,000 Francs has been provided for such institutions as the Bakossi, Kumba, Nso, and Bakweri Cooperative Societies. In West Cameroon today, we have built a vegetable, Handiwork, Cattlemen's and Women's cooperative shops societies in Mankon, Bafreng, Nso, and Ndu respectively. Voluntary work camps have been established to enlist the energy and enthusiasm of Youths in the development of the Nation. The "Volunteers for Cameroon Progress' Organization, formed in 1963, is a progressive conception which, I assure you, will help in providing inspiration for our young men in upholding the tradition of our forefathers. This Organization is destined to be part of our history, part of our identity.

Fellow citizens, as we watch the passing of this momentous hour, this hour of reckoning, I must warn you again that the agenda for our social and economic emancipation is long and the task ahead is not an easy one. Let us never for one moment do anything which would blunt our sense of hard work but let us attempt to incarnate the hopes of our people for the future, rejuvenate them, make them know that they are the architects of their own fortunes, and that for this country to march abreast with other modern countries, we must, on our own, create conditions necessary for our social progress. This progress cannot be achieved without hard and continuous work, and happily we have dedicated ourselves to this cause as evidenced by our activities in the sphere of community development. I can only hope that the youths of this country will take the challenge and avail themselves of the great opportunities which are being provided by my Government in the field of Agriculture throughout the country. A Farm Settlement has been opened in Mamfe where our young men are given a training with an agricultural bias, and one at Wum is in train, with more to come, to cater for the self-employment of our young citizens, and the production of food for our local consumption and the surplus for export trade.

The College of Arts, Science and Technology at Bambui has been created and part from its preparing our youths for the General Certificate of Education, it undertakes to give basic training to Agricultural Assistants to assist in the country's Agricultural Extension Services. But unless our people are prepared to work hard it may not be possible to gain maximum benefits from these promising institutions. I am sure you will take the challenge.

Today as we move courageously towards our national goal, it is encouraging and befitting for me to mention in an occasion like this, the great assistance accorded us by friendly overseas countries, which have provided personnel and equipment to enable the educational, social and agricultural projects to develop and progress in our land. To all these friendly overseas countries we are extremely grateful for this assistance which will help combat want and disease in our country. We shall continue for quite some time to need their advice and help and I am confident that the assistance can change with an astonishing speed the face of the world if only our philanthropic friends will cut down drastically the cost of venturing into outer space or orbiting people to the moon and redirect their efforts to help the emerging countries to develop their economic and social standards. I wish indeed to reassure the nationals of these friendly countries working among us that our purpose is definite and clear. We do not seek domination, nor subjugation, nor do we want to orbit men into space. Our task in this century of continuous peril is to create those conditions in our society, which make have, irrespective of their colour or creed, love and respect for the dignity of man. Therefore the feeling that has recently caught up the expatriates in this country that the foreigner is not wanted is without a just cause and should be discarded forthwith. This nation's great commitment to freedom and justice, shall, I am convinced find a worthy place before the bar of history and in the conscience of man. In other words, it shall leave its footprints on the sands of time as a challenge for future generations to emulate.

My fellow Countrymen, our might efforts in Education, Agriculture and all fields of national life are unattainable without a respect for Law and Order. My Government is a representative democracy, based on the concept of the Rule of Law and respect for individual freedom. These are the preoccupations on which our parliamentary system of Government is based. Our compatriots fought for years to bequeath to us a belief in the sanctity of the human individual, the right of fair and public trial, freedom of conscience and thought. To achieve and preserve these lofty ideals you will have to cultivate citizenship and assist the Forces of Law and Order in their bid to combat lawlessness. My advice to you is that rather than take the law into your hands, you should make full use of the courts whenever you seek redress. The training of Legal Personnel and the reform of our Customary Courts have engaged my Government's energy and I am glad that we are fielding in men of trust and reliability – men of sterling character. My colleagues and I are determined to infuse into our people the spirit of obedience to the law as a necessary prerequisite for the maintenance of peace and order. Freedom under the Rule of Law requires the acceptance of moral responsibility to ourselves, to our fellow men as provided by the institutions of our Republic. I have spoken at length on various issues of tremendous magnitude and dimensions. You ask: What is our aim? I will say victory in unity. We have before us the exacting task – the task of creating a true national unity. There has never been, I suppose, in all African history, so daring an experiment as the attempt to blend three cultures, the Cameroonian traditional heritage and the British and French colonial heritages, into one culture. Our only creed is solidarity. I have never believed that the existence of many tribes, many parties, religious groups, economic differences, constitute a barrier to the construction of the Cameroon Nation. National unity is therefore our current essential objective, the mortgage to be pledged before we can consider ourselves worthy sons of Cameroon Nation. No obstacle or material, sentimental, or ideological interest will hold us back from creating this unity. My responsibility to all Cameroonian people is to lead to help build in this hour of trial a lasting unity, solidarity and development. Our unity must go beyond a political unity. What is required is a spiritual unity, a unity of minds, a unity that permeates our social fabric and stands above the tribal loyalties of the day.

On this occasion of the Fifth Anniversary of our Youth Day, My Fellow Cameroonians, I wish to be assured that in facing the difficult tasks ahead, I have always to rely on the cooperation, sacrifices, and enthusiasm of you all, and that all of us shall, in concert, transform our dreams of today into the realities of tomorrow, our ills of the past into the blessings of the future, and thus build for ourselves and for generations to come, a national vessel that will defy with impunity all weathering. Cameroonians, Cameroonians, let us take the plunge while the iron is hot and pull uniaxially our country to safety.

LONG LIVE WEST CAMEROON
LONG LIVE THE FEDERAL REPUBLIC

4.5: Address by the Prime Minister of West Cameroon, Hon. A.N Jua on the Occasion of 1ˢᵗ National Youth Day, Buea, 11 February 1967

Theme: "Youth and Awareness"
Members of the Diplomatic Corps,
Reverend Gentlemen,
Fellow Cameroonians,
Ladies and Gentlemen

Today is Youth Day. And we celebrate the sixth anniversary of the Plebiscite which gave birth to what is today the Federal Republic of Cameroon. For the first time, 11ᵗʰ February is being observed by our brothers and sisters of East Cameroon as a public holiday, in order words, Youth Day has, from now on, become an event of historic significance not only to the people of West Cameroon, but also to the people of the entire Federation. The occasion is a wider context, therefore, gives me an opportunity to extend my warmest greetings and hearty welcome to you all. Although this day is usually devoted primarily to watching the activities of school children, tradition demands that advantage should be taken of every such occasion to review the past, the present and future in all fields of national endeavour.

The most objective way to carry out this assessment is to examine how the country's young people fit its economic and social patterns. This is so, for it is customary in a review of this nature to think more of the future than of the past. Because of this eminent consideration, every truly democratic Government must allocate a very special place to its younger generation, where it can give them an account of its programmes. It is for this reason that this day has been set aside as Youth Day, during which the Government, gives its youth the assurance of a sound inheritance from which they can draw their inspiration.

When I spoke to you on this date last year, I emphasized the fact that economic progress is the continuous act of a people. I warned that our programme for social and economic development was an elastic one, demanding from each of us a contribution which is not very easy to make. I am not unaware of the hardship which hit the general public and business firms as a result of the harmonization of the Customs Tariff. As a first step towards finding a solution, a brief survey was carried out by the Ministry of Development and Internal Economic Planning, to determine and assess the effect of the new measures on the economic situation of West Cameroon. Following this, reliefs were recommended in favour of some commercial firms and is hoped that, as a result of the survey, certain measures which are likely to stimulate economic growth will be introduced in the next few months. The situation created by the harmonization of the Customs Tariffs has improved considerably and full benefits of the measures are beginning to be felt. Public corporations have continued to make appreciable contributions to the growth of the State.

Countrymen, even though ours has been, and will continue to be, a difficult task, we have nevertheless made considerable progress in many fields of our economic development. Let me deal with each aspect separately.

In education, our achievements have been substantial over the year. Primary and secondary school expansion has continued at the fairly fast pace, which enrolment at both levels has been very considerable; the pressures from the primary and secondary schools have not failed to make an impact on the teacher training colleges and the College of Arts, Science and Technology, in which enrolment rose by over 50%. Unlike in the past, the proportion of girls going to primary and post-primary institutions has improved and the average age of children entering all levels of education is decreasing. To keep pace with the expansion of primary and secondary education, teacher training has been intensified by the introduction of emergency training schemes in the Colleges of Arts and certain Teacher Training Colleges. During the year, salary increases were awarded to all teachers and, in spite of a strenuous effort by the Government to absorb all the costs without raising fees, it was found necessary to introduce slight charges and reduce certain allowances in order to balance the enormous budget for education.

This brief outline of educational achievements reveals a certain pattern which will have important social repercussions in the future. Only a certain proportion of our children can be educated for the middle-level and higher level manpower needs of the society. As far as the majority is concerned, the great social and economic problem of our time is how to harness the literate youth to the demands and needs of the nation. Certainly, the introduction of vocational education and the reorientation of our educational system to the challenges facing us are absolute imperatives. Yet the problem is not simply one of education.

I must emphasize that Cameroon is principally an agricultural county; her economic growth must depend on the ability to organize and execute our agricultural programmes. Traditional farming methods must give way to scientific methods; traditional thinking about the place of women in society and economy must change. In fact, the traditional pattern of social life should ultimately evolve into a pattern where the husband is the farmer and his wife is the housewife.

Our task, therefore, is to use the literate manpower produced by the educational institutions to exploit the natural resources around us. To do this, we must provide agricultural and trade skills to school leavers. It is gratifying to mention here that my Government has already gone a long way in this direction. The Ministry of Agriculture operates an Agricultural Youth Programme by which advice is constantly given to young men and women, through advertisements and discussions, on the benefits of an agricultural career. Experts have produced figures which prove to young people that much less capital expenditure is required to begin a food production farm than for most other form of paying concerns. These figures show how farmer's income increases steadily each year and also prove, beyond doubt, that the young farmer, after a few years, is much better off than his educational counterpart in the Civil Service. Apart from encouraging schools to open up school farms and organizing school leavers into Young Farmers's Clubs all over the State, the Government established the Obang Farm Institute at Mamfe to train young people in modern farming techniques. The first set of students passed out of the Institute recently and are now settling down to organize their own farms in their own areas. These young men continue to benefit from the free technical advice of Government experts on the best ways of increasing their production and income.

In the Grassland area, work is in progress on the construction of a new Agricultural School at Wum; the Cameroon Government is being assisted in the realization of this project by the West German Government. When completed, the Wum Agricultural School will provide farmers in up-to-date farming methods in all aspects of agriculture. In order to improve the quantity and quality of production, as well as force down the cost of living, Government has launched a "crash" Food Programme for which the Federal Government made available 60 million francs which is being used to subsidize the high cost of experiments, additional staff, expert advice, advertisements and the production of seeds and seedlings for the benefit of farmers.

The co-operative Movement has continued to play a leading role in the co-ordination of the activities and efforts of the primary producers in the production and marketing of export crops such as coffee, bananas, palm kernels and cocoa. Government assists the Movement, through the Marketing Board, by providing funds for the purchase of export produce. Through the assistance of the European Development Fund, plans are afoot to install four modern Coffee Factories in West Cameroon for the benefit of the Cooperative Movement. As with the Agricultural Department the Co-operative Department has intensified its efforts to educate primary producers on the advantages of co-operation, whether it is for export or for locally consumable products. I hope that, in the coming year, a start will be made with vocational education schemes to train school leavers as carpenters, and brick layers, are contemplated. Towards this end, the programme developed to the training of women in rural areas is making a significant impact; its link with the Local Government Improvement Demonstrators is a valuable one and ensures co-operation at all levels.

In Social Welfare, the attention of my Government is being directed to those persons to whom fate has dealt a cruel blow, namely, the blind, the deaf and the crippled. Plans are afoot to start a Farm-Craft Training Centre for the blind, to provide wheelchairs for the cripple and hearing aids for the deaf.

The Council of Women's Institutes has remained a powerful social force which continues to play an important role in our society. Youth and sporting organizations, clubs and societies are on the increase, while standards of performance in sports are rising. For the first time, traditional dances will be performed by our youth on this occasion. We shall be able to judge whether they have retained or discarded the traditions of their culture in this respect. We must also not forget that what is truly Cameroonian is what distinguishes us from other nations; if we scorn our culture, we scorn ourselves. Let this demonstration of traditional dancing by the youths instil in us love of traditional history so that, whilst embracing the science and technology of the human race, we may truly enjoy that which is unique in ourselves.

With what I have said so far about education and agriculture, you will agree that given the WILL and the DETERMINATION, the fears often expressed about unemployment have no basis. With the abundance of fertile land, is it not a futile and meaningless argument to say there is no work? Energy harnessed and carefully directed creates initiative and resourcefulness and it is in this sphere that the willing hand finds something always to do. Where there is a will, there is a way!

The once unattractive Local Government Service now offers very attractive employment opportunities for educated people at all levels. Conditions of service have been harmonized with those applicable to Civil Service. In this way, it is now possible for graduates and other well educated persons to take up rewarding careers in Local Government. Recent reforms and organization of the Local Government machinery have abolished the two-tier system by the new system, the new councils are in a better position to mobilize the resources of their areas to the best interest of their communities.

Our prisons system is becoming more and more reformative and less punitive as the time goes on. Prisoners are taught various trades aimed at making them more useful citizens on discharge. In the near future, short-term prisoners will be taught farming skills on prison farms to be established at Bavenga, Kumba, Mamfe, and Bamenda. Arrangements are well in hand for the establishment of prisons at Wum and Nkambe.

In the field of transport and communications, the pressures of finance have rendered the pace of development rather slow. These pressures, coupled with rising costs, demand careful planning to avoid waste of money and human effort. With the aid of friendly nations and international monetary organizations, preparatory work has been completed on the construction of Bolifamba-Kumba, Kumba-Mamfe, Mamfe-Bamenda and Bamenda-Mbounda roads. It is hoped that, at the rate negotiations are progressing, actual construction will commence in the very near future. The construction of the Tiko-Douala road is already at the advanced stage and it is hoped that perhaps by the end of this year a first class piece of road will emerge to provide what, in practical term, may well be termed "UNIFICATION ROAD".

In spite of the financial difficulties mentioned, Government has continued to vote substantial sums of money as community development grants for the provision and improvement of transport and communications in rural areas. These grants, together with the Local Government Roads Maintenance Service, have greatly improved the lot of the rural population by providing reasonably good roads for easy movement of persons and evacuation of foodstuffs and cash crops to the urban areas. The penetration of remote and difficult areas – such as Mamfe Overside, Esimbi, Ngolo Batanga, Fungom and Bangwa Mundani is to be taken up very seriously this year.

Fellow Cameroonians, from what I have said so far, you will agree that we have like any other body politic, and our own problems in the various fields of human activity; the realization of the achievements which I have just recounted was due principally to a consciousness among us that we are one – brothers and sisters.

47

This consciousness, which formed the very basis of our reunification six years ago, materialized last year with the formation the national party – the Cameroon National Union – the foundation of which was laid the leaders of all political parties without coercion.

The advantages of national unity are numerous and are already showing themselves to the population in many ways. The organization of the new party may be slow, but we are sure that the right material is being used to provide it with a concrete foundation. Anything worth doing is worth doing well. It is in the light of this that the life of the West Cameroon Legislature has been slightly extended. I wish to assure you that the House will be dissolved as soon as the organization of the new Party in West Cameroon is completed.

Dear Cameroonians, if our political unity is to be meaningful, it must be reflected by our way of thinking, our love for one another, our readiness to compete freely with our neighbours in our continuous task of economic development. We must eschew hatred and rancour against ourselves in all forms. In brief, if we are to reap the maximum benefits accruing to us from political unity, we must learn to keep our instincts, impulses and passions under control. Cameroonians should realize that they are the children of the same parents; that they are entitled to live their lives in peace and brotherliness and that they have on inalienable right to the ownership of property wherever they live or work in Cameroon.

I cannot end this address without saying a word about the Civil Service. At the time of independence, West Cameroon Civil Servants demonstrated courage and maturity when responsibility was thrust upon them, but the emergency period is now over and they must not sit back and be content to rest on their laurels. As a developing country, the need to rapidly transform our political, economic, and social systems create inevitable administrative complications and complexities which require people of right calibre in the Civil Service. Much more is now expected of civil servants at this stage of the country's development – integrity, a high sense of devotion to duty and honesty.

With the security of their employment fully guaranteed, Civil Servants ought to express their official views on all matters referred to them with honesty and sincerity, without fear or favour. It is not my intention to pass judgment here, but I should like to make it quite clear that it amounts to official corruption for a Civil Servant, whose decisions and advice mean so much to the nation, to say YES when he or she is fully aware that the right answer is NO. Qualifications and efficiency are not synonymous, unless the former is backed by application. Unless the right persons are in the right places, the execution of the National Plan will not be easy to achieve. There is no room in the Civil Service for adventurers.

I should like to avail myself of the opportunity offered by the occasion to express, on behalf of myself and my Government our appreciation for the services rendered to the Federation and West Cameroon in particular, by the forces of law and order – the Army, Gendarmerie and the Police. I pray that the co-operation existing among the various forces of law and order will remain forever, so that they may truly fulfil their functions as the watchdogs of the State.

I wish also to take this opportunity to express my thanks to all foreign governments and missionary bodies who have, directly or indirectly, rendered assistance towards the partial realization of the economic programmes and projects I have already mentioned. The execution of the Second Five Year Development Plan has just begun and we hope that they will not fail to make their contribution.

Ladies and Gentlemen, the day's programme is crowded and I can see the children itching to play. Please have a good time.

LONG LIVE THE FEDERAL REPUBLIC OF CAMEROON!

4.6: Address by the President of the Republic, Ahmadou Ahidjo on the Occasion of the 1ˢᵗ National Youth Day, Buea, 11 February 1967

Theme: "Youth and Awareness".
Boys and Girls of this Country,
My young countrymen,
Here comes this day of 11 February that we have dedicated every year to the Cameroonian Youth. Far as I am, I did not want to fail in my duty to be at the in heart and spirit with you and to address you as it should be and as I find great pleasure to wish you a good and happy feast day.

My wishes go to each and every one of you. They also go to every locality, and every village, for we ardently want that this day be celebrated all over the territory of our federal republic and that it should really be the day for all our Youths.

Can you, dear children, through this dynamic manifestation of this day, therefore give the adults, your parents and elders, everyone of them, to understand the exigencies of your existence and their duty to prepare you for a better future.

For the public authorities and the government, and even the party, we have said the priority accorded to our youths, the Cameroon of tomorrow. At every one of our congresses, from our study days in our plans, we have never missed any opportunity to reiterate that you are our hope and the pains that we take to ensure your opportunity in life or in other terms to prepare your happy accession to the stage of been able to manage in your turn our dear fatherland with honour, in happiness and in its splendour.

That is why I want that 11 February of this year be a thinking day for the Youths, of their existence in the Nation, of their role and their duties. True, you are at an age where your main vocation is first of all only to develop your body and your spirit. You must develop yourself, become powerful, study, educate yourself, and seek all type of knowledge, books, academic, professional, sportive, religious; nothing is too much, except evidently evil. For you have before you a brilliant future and an enviable role in the Africa of tomorrow.

All our brothers of the continent, from north to south have an eye on what is happening here, which is unique and exalting at the same time. We mean African unity. It does not fall like manna from heaven. It needs people to build it. You will be these builders. Men and women of a new world with a conscience at the dimension of Africa, of its diversity, its races, its languages, its religions, its different levels of development. We need open-minded men, with large horizons, and aspirations! Yes, you will be that Africa, predestined and envied in history. But you can only be if you start by making our Federal Cameroon succeed. In the same way as one cannot love the family if he does not love the mother and the father, you should first of all passionately love Cameroon to transcend to Africa. Cameroon already offers in this composition that is loved by nature to gather in one territory all the aspects of the experience which history reserves for you, an ideal field to build the great realizations of tomorrow.

Your duty is therefore to consider your future role, its importance, and its stakes. It is not only when one is grown up that one can serve his country! Responsibility starts at the age of reasoning. This means that at school, everyone of you should see in his colleague, his brother. Are you not after all at the age where in our national anthem you should be all love to one another, but also all love for others?

Many of you do not even know their tribes! I hope you should remember that you belong to only one: the Cameroonian tribe!

But we do not address ourselves only to the youths at schools. There is an equally important number, who for various reasons live in the Republic, available, that is having left school or having been to school but who have never been employed. To these, I say that there is no small job, that the Republic is big, that on the contrary, it is not to do that is lacking, it is often the will to do something. You must be committed. Commitment means assigning yourself to one goal, become useful to yourself and to others. For its part, the government has already undertaken some realizations and projects for initiation of the Youths to the job market. It intends to continue in this direction and expand, as far as its means permits to the whole nation. It knows very well how much needs to be done in spite of its good will and its desire to do more. At least, it is time for everyone, including the Youths to understand that everything cannot come from public initiative. The time of maturity has succeeded that of the welfare state, thus the time for individual work, including the youths. And that is the way it is all over the world.

The Youth of Cameroon, on this day of your feast, is it not perhaps the day to tell you the hard truths. I want that it becomes the opportunity for an awareness of your beautiful destiny; but also of the sacrifices of a road, rough from the outset, glorified and splendid at the end. I know you are worthy of this country. I know you are apt to learn and apt also to suffer if the country and its interests so want. Rejoice in the destiny that the future reserves for you. Prepare yourselves for it! Cameroon calls on you. In its name, I tell you its confidence and its hope! I know that you will seize this opportunity.

Long live the Republic,
Long live Cameroon.

5

President Ahidjo's National Youth Day Messages: 1968-1982

5.1: Address by President of the Republic to the Youths of Cameroon on the Occasion of the 3rd National Youth Day, Yaounde, 10 February 1968

Theme: "Youth and Responsibility"

Boys and Girls of Cameroon,

My young fellow citizens,

It is my great pleasure to express to you the heartfelt wishes of the Nation on the occasion of this Youth Day which is your own festival.

This does not mean simply expressing the joy and pride that all Cameroonian fathers and mothers feel in having brought into the world a healthy, a strong and dynamic youth.

It means above all living together in periodic communion and reflection on our mutual responsibilities in this great adventure that we are living and which is called national construction.

Building a Nation means transforming mentalities, overcoming inertia, opening hearts and minds to this dynamic solidarity and this awareness of a common destiny without which the Nation could not fulfil its mission of emancipating individuals and collective civilization.

Building a Nations means also marshalling all available resources and energies to edify a society that offers to each and all the minimum conditions for existence compatible with human dignity.

This is to say that, in the long run, the success of national construction, whilst it implies a strict planning of resources and efforts, depends above all on our desire for progress, our capacity to place ourselves in the service of the community, in a word our faculty for enthusiasm and devotion to duty.

And who better than the youth who contemplate the world with new eyes and a mind that is receptive to the solicitation of change, who better, I say, than youth whose will for progress is not yet curbed by the crippling burden of prejudice, is capable of this enthusiasm, this devotion, this faith that is essential to the success of great design?

Young citizens of Cameroon, when we tell you, as we have repeatedly done in the past, that you are the Nation's future, that we place our hopes in you, it is precisely because we want you to become conscious of your special responsibilities towards the Nation.

You are young, this means that, departing from the context of regional particularism, you must be the incompressible leaven of National Unity.

You are young, this also means that, having the opportunity to benefit from modern knowledge, you must be the spear-head of the country's progress.

You are young, this again means that you must, in town or country, place in the Nation's service that capital of drive and enthusiasm which is a property of youth.

You are young, this means finally that the future of the Nation will be in your image, that tomorrow will be made of the stuff you have woven today, that the seeds of the present are unfailingly preparing the harvest to come.

This is a particularly heavy responsibility to burden your young shoulders. Through the accidents of history, you have been born in a country that has need of you to fulfil itself. This situation has created for you constraints and obligations at an age when one is generally unrestricted and care-free. But what an opportunity this is to dedicate yourselves to a great cause, to feel that you are useful.

Serve your country, therefore, with serious intent and discipline! Deploy your enthusiasm and devotion in all the battles that are preparing the Nation's future, which is above all your future! In this way, and this way only, will you raise yourselves to the dignity of men, of free and responsible men who are masters of their own destiny.

It is our duty to prepare you to assume your responsibilities as men. The constant development of general and technical education in our country, the creation of the University, the extension of youth centres, pioneer villages and cultural centres as well as the development of sports facilities and the promotion of youth movements, bear witness to the government's determination not to fail in its highest mission, that of training today the men and women who tomorrow will take over and continue, with the greatest chance of success, the work begun under often difficult conditions.

It would be a serious mistake, however, to think this task of training is the responsibility of the State alone. Man's education is not confined only to the institutions which I have just mentioned. It begins within the family and it cannot be complete without the constant participation of this basic cell of the nation.

That is why it is of the utmost importance that parents become more and more aware of their duty in this respect. Too many parents, indeed, tend to think that their responsibility lies only in sending the child to school, giving him the opportunity to receive instruction which will pave the way to his social advancement. They forget that instruction is only one aspect of man's education. It is said with good reason that "learning without conscience only destroys the soul". A man's worth is not only measured by the sum of his acquired knowledge, but also by his moral qualities. Moral education is essential to man's equilibrium as it is to that of the nation. It is up to the parents, within the context of this school of life, the family, to see to the moral upbringing of their children, to shape their conscience, to instil in them the cardinal virtues of the sense of duty, honesty, honour, responsibility, discipline, love for one's neighbour and loyalty, without which they cannot fully become men.

I have said on many occasions that men are a Nation's most precious asset. But they are this only if they combine with their competence a moral worth which allows them to overcome their egoism, to raise themselves to the level of the general interest, if they have enough faith and self-denial to make their Country's destiny their own.

I am firmly convinced that by our joint efforts we shall be able to make of Cameroon's youth the men called for by the Nation's destiny. To all the young people of Cameroon, I repeat my assurance that the Government will leave no stone unturned to fulfil this fundamental need.

Long live Cameroon.

5.2: Address by the President of the Republic to the Youths of Cameroon on the Occasion of the 4ᵗʰ National Youth Day, Yaounde, 10 February 1969

Theme: "The Youth, Seeds and Actors for National Unity"

Boys and Girls of Cameroon,

My dear young fellow citizens,

This year again, I am faithfully keeping our appointment of the 11ᵗʰ February, the appointment of Youth Day, your own Day, that I may bring you, as in the years past, the most heartfelt wishes of the nation.

This faithfulness, were it still necessary, bears witness to our affection, to the special interest we take in your material and spiritual well-being, and to the privileged place which henceforth is yours within the Cameroonian Nation.

This affection, this interest and this place are rightful ones for, it must be repeatedly reminded, on your young shoulders rests the hope of the entire Nation. It must be repeatedly reminded for it matters to the Nation's future that you should be fully aware of your responsibilities and of the special position that is yours in a world in full process of change.

The advances of science and technology, and in particular the prodigious development of communication and information media, are narrowing more and more the dimensions of the world in which we live. This phenomenon has the advantage of bringing out mankind's profound solidarity and its common destiny in the universe. It also carries a threat against our personality, by which I mean against the original character of underprivileged peoples who thus find themselves unarmed in the presence of external influences which often are not in keeping either with their own situation or with their moral or cultural aspirations.

This threat, however insidious, is nonetheless a fact noticeable everyday in many African countries – to mention only our continent – especially among young people whose very youth and accessibility render them particularly vulnerable. It finds reflection in mimicry in dress fashions, in dubious taste for a kind of music of which the least that can be said is that it is far from making for gentler manners as a well-known saying has it, in a disrespectful behaviour towards their elders and imitation, here and there, of that spirit of protest which is by the way of becoming an epidemic in university institutions.

Such attitudes may have a significance in highly developed societies. They no doubt aim at drawing attention to the moral crisis of a youth which finds itself cramped for room within structures functioning without it and more concerned with technical perfection than human problems; to a youth which desperately seeks to place its intelligence, its enthusiasm and its dynamism in the service of a society often too old and too satisfied to fully understand its hunger for participation and responsibility.

What resemblance is there between that embittered youth seeking a place in the sun and the fine and vigorous youth of our countries, no doubt underdeveloped, but engaged in the most exciting of adventures, that which offers the highest satisfactions and the most favourable opportunities for self-realisation in the fullness of a life in the service of the nation?

National construction, in fact, is in itself the most radical protest there is: at home, a protest against mental attitudes and social structures maladjusted to progress; abroad, a protest against age-old prejudices and the inferior position that the world intended to reserve for Africa.

In the presence of this gigantic and revolutionary task, what is needed is participation and responsibility, as we are repeating increasingly. Responsibility and participation of the whole people and of every citizen conscious of the fact that the nation's destiny rests on our faith in the future and on our own efforts in discipline and unity. But, above all, responsibility and participation of youth which, by its ability to place itself in the service of great causes, is the leaven of the future and our most sacred hope.

The youth of Cameroon has the outstanding privilege of not having to find its own place in our society. In this society, everything, to be sure, has got to be created, but everything is already being created for our youth and by our youth within a dialogue that is free but wishes to be well-ordered and respectful of authority. That is why we must sternly condemn any slavish imitation of foreign fashions which, being out of tune with our own situation, cannot but lead our youth astray from its duty and so interfere with our will to progress.

That is also why it is necessary to remind all those persons, whether Cameroonians by birth or by choice, who have the delicate mission of educating our youth, that their role towards our youth is not to act like outposts of other societies, however admirable and exemplary, but to equip our youth both intellectually and morally for its historic responsibilities.

For indeed the problem of our youth is none other than a problem of education, of a judicious education so oriented as to make it more easily adjustable to demands of national construction. As you know, this problem is, within the limits of available resources, one of the main concerns of the Government and Party, as is eloquently shown by the development of primary, secondary, technical, and agricultural education and of university and other advanced types of education.

Our aim is to prepare our youth for its future tasks to increase the effectiveness of its immediate and future action for development, to meet better and better the Nation's needs both in the public and private sectors, both in the towns and the countryside. I insist on the word "countryside", for there is no doubt that to a keen and well-equipped youth, agriculture, which remains the basis of our economy and will so remain for a long time yet, offers great opportunities for social promotion.

That is why the Government and the party regard the drift from the countryside, which deprives our villages of the beautiful dynamism of its youth, its spirit of enterprises and desire for progress, as a scourge which must be halted before it becomes a brake upon our national drive for development. That is also why a more efficacious planning of education has become imperative.

Contrary to what is generally believed, educational planning does not aim at constraining the spirit of liberty which is the basis and ferment of any education worthy of the name. Its ambition – the legitimacy of which seems to be self-evident, is to help in adapting it to the needs of society and the exigencies of progress.

In point of fact, everyone today agrees, as the Director General of UNESCO recently said, that education is one of the most essential, if not the most essential, of pre-investments since the exploitation of natural resources is subordinate, as experience has shown, to the development of human resources. So important is this investment which accounts for a respectable part of the national income that its profit-earning capacity must be controlled and a satisfactory out-turn must be provided at all times by this educational enterprise. But such a result can only be achieved if this rapidly expanding enterprise is managed by appropriate methods, including a mechanism to provide estimates and co-ordination, in other words, only if it is subject to planning, within the framework of the general planning of the Nation's development. In this field, as in others, just as strict as too strict a control will be dangerous, so a policy of laisser-faire will be inconceivable.

Whilst, as I have said, the fundamental aim of education, must be to prepare young people for their present and future responsibilities, it is nonetheless true that they must not remain oblivious of the contribution they can make to the consolidation of national unity. The latter is in fact, nothing else, in the final analysis, but the acquisition of a common social culture, a common mentality, and a common language in spite of the material differences. And this patrimony which is common to all the community can only be the result of education, the basis of which is the same to all the citizens. The progress achieved by education satisfies in this way not only an economic need and a desire for social justice but also the necessity to instil a new spirit of patriotism in a country that is still hide-bound with particularism.

However, if education is to play the dual role effectively, it must further be adapted to the living realities of the Nation and the culture which nourishes it must be authentic, that is to say, rooted in the living springs of popular life, in those negro-African values which vitalize and impart a meaning to its existence.

This means that the rediscovery of our traditional cultures has now become an imperative necessity. It also means that a stirring mission beckons to our youth. A people's culture is the ear-mark of its personality, its identity card in the forum of nations. Let us miss no opportunity than to proclaim our culture in all its force and richness. At the World Festival of Negro Art in Dakar, Cameroon obtained a well-deserved success. The Pan-African Cultural Festival instituted by the Organization of African Unity, the first of which will shortly be held in Algiers must also be for us the occasion for an even more glittering triumph.

My dear young citizens, I must however say a word about the very special nature of the Algiers Festival. Dakar was a world-wide event. That of Algiers will be Pan-African. For the first time on African soil, African unity will be the subject, not only of charters and resolutions, but of a triumphal celebration with the participation en masse of the African people themselves. Yes!, at Algiers, we are going to sing and dance, and celebrate with the thousand voices of every African instrument the unity of Africa so painfully born in the cradle of our independence.

Cameroon, this Africa in miniature, this land of dialogue, of meeting and union, is also by nature and by vocation the cultural synthesis of our continent. The call from Algiers is therefore like an inescapable summons for Cameroon. The answer that our county must give to this call – for it will be the overwhelming voice of Cameroon in all its unity and diversity – must be worthy in its amplitude of the significant page of history that Africa is living.

I therefore invite the entire Cameroon people to prepare for the Algiers Festival as they would for an occasion of national importance.

I address a special invitation to the Youth of Cameroon who will certainly find in this effort to rediscover our cultural heritage a source of enrichment and nourishment for its pride and need for authenticity, the strength to resist the hollow attractions of a wanton and sterile agitation and the force to continue to work with devotion, enthusiasm and discipline for national progress. In this way, Cameroon will continue to proclaim its maturity and national vocation to the world and will always be deserving of the select place which is hers in Africa.

LONG LIVE THE YOUTH OF CAMEROON
LONG LIVE CAMEROON

5.3: Address by the President of the Republic to the Youths of Cameroon on the Occasion of the 5th Youth Day, Yaounde, 10 February 1970

Theme: "Responsibility and Participation in the Face of the Requirement of Nation-building"

Boys and Girls of Cameroon
Dear Young Compatriots,

It gives me special pleasure on the eve of the new decade which we are starting as an independent people, to take the opportunity offered me by the Youth Day to convey to you, as in previous years, but this time in quite a different way, my personal wishes and those of the entire nation.

A month ago we celebrated with solemnity, enthusiasm, and pride the tenth anniversary of Cameroon in the presence of numerous friends and representatives from all the continents.

For us it was a milestone in the long journey towards progress upon which we have been engaged for a decade and an occasion to measure the road covered during the first ten years of national independence.

I think we have honourably passed this kind of test which we set for ourselves under the eyes of international observers.

The various manifestations organized to mark the tenth anniversary celebrations will have enabled the world – and also many Cameroonians without doubt – to take an objective look at the progress accomplished by our country in spite of initial difficulties.

Through the march past, it will have been obvious that here was a nation concerned with order and stability, anxious to ensure its own security: a people in their diversity, profoundly united within the CNU, and spurred by the same ideal for progress, by the same attachment to the fatherland and by the same confidence in the future.

The national fair on its part, has been a manifestation of the many successes obtained in the field of economic and social development, with special emphasis, as it ought to be, on the rapid development of our agriculture within the variety of its resources and on the great vitality of our young industry which has the best prospects.

This same impression of vitality was evident in the cultural manifestations the importance of which we continue to stress in the shaping of national consciousness: the vitality of a people asserting its personality more and more in a great effort of modernization and faithful to its most authentic traditions.

On the whole, the manifestation of the tenth anniversary confirmed that Cameroon is a country that is stable undergoing full development and which is already in the vanguard of those African countries seriously pursuing their development and having the best potentials for a rapid take-off.

As I said in my last message to the nation, we have throughout the past ten years been constantly anxious in our desire for social justice, to ensure that the progress achieved through the collective effort of all Cameroonians should serve equitably in the advancement of all the regions of the country and of all categories of the Nation's people.

There is no doubt that the youths have always been at the centre of this anxiety and that their well-being in the present and their development in the future have always constituted one of our major preoccupations - notwithstanding the numerous problems experienced in general by young states acceding to independence and those experienced by our country in particular – as shown beyond doubt by the important resources devoted to education and training in all fields and at all levels as well as to cultural, civic and sports activities.

It is not saying little to stress that our country, with 70% of its children attending school, at the end of the first decade of independence, is one of the countries on the continent with the greatest number of children going to school and one of those that have the largest number of highly trained national cadres.

You are aware of the tremendous confidence which I have always placed in our Youth, by facilitating in every way possible, their harmonious integration into the national, public and private life and the by enabling them, whenever they deserved it through their competence and their conscientiousness, to assume the highest responsibilities in the state.

I must admit that the confidence has not been abused. In most cases indeed, the Cameroon Youth has proved to be serious, shown a high sense of duty and efficiency, qualities which fully justify the hopes which we continue to place in it and which augur well for the future of the Nation.

Who possesses You possesses the future is a popular saying. No doubt this saying is just true today as it was yesterday. The population explosion which humanity is experiencing has however, at different degrees modified the youth situation in the world. I have already pointed out that, with regard to Cameroon, the number of young people below 20 years of age has reached the three million mark. That is to say that youth represents more than half of the population of the country. This is also equivalent to saying that it is no longer the future of the Nation only, but that it is already the Nation in the present.

Finally and especially, this means that the next decade even more than the one that has just ended, will consequently be the decade of Youth. It will be because increased efforts will be made to better prepare it for the tasks that await it. It will be because it is the nature of things that greater and greater responsibilities be entrusted to it in all the sectors and at all levels of National life.

This is in the nature of things, I repeat because Youth is already in the present. But this is also in the interest of the entire nation. Indeed we are living in a period of profound changes and acceleration in history. The new problems facing man today can no longer be solved through the experience of the past only. Henceforth these solutions can only be found through the greater use of new scientific and technical knowledge and through a capacity for adaptation, which Youth because it is uncommitted and receptive will alone possess more and more in the modern world.

It goes without saying that this does not at all mean that the older people no longer have a role to play in the Nation. Their experience will continue to be a reservoir of wisdom and a valuable factor in individual and collective balance. That is to say that the entire Nation must open itself to this process of rejuvenation unreservedly convinced that this corresponds to the profound requirements for its rapid and full development, certain that this constitutes a determining factor in a complex civilization undergoing a rapid process of transformation.

This being so, Boys and Girls of Cameroon,

Dear young compatriots, it is only natural that I should turn to you and emphasize once gain the heavy responsibility which is yours. The destiny of the Nation rests, and will continue to rest more and more on your shoulders. For our part, we are doing everything in our power, and as far as possible to make worthy men of you duly shaped to assume the tasks which will be yours in the society. It is your duty to prepare yourselves to take over with seriousness and application, in town as in the countryside, in the public sector as in the private sector, so that Cameroon may continue to occupy the position which is henceforth hers in Africa and the world.

In order to achieve this aim, you must remain realistic. The value of a man is not only assessed by the ease with which he handles general matters, but also and especially through a specialized field and the skill which he places at the service of the community, through his ability to understand the complexity of the problems of his time and to contribute in solving them. You must always remember what Manzoni said "There is no just superiority of a man over the other, except at their service". The social promotion which is bestowed upon you makes of you the first servants of the Nation.

It is through the clear understanding of the mission which is yours and the unbending will to fulfil this mission loyally that you will become fully accomplished while discharging the noble vocation assigned by history to the new Cameroon in a new Africa.

To conclude, how can we help recalling here what Emile Zola said to the Youth of his time?

"On youth! Think of the great task that awaits thee. Thou art the future workman, of this we are more than certain. We the elders are ready to remit into thy hands this Nation which represents the sufferings endured by thy fathers; terrible battles which they had to win; in fact, a passionate effort towards light; this Nation which thou must continue to build for thine honour and for thine happiness. We are only making you to be more generous, to transcend us by your love of life normally lived, by your effort which you entirely devote to work, this fecundity of men and of the earth which shall yield finally abundant harvest of joy under the bright sun. And we shall fraternally yield to you your place, happy to disappear and to rest from our share of the task well accomplished in the sweet steps of the earth if we are certain that you are carrying on with our work and that you will realize our dreams for us!

Long Live the Youth of Cameroon!
Long Live Cameroon!

5.4: Address by the President of the Republic to the Youths of Cameroon on the Occasion of the 6th National Youth Day, Yaounde, 10 February 1971

Theme: "Youth and Development"
Boys and Girls of Cameroon,
My dear young compatriots,
Once again the time has come round to this day, the 11th February, which we have dedicated to you and which, to mark our special interest, deep affection and hope, we have decided should be a festival for all the young people of Cameroon.

Wherever you may be at this moment – at school, in the factories, or in the fields, in town or country – be sure My Dear Young Compatriots, that my thoughts go out to you, who are the Nation's hope, to bring you on behalf of all the people of Cameroon, my best wishes for your health and happiness and to assure you once again of our determination to work untiringly to promote your full development in a Nation making constant progress in peace, justice and brotherhood.

In past years, I have addressed myself to youth in general, emphasizing what we expect of them in our struggle, at once difficult and exhilarating, to achieve national construction and the well-being of the Cameroon people.

On these occasions, I have often stressed the special responsibilities resting upon the young at school, the special duties that fall on this section of young people, who benefitting from the sacrifices of the whole Nation, find, in their school or vocational training centres, a privileged means of social advancement.

Today I address my message to the unoccupied youth, to you in the towns and villages who as luck will have it, have been obliged to leave school early or have not had the chance to go at all and who, ill-equipped to confront modern life, have not yet started work.

Today I feel I must address myself especially to you to let you know that you are not forgotten, and that, as much as if not more than other sections youth, your particular situation is a source of constant concern to me.

I also feel I should speak especially to you at a time when at the dawn of our country's second decade of independence, we are preparing to embark upon the Third Five-Year Development Plan of economic, social, and cultural development and when the Second National Council of the Cameroon National Union which has just ended has forcefully underlined the need to mobiles all national resources and energies in the interests of the Nation's rapid economic take-off and the well-being of all Cameroonians – the imperative need to make development the task of each and everyone a national task.

It is in the nature of things, my dear young compatriots, which in the towns, which are the result of our progress towards development, should attract large numbers of young people in search of better living conditions than those they find in the traditional environment.

Unhappily, every picture has its dark side. Although considerable progress has been made in all fields since independence, it is not yet sufficient, alas, to enable the administration, industry and commerce put together to provide full employment for the available labour force in the towns.

The unfortunate result of all this is that our youth, despite their intelligence, vigour and dynamism, live crowded together in insanitary districts in the towns, unemployed and exposed to the evils of alcoholism, juvenile delinquency, and dissolute living.

The state of affairs is injurious to the Nation in two ways. First, it constitutes an obvious danger to its moral health, sustaining as it does a harmful and contagious climate of idleness, immorality, and social parasites among the younger generation on whom, as I have said over and over again, the Nation's future depends.

And inasmuch as it is a result of the rural exodus, there is no doubt that this state of affairs acts as a brake on development. In leaving the rural districts, young people are in fact abandoning the countryside to older men, those who are less suited to the task of production and productivity without which there can be no economic growth and less prepared for change, innovation and new ways of thinking, without which development cannot assume its full social and human significance.

Needless to say, the Government has not remained indifferent to this double threat to its national construction effort. Cultural centres, youth clubs and sports facilities, soon to be completed by mini-sports stadium at Douala and Yaoundé, have been established with a view to encouraging the young to pursue healthy physical and intellectual activities and to providing the civic and moral education they need if they are to have a clearer understanding of the their responsibilities within the Nation.

But the chief problem remains that of finding work for the young unemployed so that they can improve their own living conditions while making the necessary contribution to national development. Notwithstanding the Government's policy, which is to create more and more jobs every year, we must not delude ourselves: at our present stage of development, finding work for young people means, in most cases, firmly asking them to return to working on the land.

Young people without work, particularly those living in the towns, must indeed convince themselves of the dignity of work on the land, which is the source of all wealth and civilization; they must convince themselves that agriculture, like the rest of the Nation's activities, when practiced with love, conscientiousness and efficiency can provide considerable personal satisfaction and just as sure a means of social advancement.

Of course, mere exhortations are not enough to instil these convictions, to halt the drifts to the towns and to start a significant movement back to the countryside. What is also needed is a policy which will provide young people in rural areas with the means of earning a good living and the amenities now essential to modern life.

The Government is continuing to implement the essential aspects of this policy; the YABASSI-BAFANG OPERATION, for example, is a demonstration of how large, uncultivated areas could be developed with the help of people coming from overpopulated districts whilst pioneer villages are introducing young people to agricultural work by showing the benefits they can derive from it.

Another aspect is the continuing improvement in the technical and scientific guidance staffing of farmers provided by engineers trained at the Advanced School of Agriculture and the trend towards the ruralisation of primary education so as to better equip young people in rural areas for the tasks ahead of them and render them more susceptible to innovation and progress.

And, lastly, an important drive has already been started to develop rural areas by piping water to large built-up areas, improving housing, developing rural medical facilities, strengthening administrative staffing and constructing more roads to facilitate contacts with urban areas. All these efforts are aimed at stepping up the process of urbanization of rural areas and the progressive fulfilment of the legitimate aspirations of all Cameroonians towards a decent standard of living.

This policy undoubtedly receives effective backing and new impetus in the development of agricultural credit which has been decided upon by the Government.

However, MY DEAR YOUNG COMPATRIOTS, the success of this policy which is so vital to the harmonious development of the nation, depends on you,

61

on the awareness you have of your own interests and the national interests, on your patriotism and sense of duty, and above all and else on your conviction that such a policy has only one aim – that of your well-being and social human advancement ; I a few words its success depends on your voluntary, whole-hearted and effective participation.

This is why the party must, in accordance with the recommendations of the recent National Council, mobilize itself for a campaign to explain our economic, social, and cultural development objectives and the responsibilities of every Cameroonian citizen in the realization of these aims.

I call upon the YCNU especially to take a resolutely active part in this campaign in conjunction with the party and the WCNU. It seems to me to be in the best position in point of fact to start an effective dialogue with the unemployed youth. It surely it because it shares the same idealism, the same desire to serve, the same will for progress devotion to the independence and greatness of the fatherland.

I also call upon the National Youth Service which must provide the young men and women of our country with the opportunity to undertake together – economic, social and cultural activities in a healthy climate of cooperation and mutual assistance.

The aim, when all is said and done, is to help young people with no education – those who left school too soon and those whose youth has been handicapped in any way – to organize themselves in order to produce goods or supply services, in short, to assume responsibility for their own destiny.

Yes, MY YOUNG AND DEAR COMPATRIOTS, that is the real secret of all true progress; to assume full responsibility for one's own destiny. A people not capable of accepting responsibility for one's own destiny is not worthy of being formed into a nation. And a Youth not capable of shouldering the responsibility for its own destiny can never be worthy of its fatherland. Knowing as I do the priorities of Cameroonian youth, its dynamism and its desire for progress, I am convinced that you will prove equal to history's challenge; that is to say, through the work of each and every one of us, through our dogged, unremitting efforts, achieve the great task of national construction and build in peace, justice and fellowship a united, strong and prosperous Nation, a Nation in the vanguard of the New Africa, effectively helping it to give the world the full benefit of the creative genius of the Negro-African peoples in the concerted construction of a universal civilization.

LONG LIVE CAMEROONIAN YOUTH
LONG LIVE CAMEROON

5.5: Address by the President of the Republic to the Youths of Cameroon on the Occasion of the 6th National Youth Day, Yaounde, 10 February 1972

Theme: "Youth Permanent Tool for Dialogue and Multiplying Factor"
Boys and Girls of Cameroon,

My Dear Young Cameroonians

In keeping our rendez-vous of 11 February, I am this year as in the past years on the eve of the sixth National Youth Day, the bearer of our heartfelt affection and confidence and of our earnest wishes for your health, happiness and prosperity.

In my message to you after the celebrations marking the tenth anniversary of national independence, I did particularly emphasize the prominent position which you will, henceforth, be occupying within the Cameroon Nation. I stressed, with all the emphasis it deserves, the fact that the Youth of Cameroon, forming as it does, more than half the country's population, has even now become the very Nation of Cameroon with whose concerns and aspirations it can be more and more closely indentified.

With this major fact in mind, I called on the Nation as a whole to awaken to the truth that the second decade of national independence, even more than the first, will be a decade of Youth. For our part, as the authorities responsible for the future of the Nation, we shall continue, as in the part to make untiring and ever-increasing efforts so that the needs of Cameroon's fine youth can be met more effectively.

The third Five Year Development Plan is a forceful expression of this determination. Intended to create the conditions necessary for the rapid economic take-off of the Nation, it urges the people of Cameroon on to greater effort towards progress in the economic, social and cultural fields. It goes without saying that Cameroonian youth with all our concern behind it, will in the future, just as it was in the past, be the principal beneficiary of such an effort. This is part of the realities of our nation; it is also in the interest of the Nation as a whole, of our Nation's future which we want to be more secure than ever in solidarity, unity, peace, and fraternity.

Thus, over the next five years our policy of industrialization will be progressing with the threefold aim of accelerating the growth and diversification process of the National economy, strengthening even more our sovereignty and offering still greater employment opportunities to youth.

Thus we shall also continue to develop at all levels, taking into account the actual needs of the Nation, the educational and vocational training institutions in order to train young people more effectively for the tasks awaiting them in the great struggle aimed at building the nation.

And lastly, the health and sports structures of the Nation will continue to be given all the attention they deserve. A healthy mind in a healthy body as the saying goes, and rightly so. The full use of one's mental faculties is in point of fact dependent on a healthy body. But a sound body is not only a body which is healthy and free from disease. It is also a vigorous, full-developed body, prepared by appropriate training to undertake all its functions with ease and thus to contribute to the development of the human being.

I shall not dwell, my young compatriots, any longer on the importance of practicing a sport for the development of the individual. I shall simply add that it was because of this that the Nation gladly agreed on the sacrifice required to give you two multi-sport stadiums in Douala and Yaoundé. On behalf of the nation, I offer to you these two fine architectural structures on the occasion of the sixth anniversary of the Youth Day, your day, with the hope that you will make the best possible use of them, both for yourselves and for the country. In fact, sport is not merely a way to physical development and the good functioning of the human body. By the manner in which it is practiced and which requires team work, endurance and loyalty, it is also a school which eventually, through solidarity and fraternity, regardless of any differences and through its essential moral qualities, will lead towards complete success in nation building.

Boys and Girls of Cameroon,

My Dear Young Compatriots,

I have said before that the youth, from now on, constitute the present-time Nation and that its anxieties and aspirations become increasingly identified with those of the nation as a whole. This means, obviously that national problems should henceforth, as we are wont to do, be examined and resolved in the light of this important factor. But this means above all that these problems, for which there are no miraculous solutions, cannot be successfully solved if there is no contribution on the part of the entire youth, prompted by a true desire for progress. This means in a word, that you, my dear young compatriots, should fully assume your responsibilities in the Nation if you want it to continue its forward march with full confidence in ultimate success.

You must first of all take your responsibilities by actively endeavouring to seek, in a spirit of constructive dialogue and of patriotism, those solutions that are called for by national problems and to implement them in thorough discipline and by conscientious unrelenting and efficient work.

You must also assume responsibilities in the fields of public morals. You must constantly fight against all the scourges that threaten the youth, fully aware that the building of the nation for which you will become increasingly responsible, can only be achieved in an atmosphere of absolute moral health, that is to say with respect for the laws and values which are essential for social peace, guarantee human dignity and make for genuine patriotism.

I am fully confidently in your victory – in our common victory – in this struggle which the Nation shares with you. I am confident because I am aware of your qualities of courage, devotion and loyalty and your deep attachment to the progress of the Cameroon fatherland. I am also confident because you live in an age when the young have more to offer than to receive. In fact, it is through you, who are as it were, the most sensitive and most open part of society, that society becomes aware of itself, of its weaknesses and needs.

All the active forces of the Nation will help you wage this decisive struggle. In particular, the various religious denominations to which our country offers a most favourable climate for their spiritual activities have a useful role to play in this field, a role which is vital for safeguarding the interest of the whole national community.

The most propitious framework enabling you to discharge your responsibilities in the building up of the Nation – responsibilities which are both civic and moral – is still our Great National Party within which the YCNU was specially entrusted with preparing you for your task. You are aware of the special interest I attach to the militancy of the Youth. In the near future, the structures and activities of the YCNU will be accorded a national standing so that it can carry out its mission with greater efficiency.

However, even now, I am happy to note that the party can boast the active membership of the great majority of Cameroonian Youth who realize full well that our Great National Party is the irreplaceable momentum behind the progress of the nation.

Sons and Daughters of Cameroon,

My dear young compatriots,

In point of fact, your responsibilities in the great struggle for national construction can be encompassed in one single responsibility: the building of a strong and prosperous Nation that might offer to all men and women of Cameroon the conditions for full development in peace, unity, and justice, in other words: the building of a new Cameroon. In the final analysis, it is this supreme responsibility which should consistently guide your ideas and actions. My wish, on the occasion of the sixth National Youth Day, is to see the Youth of Cameroon adopt the oath that young Athenians used to take: "We vow to leave our country better than we found it". There is truly no assignment or difficulty that could withstand either the passion for progress of the Youth or its faith in the future.

LONG LIVE THE YOUTHS OF CAMEROON!
LONG LIVE CAMEROON!

5.6: Address by H.E the Vice President of the Republic, Prime Minister of West Cameroon and Chief Scout of the Boy Scouts of Cameroon, 8 February 1972

The Hon. Minister of Youth and Sports,

Honourable Guests,

My Dear Brother Scouters and Sister Guiders

Ladies and Gentlemen,

I welcome you all to this social evening of the National Federation of Scouts and hope we shall enjoy ourselves. It is not customary that addresses are made at receptions. All the same, it does not appear inappropriate to say a word or two on the significance of the reception here tonight.

This reception is intended to highlight the ceremony of handing over certificates of recognition by the Boy Scouts World Bureau to our Cameroonian Scout

Movement, "The National Federation of Scouts" as the 99th member of the World Scouts Conference - a testimony that scouting in Cameroon today has achieved high international standards.

As you know our boys recently returned from Japan where they participated in two great world events, namely: the 13th Boy Scouts World Jamboree "For Understanding" and the 23rd World Scouts Conference.

The Scouts movement is now forty-eight years old in Cameroon; only two years for the movement to celebrate its golden jubilee.

Scouting was introduced into West Cameroon in 1924 and into East Cameroon in 1937. With the realization of reunification, our Scouts saw the need for great family. So on the 19th of July 1969, the various Scout Associations in the Country met together and gave birth to what we now call the "National Federation of Scouts".

Working then as a unit, the movement began to gain momentum and to make an impression on the Scouts world. In the same year (1969) the Boy Scouts world Bureau – Africa Region – invited our Scouts Leaders to participate in a West African Inter-state Woldbage Course in Dahomey; they even paid the fare for some of them. In 1970, the National Federation of Scouts applied for membership of the World Scouts Conference.

Following this application, the Boy Scouts World Bureau – Africa Region – ran a preliminary Wodbadge Course at Victoria to test the standard of scouting in this country. Our boys impressed the Boy Scouts World Bureau, and the Africa Scouts Committee favourably recommended the Cameroon application to the World Scout Committee. This Committee conveyed its approval on the 26th of March 1971 and the same at the same time communicated this good news to all the 98th member-countries of the world scout conference. Our Scout Movement had become of age!

As a result of the this approval the Chief Scout of Cameroon was officially invited by the Headquarters of the World Brotherhood Movement in Geneva to the 23rd World Scouts Conference holding in Tokyo, Japan in August 1971, to receive the certificate of recognition of the Boy Scouts of Cameroon our National Delegation was composed of the Chief Scout, the Honourable Minister of Youth and Sports, the President and Assistant Secretary-General of the Scouts Federation.

Animated by the news of our recognition, our Head of State and National Patron of the movement, His Excellency EL. Ahmadou Ahidjo, graciously honoured members of the World Scout Committee. The Honours were conferred upon the beneficiaries by me on behalf of the President. This was during a reception accorded by our Government after the presentation ceremony in Tokyo. Among the personalities decorated were:

- Lady Olave Baden-Powell, 1st Honorary Vice-President of the World Brotherhood of Scouts and World Chief Guide – decorated in abstentia,
- Mr. William D. Campbell, 2nd Honorary Vice-President of the Movement;
- Mr. Charles D. Green, retiring Chairman of the World Scout Committee;
- Honourable Emmett Harmon, Chairman of the African Scout Committee and member of the world committee.

Our boys were also invited to the 13th Boy Scouts World Jamboree in Japan in August 1971. I am sure you will be pleased to learn, Ladies and Gentlemen, that the Boy Scouts of Japan paid their fare from Lagos to Japan and back to Lagos. On Government took care of their upkeep during their stay out of the country and their transport fare between Cameroon and Lagos, Nigeria. Our Jamboree Contingent was six strong. The boys ably projected our country abroad.

But what does all this means? Or, in other words, what is the meaning of scouting? Ladies and Gentlemen, Scouting is a movement which aims at developing the young into self-discipline citizens, with sterling qualities of character to make them patriots of their country in particular and the world in general. It is a movement of national, international and universal character, the object of which is also to endow each separate nation and the whole world with a youth which is physically, morally, and spiritually strong; it is national in that it aims, through national organizations, at endowing every nation with useful and healthy citizens; it is international in that it recognizes no national barriers in the comradeship of the Scouts; it is universal in that it insists upon universal fraternity between all scouts of every nation irrespective of class or creed. The Scout movement has no tendency to weaken but, on the contrary, to strengthen individual religious belief. The Scout Law requires that a Scout shall truly and sincerely practice his religion, and the policy of the movement forbids any kind of sectarian propaganda at mixed gatherings.

The youth of today are the leaders of tomorrow – our Head of State has said this again and again – and it is our duty to prepare them for adulthood, or the day when they will be responsible for steering the ship of the destiny of our fatherland. Let me remind you of what His Excellency the President and Patron of the Boy Scouts of Cameroon said during his inaugural ceremony of the launching of the 11th February Youth Day in this country. In 1967, because of his personal commitment to the cause of the youths, His Excellency addressed a far-reaching message to the youths and the population as a whole. He made it quite clear that, as far the public authorities in Cameroon are concerned, the youth and the Cameroon of tomorrow have a pride of place. My dear fellow citizen, listen to what the President said:

"At each of our party congresses, at every study sessions, and in our national plan, we have never failed to declare, on every possible occasion, that you – the youth - represent our hopes, and that it is our concern to make sure you have a chance in life. We have never, in other words, missed an opportunity to prepare you for adulthood, to prepare you for the day when you yourselves will be responsible for the fortunes of our dear country, honourably, in its prosperity and resplendence … You are men and women of a new world, he declared, conscious of Africa's dimensions, its diversity, its many races, languages and religions, and its varying degree of development. Men with breadth and vision, limitless horizons and noble aspirations".

We have a Scouts movement of which we are very proud and to which we can as responsible citizens make a contribution. We do not need to be trained Scouts to make that contribution. We have amongst us many people with special skills and expert knowledge in various fields of specialization who can pass on a little of their knowledge to the Boy Scouts and Girl Guides. For instance, as a forester you can assist as an instructor in the conservation of nature; as a medical person you can assist in teaching of First Aid. Of course there are other ways and means of contributing – financially and so on. I want to assure you that whatever support you can lend will be most welcome by the Scout Movement.

When our boys were to proceed to Tokyo for the Jamboree, companies such as Bata Shoe Company, Brasseries du Cameroun, Air Afrique, and a few others provided encouraging financial assistance. If the Scout and Gide Movements in our country are to achieve their aims and objectives and to meet world standards, we would require the assistance of the Cameroonian public as a whole financially and materially.

The Government is already doing its bit. The Movement receives annual subventions and other assistance in the way of transport for members of our National Scout Committee to attend meetings and conferences in the country and abroad, and for running training courses. The Scout and Guide Movements have two full-time officials who are civil servants but have been seconded to the movements to assist those who help as part-time workers. The movements need your moral and financial support, and I appeal to fellow citizens and institutions to lend support to the movements. If fellow citizens helped in this way, I can assure you, Ladies and Gentlemen, that the Scout and Guide Movement in our country will grow from strength to strength.

Lastly, I should like to take this opportunity to thank all those who have helped the Scout movement in one way or the other and especially the Federal Government for the financial support which the Movement has continued to receive. Without the help, the guidance and inspiration the Movement would not have attained the present standards. Let alone international recognition.

I will now call on my Brother Scouters and Sister Guiders to step forward and reaffirm the Scout and Guide promises before receiving the certificate of recognition as members of the world-wide brotherhood of Scouts. Please step forward!

(Ceremony of handing over of World Brotherhood Flag and Certificate of Recognition)

LONG LIVE THE NATIONAL FEDERATON OF SCOUTS;
LONG LIVE ITS PATRON, THE HEAD OF STATE;
LONG LIVE THE FEDERAL REPUBLIC.
S.T MUNA
CHIEF SCOUTS OF THE BOY SCOUTS OF CAMEROON
National Scouts Headquarters, Yaoundé, 8th February, 1972.

5.7: Address by the President of the Republic to the Youths of Cameroon on the Occasion of the 7th National Youth Day, Yaounde, 13 February 1973

Boys and Girls of Cameroon,

My young and Dear Compatriots,

Tomorrow will once more be the Youth Day, your festival. I am profoundly delighted to wish you, on the occasion of this Day that the Nation has dedicate good health, happiness, and prosperity.

In addressing these wishes in my name, and on behalf of the entire nation, I cannot help thinking about the great Peaceful and Democratic Revolution that the Cameroonian people had accomplished with method and realism since 20 May 1972, since the historic act by which it signed the birth of the United Republic of Cameroon.

At this decisive moment of our national history where the state has accepted to grow in the diversity of its structures to rebirth in the unity of a one and indivisible Cameroonian Republic, more rational and stronger, it is necessary, my young compatriots, that you become conscious of your responsibilities within this new Republic, like you, young and full of promises.

The promises of the United Republic of Cameroon, if they are for the entire nation charged with the heavy responsibilities and the immense tasks, could be summarized in a few words: a national unity definitively sealed and a greater efficiency in the action for development.

I know your commitment to the Cameroonian nation and your pride for being Cameroonian. I know that within the YCNU, most of you have contributed through your devotion, enthusiasm and patriotism, your contribution towards the permanent consolidation of the conscience. I do not doubt your availability for the tasks that await us if we want that the United Republic of Cameroon meets its promises.

What needs to be underlined here hear is that the increasing efficiency to which we aspire is not based only on a good display of national institutions. It is also a function of our will to progress and of our fervent will to work.

The nation, in effect, could be constructed only through work by everyone. That is why, each one of us, to borrow a celebrated phrase, should henceforth be to ask, again not only what the new republic could do for it but above all what it could do for it.

What it can do for every one of us is very easy to determine: more security and dignity, more opportunities for progress and human promotion. What we could do for it is more difficult to apprehend for human nature, as a universal truth, is more inclined to receive than to give.

But, my young and dear compatriots, you still have the generosity of youth and her capacity to commitment to the ideal. It does not necessarily mean that at your age, you are expected to make big things. It means first of all for each an everyone of you to be animated with the strong determination to serve your country and to bring, whatever your age, her small stone to the construction of the nation.

The manual work under human investment, which you have realized throughout the just ended Youth Week in the entire the country, have permitted an appreciation in a more concrete manner, modest as it is, which could be yours in the construction of this country, your country.

Allow me to congratulate and wish you for this experiment, which you have undertaken with enthusiasm, could be renewed incessantly and to permit you to contribute your hands to your parents for their private work, no doubt, but also to the authorities of your different localities for the work of general interest, whose utility and necessity are evident, but which could not be implemented for lack of means.

The Government, you know does not neglect anything to ensure the development of the nation and transform the living conditions of the Cameroonian people in both the cities and the rural areas.

You will doubt: this immense undertaking demands means that the situation in our country as a developing country does not always permit us to have in a world where self-interest weigh heavily on our efforts for your progress.

In face of this situation, we nave the obligation to utilize to the maximum the immense capital which we have: the productive force of our hands and notably the infinite reserve of energy which the Cameroonian Youth possess.

It is not only a problem of neither the rural youth nor the disadvantaged urban youths. It is a problem of all the Cameroonian Youth. It is true in the entire youth milieu and notably in the scolarised youths, who have the responsibility to restore the dignity of manual work and to generate the permanent passion to be useful in the society.

The United Republic of Cameroon does not need a contemplative youth. She needs a youth oriented towards the public service, of a youth disposed to integrate, without reticence, towards the national effort for a rapid progress accomplish in social justice and in the balance of provinces.

To make all the Cameroonian youth a youth oriented towards the service is a task which requires a radical transformation of mentalities – a human revolution which will be the pendant of the institutional revolution which is the product of the United Republic of Cameroon.

This revolution of mentalities is necessary. It constitutes, my young and dear compatriots, the seeds which will permit the United Republic of Cameroon to give fruits, the energy, without which our national ambitions will remain at the level of dreams, because I have already said, you are not only the future of the nation, but the nation in the present.

You should however emphasize: this delicate mission, without doubt requires to accomplish happily, the action conjugated by the state, the party, the institutions of training and all moral forces of the nation, each of which have their role to play. It also requires the sincere and active collaboration of families, whose role in the education of youths is determinant.

In this regard, how can one avoid thinking that there are many parents who, consciously or not, encourage among their children a negative attitude towards manual work, preoccupied only to make them have knowledge and degrees which will make them bureaucrats.

Such a conception of life, is evidently, nefarious to the nation. In effect, if the ambition for social promotion through Degrees is legitimate, it however remains that in a country like ours, it is important that intellectual training is closely associated to manual work for the efficient transformation of the environment. I therefore call on all the parents to become the first guides of their children in the noble path of manual work, notably in agricultural work.

I will insist on this because agriculture, which will remain for long the main source of revenue of the majority of Cameroonians, merits that one, should start loving it at a young age. It is only at this price that we could find a solution to the preoccupying problem of rural exodus and accelerate the process of development by making the Cameroonian youth the real engine of progress of the nation.

The Youth should learn to behave themselves no longer as spectators but also as actors of development. They must be actively integrated in the national effort for progress. This imperative is bestowed primarily to this fraction of young university students, particularly favoured, because it benefits from an education which is always more expensive. To this youth we demand always live to the expectations of the Cameroonian society and to be realistic. That they should be open to the national realities and to penetrate the exigencies of the development of the nation which conditions the social promotion of the welfare of everyone.

That it should above all imbibe this truth that, in a society like ours, the training which it receives does not only involve rights. Because these are provided at the price of heavy sacrifices by the people, they also imply obligations: obligation to put the knowledge acquired to the service of the nation; obligation to go towards the people and to participate in the daily tasks to enable them for example to better understand and better implement them; obligation to assist, through an intelligent participation in the life of the people, the indispensable transformation of mentalities towards an authentic progress.

It is in the realization of these obligations, the obligations which are incumbent to the Youth of the nation, which reside the true sense of juvenilisation which should constitute a positive response to the peaceful revolution which the Party and the Government are pursuing, and which could not be complete without the rejection of all cultural alienation.

For, to consider only the Degree and knowledge which accompany it as the sources of privileges is a mental attitude which calls for cultural alienation because they are attached to values stemming from historic contexts different from ours and in adapted to the real exigencies of our own society. It is left on you to show that through your desire for realism and authenticity, through your desire for service, the juvenilisation is, after everything, the expression of a profound cultural renewal and the solid foundation of a national personality.

In this way, you will fully merit the great solicitude which the nation will give you and the heavy sacrifices that it provides for your education.

O Cameroonian Youth, all the generosity and commitment! At the dawn of great historic events which have ever marked the seal of destiny of our fatherland, here is the young United Republic of Cameroon calling you to serve her. By doing this, it is not asking you to illustrate by heroism the great achievements. But to everyone it gives, in the daily accomplishment of their tasks, modest as they may be, the possibility to serve it fully. The nation is calling on you to be aware of what you could give her. True, at your age, you can only receive more than you can give. But to serve your country is a state of mind which one can adopt at any age. If to serve should therefore, as it should be your motto, then we could hope for a future with serenity and confidence, persuaded that by your work and your sense of duty, tomorrow you will ensure with dignity, the succession for which the Cameroonian nation lives in unity, prosperity, and fraternity.

5.8: Address by the President of the Republic to the Youths of Cameroon on the Occasion of the 8th National Youth Day, Yaounde, 12 February 1974

Boys and Girls of Cameroon,
My Young and Dear Compatriots
Always faithful to our rendez-vous of 11 February, I am delighted this year, like in the previous years, to address you my fervent wishes of good health and prosperity on the occasion of the 8th Youth Day and to bring, once more, the assurance of a permanent interest of the nation and hope that it legitimately places on you.

In doing this, how can I forget to think, my young and dear compatriots, that you and your parents and your elders a certain and inestimable advantage: You are the men of tomorrow, that is to say those who will be deciding and implementing tomorrow.

But this advantage, one should stress, implies a heavy responsibility: men of tomorrow, you will also confront difficulties in the future. That is why the Youth Day should be to you, each year, the occasion, of serious reflection, the opportunity to be acquainted with the exigencies of progress of the nation and the imperative of their survival in a world that has become very difficult every day.

At the beginning of the year 1974, the least I can say is that the world is divided between uncertainty and hope: Uncertainty of all the countries, rich or poor, compelled by the increase in the price of energy, to review their conception of development; hope of the Third World to see, by the re-evaluation of the cost of raw materials, which is the first supplier, develop commercial relations between the developed and less developed countries, in a manner to reduce, if nor eliminate, the constant degradation of the terms of trade which, not only is the concrete expression of inequality and of injustice in international economic relations, but still weigh heavily on the efforts towards progress.

The big lesson of the present situation is that the world is profoundly united and there will be no real progress of humanity than in cooperation, equality, and justice. One should however not be discouraged: this situation, from every indication will benefit first the countries of the Third World which, from now henceforth have important mineral resources. This, you know, is unfortunately not the case with Cameroon.

Certainly, our country disposes of certain potential and is resolutely pursuing an important mineral research programme, some of which have produced promising results. It does not remain today, an essentially agricultural country. That means, in the present context, Cameroon should construct her development, no doubt, always taking into consideration her own means and in concentrating her efforts towards the development of agriculture.

This situation shows the importance given to the Green Revolution, to which I call in an emphatic manner, the Cameroonian people since the Buea Agro-Pastoral Show. In effect, a greater agricultural productivity signifies, for each and every one of us, the possibility of a constant improvement of the standard of living, and for the entire nation, the greatest opportunity for rapid industrialization, creation of new jobs, and social progress.

It is necessary, my young and dear compatriots, to give during the present Youth Day, her full dimension to the Green Revolution in the frame of national construction in which we are resolutely engaged. It is placed first within the Peaceful Revolution of 20 May 1972 which the fundamental objectives of strengthening unity, consolidation of the independence, and affirmation of the national personality have as the final outcome, a greater efficiency of the state for a rapid development, balance, and mainly focused on the needs and the aspirations of the Cameroonian people.

The Green Revolution, as the cornerstone of a self-reliant economic development of the nation, contributes in return to confer to the 20 May Revolution a more positive content. It is henceforth evidence that independence and stability of the state mean an equally independent economy and constant expansion.

Green Revolution must, among other things, serve the foundation of a cultural renewal by the transformation of mentalities which require our full splendour as a nation. This is not only so because culture needs economy as the force for its development and flourishing. It is more fundamentally so because the first sense of the word culture, is agriculture work, which means the transformation of the natural environment which constitute the essential element of subsistence and the emergence of man and nature.

Thus, the Green Revolution does not only give a content to the National Revolution of 20 May, it also give it its orientation: every revolution becomes an illusion and degenerates to raw dreams, if not cultural alienation, when instead of recognizing its own sphere of belonging, that means the realities on the ground of the fatherland which it must transform, it becomes empty reclamations and interests – reclamations of rights without corresponding real and concrete obligations.

The true revolution, on the contrary, is that which, desirous of transforming the environment does not know empty visions, but the hard work of every day, efforts for research and changes to operate – necessary changes for the development of the country.

If I thought it necessary, my young and dear compatriots, to talk to you more particularly today of the profound implications of the Green Revolution, it is because I consider that the Youth, which still have all the energy should be the

73

avant-garde of this revolution. Consequently, I hope that the 8th Youth Day should be for you, an opportunity for spontaneous and general mobilization with a view to actively participating, with determination and enthusiasm, to the Green Revolution, notably through the channel of the National Civic Service for Participation in Development destined to become one of the main instruments; in short, the opportunity to create an awareness of your responsibilities in the task, which without doubt, will determine the future of the nation, thus your own future.

You have in effect, my young and dear compatriots, special responsibilities in the success of this enterprise of national interest, not only because of the physical and moral forces which reside in the youth but also because of the knowledge which you possess and which, everyone of you, is particularly apt for changes.

It means at the same time to physically show the tenacity and commitment to work and to demonstrate, by relying on the knowledge acquired, the means to always do the best and to progress. It means to show that the Youth, which is the leitmotiv of the nation, becomes effectively the engine of its destiny by becoming, through the ownership of the Green Revolution, a catalyst of the country's economy.

You can see: the call is addressed to all the components of the Youth. You can see also, a special role is bestowed on those who have the opportunity to accelerate a modern training and who by this fact, have the duty to show that for example and by a permanent and efficient supervision of the peasant masses, the knowledge acquired will permit them have modern forms of agriculture as well as diverse industrial and scientific achievements which are necessary.

My young and Dear Compatriots,

Girls and Boys of Cameroon,

That is the orientation which henceforth we should concentrate our energies. Our country is engaged in a triple revolution: a political revolution by which it is constructing an independent, strong, efficient state; an economic revolution, through the Green Revolution, whose goal is to promote progress for all in equilibrium and justice; a cultural renewal, which aims at restituting to the Cameroonian people the sense of her dignity and creative initiative, in short, to make of the Cameroonian people, fully, the subject of her own history.

In reality, these three fundamental revolutions which we are accomplishing peacefully, but with method, realism, and efficiency and without empty agitations, will resolve in one and unique ambition: promote Cameroon to the rank of an authentic nation.

We do not want to realize this ambition only for the Cameroonian Youth, which is already the nation at present, but for, with and by the Youth. Which other more exalting task could be offered to a committed, vigorous, and intelligent Youth like ours, than that to build its own destiny?

But the successful accomplishment of this task demands of you, my young and dear compatriots, a high sense of civics, an open mind for solidarity and a voluntary and fervent participation to actions of the national programme, conceived and put in place by the Government for the progress of the nation, in a manner as to become the true agents of a development based on the welfare of the people.

It also requires patriotism, discipline, a sense of public interest and above all the permanent desire for national unity, the revolution signifies nothing, for it does not mean that your entire nation should be involved in the movement for renewal that it has initiated. Only the awareness for national unity could give meaning to any revolution.

The Youth, which should be the avant-garde of the regeneration of the state, in short of progress, should find its efforts expended at a total loss, if not to benefit special interests and without a future, if it does not work before all in the interest of the nation, in other words, for the consolidation of national unity under which henceforth all our actions should be directed for the destiny of the same country.

To say that the efforts that the youth is called to make for the general progress of the nation should, consequently, to be useful and efficient, in conformity with the objectives of the plan, which is the "Plan for Production and Productivity", but also and above all in conformity to the objectives of our great national party, the Cameroon National Union, which is the irreplaceable instrument for our national destiny.

In this way, these efforts are harmoniously directed within the frame of the main preoccupations of national construction, which demands, through an a general awareness of the dignity of manual work and notably agricultural work, a radical transformation of mentalities which risk to alienate the abandoned structures, or in the theoretical knowledge, with a view to impacting on the requirements of development. Thus the Cameroonian Youth will show prove that it is finally committed in the national revolution, in this revolution of multiple faces of which the final outcome is to make our dear fatherland, a strong and prosperous nation and a centre for the radiation of an authentic African civilization.

Long Live the Cameroonian Nation,
Long Live the United Republic of Cameroon

5.9: Address by the President of the Republic to the Youths of Cameroon on the Occasion of the 9th National Youth Day, Yaounde, 10 February 1975

Theme: "Unity among the Youths of the Cameroon National Union"
Young People of Cameroon,
My Dear Young Comrades,
On the eve of youth Day, 11 February, which falls this year during the Party Congress of the Cameroun National Union, it gives me particular pleasure to speak to from Douala in the midst of the Nation's wholehearted and enthusiastic commitment to the Congress of Maturity of our Great Party.

I should like to take this opportunity, which I Feel is something more than a coincidence, of course to wish you good health, happiness and success in all that you undertake, but above all that you undertake, but above all to congratulate you on your share in the party's activities and your commitment to its ideals, both ever more tangible and manifest. I am bound to say how highly we value your participation in very large numbers in the basic organs of the YCNU, as has been the case in Douala for instance. It is with similar pleasure that we acknowledge the wish recently expressed by the students of the University that their activities should henceforth be involved with the movement of the Cameroon National Union Party.

This decisive turning point in the Nation's history, corresponding as it does to the maturity of the party and the State, comes hand in hand so to speak with the coming of age of our youth, who have fully grasped the role which the Party has to play in building national awareness and developing the Nation. This coming of age, which is a great satisfaction to all, shows that Cameroon is on the right road, yet it does call for a realization of the major direction in which our mature youth should deploy their energies to help constructively in nation building.

There is one principle that should govern all our activities over the next few years in the framework of the National Revolution whose aim is to promote Cameroon to authentic nationhood. This principle rests upon the need to ensure that Cameroon becomes the motive force behind its own development because, as I have said before, progress can come only through a people's own efforts.

In fact, we have to define the part to be played in all this by the most dynamic section of our people, the section that can ensure that the Cameroonian people become the motive force behind their own development. You know of course that this dynamic section is the young people, who by their numbers, make up over half our population. It is the young people who, by their potential, have a wealth of physical, moral, and intellectual qualities to offer. That is why I have in the past called our young people the Nation of the present.

This means that our young people, who are the soundest, readiest and most forceful part of the Nation's strength, must be in the forefront of the struggle which the Party and the Government are waging to achieve National Unity and enhance our independence in every sphere. In other words, the nation's drive to win full mastery of its destiny will not attain its full magnitude until there is a feeling among young people that they are mobilized for the construction of a strong, prosperous and independent Nation.

I issue here a solemn call to our various categories of young people, the vital forces of the Nation, to unstintingly weigh up their responsibilities at this decisive turning point in our history and mobilize all their energies to give a true and tangible content to the National Revolution for the well-being of the Nation by development which we have ourselves conceived and ourselves carried out, development that is the work of our own hands.

In these circumstances we must decide which ways and means will most surely lead you to this supreme aim. It is clear, MY DEAR YOUNG FELLOW COUNTRYMEN, that the first duty is for young people to organize themselves, and the sole basis for this can be Unity within the Cameroon National Union Party, whose supreme aim, precisely, is the unity of all Cameroonians. By doing so we shall avoid all dispersal of energy, indifference and apathy, which can only hamper the realization of national unity and the mobilization of the vital section of our people who will become masters of their destiny through the efforts of our youth. Accordingly, your foremost watchword must be: UNITY WITHIN THE YOUTH ORGANISATION OF THE CAMEROON NATIONAL UNION.

However, the unity and solidarity of the young people will be significant only if they are active and efficacious. By that I mean that you must ensure that Cameroon truly becomes the motive force behind its own development, and this can only be so if each one of you works actively for development by striving to carry through the projects defined by the Party and the Government for the construction of the authentic Cameroon nation.

These projects, you already know, have been given particular definition in the Green Revolution and the National Civic Service for Participation in Development. As you yourselves can see, mobilization under the banner of our Party's noble ideals basically entails a commitment to service our country by action, by dynamic and enthusiastic participation in the specific tasks but also in the concrete deeds defined by the Party to secure victory for our political, economic, and cultural Revolution, to secure victory for the Revolution that will strive to ensure that our country becomes a self-reliant Nation on the basis of its own potential.

Unity within the YCNU, mobilization for the Green Revolution – this commits you to the true revolution which, in its concern to transform the environment, does not engage in facile dreams but in hard, day-by-day toil, in striving to find the changes to be made, the changes needed for the development of the country. And this commits y you to making your comrades realize the scope of this task, the demands of the task of National construction which first requires a conversion of attitude and a creative approach to conceiving how to reach the manifold objectives we have set.

DEAR YOUNG PEOPLE OF CAMEROON,

You are thus called upon to provide motive force for of the future of the nation in the pursuit of the objectives of the threefold political, economic and Cultural Revolution in which the entire nation is engaged since 20th May 1972. You can fully do so only by your commitment to the Party's activities for the country. It is within this framework that you will be best prepared for the urgent tasks dictated by the circumstances of a developing country and the need for young blood in all fields.

It is by effectively proving our determination to supply this motive force in building the nation that you will climb to ever-growing responsibilities in every sector of national life. Young blood will then be infused in the way most worthy of the Cameroon people, since the dynamic element, young people, will have shown their resolve not only to carry on the work of their elders, but also to forge ahead with the building of a nation that is master of its own destiny.

Knowing as I do your high sense of patriotism and your maturity of mind, re I am convinced that you are ready to give the best of yourselves, to display your creative imagination in giving the National Revolution a true and tangible content, a content drawn from the original genius of Cameroonian people, that is, from you yourselves in fact. In this context, it is important that you should be mobilized and committed as one in the daily struggle for the progress of the nation, whose potential you must increasingly develop for the well-being of our fellow citizens, whose values you must unceasingly protect against any alienation, so that our personality is more and more clearly asserted.

Dear Young people of Cameroon, the whole nation is behind you in this revolutionary struggle! The whole nation expects you to bring back the trophies of victory!

LONG LIVE THE YOUNG PEOPLE OF CAMEROON!

5.10: Address by the President of the Republic to the Youths of Cameroon on the Occasion of the 10th National Youth Day, Yaounde, 10 February 1976

Theme: "Youth and Green Revolution"
Young People of Cameroon,
My Young and beloved fellow countrymen,
Tomorrow is the tenth anniversary of our country's Youth Day, the holiday we hold each year in your honour, and so joyfully look forward to celebrating with you.

It is the occasion once again for me to express all the love and confidence we feel, and all our fervent good wishes for your health, happiness and prosperity.

Let us, however, go beyond the proud and joyful feelings aroused throughout the country by the vigour, the enthusiasm, and the vitality of Cameroon youth.

Most important of all on this day is our chance to reflect and meditate profoundly on the mutual responsibilities we have accepted, and which we are called to accept ever more firmly in the future, in the name of our National Revolution through which we are to build up an authentically Cameroon National, going on from strength to strength.

This day must also be the special celebration of your commitment and your determination to serve your Fatherland wherever you are, in town or country, with utmost devotion, exertion and faith for the triumph of the National Revolution.

I never cease to stress the major role that youth must assume in building our Cameroonian Nation, and to call for that special solicitude which all the vital forces of this Nation must have for young people as they carry out their tasks.

It is an absolute fact that youth is central to all the main concerns of our Great National Party just, indeed, as youth is central to all the activities of the Government.

At the last Congress of the Cameroon National Union, describes as the Congress of our youth's maturity, we concentrated on the necessary revitalization of the YCNU.

What I said then was that "the revitalization of the YCNU must take into account the fact that young people.

What must be achieved is genuinely effective integration of young people into the wider movement of the work of the Party, and this can only be done if youth is organized, ideologically educated and politically committed.

The party authorities, with this in view, have now completed arrangements which will enable young people to meet and organize in the framework of the National Youth Conference: a huge programme is being prepared and you will be informed of it very shortly.

Furthermore, in the next few days the Political Bureau will be considering how our young people at University can be effectively integrated within the Party, as they asked to be last year.

But organization is not enough if the young are not ideologically trained and politically committed, and this means that they must have a keen sense of their actual role in the great work of national construction.

This role consists essentially in the efforts that young Cameroonians must unremittingly make towards the consolidation of national unity and in working without stint for the objectives of the objectives of the threefold Revolution of 20 May.

For the youth of Cameroon must be the spearhead of our political Revolution of an independent state which, day by day, consistently upholds its sovereignty and its influence abroad.

The youth of Cameroon must be exemplary of commitment to the Green Revolution which summons the Nation to ensure the progress of the people in equity and justice.

The youth of Cameroon must be the vanguard of the Cultural Renewal which is restoring to our people that dignity which makes them matters of their own destiny.

The Government, for its part, has spared no effort to ensure that young people should adequate scope for exercising their responsibilities, and also the wherewithal to make their endeavours a complete success, and the high proportion of our resources allocated for the education, training, health, and recreation of young people is proof of this.

Since our country gained its independence, while we have never ceased to consider agriculture as the first of priorities, we have carried out a policy of industrialization with the aim of accelerating the process of growth and diversification in our national economy and providing more and more jobs for young people.

We have also endeavoured, in the light of the real needs of the Nation, to equip it with institutions for education and vocational training of a kind to prepare the young people of Cameroon more effectively for the tasks which fall to them in the great work of national construction.

We have continued to develop the facilities for health, sports and recreation that can bring about the ideal of a healthy mind in a healthy body in our youth, thus contributing to their full development and enabling them to discharge properly the obligations that are theirs.

All the activities and resources provided for the youth of the country should enable them to commit themselves unreservedly to this threefold revolution which the Government and our Great National Party are realistically and methodically conducting.

The young people of Cameroon ought each day to put their commitment into practice, through acts which will give to our economy the means to develop, to our culture the chance to flourish, and to our country the power to assert itself as one Nation solidly united by shared aspirations and a common destiny.

Acts like this, conducive to the fulfilment of our noble and just ambition to build up modern and authentic Nation, can never be achieved without the unanimous, zealous and resourceful participation of the young people of Cameroon.

Thus the Tenth Anniversary of Youth Day must be an occasion for you to demonstrate clearly your firm desire and your fierce and unswerving determination to mobilize yourselves from now on behind our Great National Party in order to ensure the success of the Green Revolution – that dynamic and realistic undertaking for progress that must put to work, actively and clear-sightedly, the immense physical, moral, and intellectual potential of our young people.

Consequently it is the responsibility of all young Cameroonians, at this decisive moment in our history, to assess the weight of the responsibilities devolving upon them in the Nation's drive to become master of its own destiny.

In other words, the young people of Cameroon must be above local particularisms, shun apathy and indifference and avid the dispersion of efforts. They must, in a glow of solidarity and responsible and enthusiastic participation, come forward as activists for the progress and development of their country.

The progress of the Nation, and its transformation into a truly modern entity that guarantees happiness and security to everyone on a basis of harmony and equal opportunity, is a joint endeavour that requires hard work, responsible participation and faith in the future.

I also affirmed during the Douala Congress that the National Revolution will not succeed unless the people in their entirety are ready to become the motive force behind their own progress. This means that all development programmes defined by the Government and the Party must be undertaken and carried out by all the vital forces of the Nation.

Above all, this means that young people, who are the most dynamic and readily available group among the vital forces of the Nation – being more enthusiastic and better prepared for these development programmes – constitute the force most likely to make the National Revolution a success.

It pleases me in this regard to join the entire Nation in welcoming the vigour that our young people are bent on giving to our national culture, which remains above all an essential factor in the affirmation of our national identity and forms our people's message of friendship and brotherhood to the world.

This new dimension added to our cultural renewal is a perfect reflection of the vivacity of the creative genius of our people and their ability to participate actively in the moulding of the universal culture.

The same is true of the development and expansion of national sporting activities which, in addition to their physical benefits to our young people, provide real training in good citizenship, are invaluable in cementing national unity and remain a pre-eminent means of bringing peoples together more closely.

Bur we have always thought that, while the success of the National Revolution necessitates the affirmation of our cultural identity and the consolidation of national unity, that revolution can have no real meaning or success unless it is sustained by harmonious development of the nation's economy which will guarantee a certain level of material wellbeing and happiness to every Cameroonian.

It was with this major imperative in mind that we launched the Green Revolution, convince that agriculture will for a long time remain the most important sector of our economy.

Through the Green Revolution, viewed in this way, our people should be able to carry through with courage and lucidity the profound changes that are necessary if our rural areas are to advance; and our National Revolution should focus on these areas where our young people are called upon to deploy their vast resources of ability and energy.

While the development of our rural areas, which is perfectly in line with our fundamental choice of self-reliant development, can today be seen as a vital necessity for our people, bringing it about implies not only a radical change of attitudes among the masses and among our young people in particular, but also above all a clear awareness of the dignity of work on the land.

In fact, it is through the rational and methodical exploitation of that inestimable treasure, the land of our ancestors, that our people will equip themselves with the means of improving their material living conditions.

We must therefore exert all our efforts to accelerate the development of our rural areas and to ensure their advancement.

We are thinking here of measures and steps aimed at integrating our educational system in the national production process through the ruralisation of teaching, the development of vocational training and the setting up of a University of Technology.

We are also thinking of the National Civic Service for Participation in Development, a real vehicle for civic, moral, and vocational training which is intended to foster and restore to our people the mystique of manual labour and show our young people that we can honestly earn our living and ensure our own social advancement through the seat of our brows and, in so doing, play a worthwhile part in nation building.

At a time when the whole world is searching of new balances and when developing countries like ours are engaged in a merciless struggle to survive, our fine and energetic young people, have in the National Civic Service a precious means of accelerating the development of the national economy.

By contributing actively and with determination to programmes aimed at giving real content to the National Revolution, our young people will once again demonstrate both their high sense of patriotism and their spirit of maturity.

And what is more, they will show firmly that the passion and enthusiasm displayed at the launching of the National Civic Service really derives from their firm desire and unswerving determination to participate in concert with the other vital forces of the Nation in the building of a truly stronger and more prosperous Cameroonian Nation.

My Dear Young Fellow Countrymen,

As you can see, the Party and Government are making immense efforts and Nation is making many sacrifices to secure your future.

Why these efforts and sacrifices? Because we are aware of your right to a decent life that gives everyone the opportunity to develop fully.

What has already been done is immense. But we know too that what remains to be done is equally immense. We should bear in mind, first of all, that the resources of the Nation are not limitless, and this means that things be only done slowly and patiently.

We should also remember that no category of citizens has only rights to ask of the Nation. Not only must all citizens, in the legitimate interest of social justice, consider the rights of others; above all else, they have responsibilities as well.

Consequently, we must not simply claim our rights. In order to deserve the great sacrifices made by the Nation, we must fully assume our responsibilities towards the Nation in order to accelerate its development and make the climate for progress for all favourable.

Thus, my dear young fellow countrymen, if you always remain at the forefront of the National Revolution, you will have shown by your discipline, your dynamism, your competence and your unshakeable commitment that you are truly capable of taking over from your elders and of securing a better future for the Nation.

LONG LIVE THE YOUNG PEOPLE OF CAMEROON!
LONG LIVE THE UNITED REPUBLIC OF CAMEROON!

5.11: Address the President of the Republic to the Youths of Cameroon on the Occasion of the 11ᵗʰ Youth Day, Yaounde, 10 February 1977

Theme: "Youth and National Culture"
Girls and Boys of Cameroon,
My young and Dear Compatriots,

Together and with a perfect communion in thought and sentiments we will celebrate again tomorrow as the Youth Day, your Day.

It gives me pleasure to once more take this opportunity to address to you, as in the previous years, my personal wishes of good health, happiness, and prosperity as well as those of the entire nation.

As you will no doubt remember, my present tenure at the helm of the state is based on a contract of progress with the Cameroonian people for a society which is authentically Cameroonian, that is to say which plunges the roots of the national territory, is nourished on the aspirations of the people and is apt to ensure the development of the nation and its radiance in Africa and in the world.

This means that that the envisaged objective is to construct a new Cameroon. The accomplishment of this high and legitimate ambition by our people supposes constantly concrete projects in the area of development. These projects as you know, have just been defined by the Fourth Five Year Development Plan, baptized, and justly too, as the Plan for Self-Reliant Development and which, based on a general system of democratic consultation at the local, regional, and national level, expresses at the same time the future needs of national collectivity and the present aspirations of the Cameroons.

It demands, from now on wards, to engage a big campaign on general mobilization and the radical sensitization of all the country's stakeholders for the effective and progressive implementation of the actions envisaged in the Plan.

The self-reliant development, which signifies after everything the development of the people by the people, responds to this necessity to mobilize all the national resources and energies for development for, as I have always said, authentic development, is that which is based on the productive and creative efforts of the people themselves.

What element of the Cameroonian people, other than her dynamism and youth, could bring, with efficiency, faith, enthusiasm and determination, a more decisive contribution towards the realization of our noble and legitimate ambition?

The achievements of these actions prescribed in the Fourth Development Plan and which should permit the building of a new Cameroonian society capable of responding, in the shortest possible time to the aspirations of the masses therefore calls, on the part of the youth an awareness of its responsibilities in the progress of the country and her active participation in all the sectors of national life.

This signifies that the Cameroonian youth, which is already the nation in the present and constitute the most dynamic element the most dynamic social forces of the nation, because they are most available and better prepared for development activities, should be the leitmotif of national revolution in which we are resolutely and irreversibly engaged.

This also means above all, that the Cameroonian Youth should be the model for the engagement in the road and pursuit of our self-development policy which aims at the promotion of a new person, capable of constantly improving her own living conditions and affirm, with more vigour, her identity at the political, economic, social, and cultural levels.

My young and dear compatriots,

I said it recently during the National Council of the CNU: the success of self-reliant development supposes a strong government and party action aimed at the technical supervision of the efforts undertaken in all the sectors of national life and also and above all the ideological supervision of the masses and especially the youth with a view to mobilizing the desire for progress through personal effort and to make every citizen an efficient agent of progress.

It is in this perspective that the recent National Council of the Party, applying the resolutions of the Congress of Maturity, took appropriate dispositions for the transformation of our administration and the CNU into a development administration and Party and to revitalize the YCNU in its structures and its activities.

It is equally in this perspective that we have decided to readapt our educational system and the university institutions to the imperatives of national development as well as to the realities of our country and that we put in place the necessary structures for the massive and rational exploitation of the national resources with a view to the edification of a stronger and more prosperous nation.

Cameroon, our beautiful country, has a rendezvous with history, as a model which within reinforces her unity, consolidates her economic achievements confirms her personality and identity and, abroad, ensures the radiance and brings to the world in full sovereignty, but in friendship and cooperation, her message of fraternal solidarity.

It is to our youths that we have always considered as the spearhead of the Cameroonian nation that the most important mission of ensuring the construction of the new Cameroon nation. Endowed with the proven experience of preceding generations and the solicitude of the public authorities in the efficient management of our grand national party, the Cameroonian Youth, because of its disposability and preparedness to exercise responsibilities, should put itself at the forefront of all the sectors of activities of the country and put at the service of the nation her immense capital of energy and knowledge, her talents and intelligence.

But my young and dear compatriots if self-reliant development calls for the permanent mobilization and active participation of all the national resources and all the active forces of the of the country and especially the youth in all the sectors of the road to national construction, the success of our action is conditioned, for a large part, by the promotion of our rural sector for, as I have always said, agriculture is and will remain for a long-time, the key sector of our economic development.

Self-reliant development signifies that we most first of all count on our available national resources to ensure the development of the country, it therefore imposes on us the necessity to utilize to the highest, for the work of the earth, the immense capital of energy which our country possesses and especially her good and dynamic youth.

This fundamental preoccupation has led the government of our grand national party to undertake a vast campaign for green revolution and to take appropriate measures, in creating the structures of animation and supervision, for the promotion of the rural world.

It is in this vein that the national civic service for participation in development was instituted after a large consultation of all of the county's sectors of opinions and decision-making, with the objective of civic, professional, and moral training, to insert the young Cameroonian girls and boys in the production cycle and to ensure their supervision for the execution of the work of general interest in relation with the imperatives of development.

Conceived in this way, the Civic Service, a real school for civic and professional training and economic action should be one of the privileged structures for implementing our self-reliant development. It is therefore for our youths to mobilize themselves actively around the civic service and to bring the immense force of their hands and the immense treasury of their talents, of their knowledge and intelligence, for the transformation of our rural world to a privileged road for national promotion.

It requires, however, good institutions adapted to the realities of the county and to the imperatives of our time. But it requires above all, an ardent youth, men capable of doing their work with character, animated by the passion of progress, of justice, of unity and the unity of the efficiency, the men capable of responding positively to the appeal of the ideal.

These men, we are bound to make them by an appropriate education within the party as in the frame of the state training institutions. It is high time to remind the role of the responsibilities of parents. It is in effect within the family that that the child should mainly receive his moral and civil education which will make him a man and a citizen with sure and apt moral values to plays their roles in the society. To abdicate this basic responsibility is on the part of the parents a serious deficiency of fundamental responsibility towards the nation and deprives the youth of her potential.

Why not tell the youth of this beautiful country full of a bright future? You have an inestimable opportunity to be called to implement for a grand design, to implement a big dream of a project of a new society, in a word, to participate in the edification of this radiant future.

But preparing for the future implies a permanent will for action and initiative and a big capacity to dream, that is to say, creative imagination. The dream, in effect, is the force of the people because it evokes the hope which is a powerful engine of history, a strong stimulus for active participation.

In this regard, it gives me pleasure to send my warm congratulations to all the boys and girls of schools who by registering the names of their schools in golden letters in the Grand Prix du Travail Manuel that we have instituted, have shown that the work book in general, and the practical work in particular, because of they are noble and enriching, are worthy of their interests because they could, as other branches of activities, contribute in a decisive manner to the promotion of the Cameroonian person and the building of the new society which guarantees everyone the best conditions of existence and development.

This clear awareness of the avant-garde role of the Cameroonian youth in the pursuit and the full accomplishment of the triple political, economic, and social revolution that the nation has undertaken merits to be highlighted with satisfaction because it constitutes a determining factor in the progress of the nation.

I am persuaded that in this committed participation in the task for national construction, our youth will find a deep personal moral satisfaction. In effect, the real and responsible participation , the success of the common enterprise, the victory on the adverse forces, constitute without contest, an affirmation of the self and brings to those who give it the satisfaction of being and of useful knowledge to the national collectivity.

Girls and Boys of Cameroon,

My young and dear compatriots,

The world is at a time of profound changes and acceleration in history. The problems confronted by man today, as I have said, do not find their solutions only in past experiences. They require new scientific and technical knowledge and in the adaptive capacity of the youth, because of their availability, their receptiveness and training, become more and more the only ones to possess in the modern world.

This new situation implies that the youth, without despising the reservoir of wisdom and the precious individual and collective balancing factor which is the experience of the adults, nonetheless, make the originality and cultural authenticity of a nation, will take in their hands, progressively in all conscience, dignity, responsibility and realism, the destiny of the country.

In doing this, the Cameroonian Youth, that we prepare to take over with seriousness and application, in the urban and rural areas, in the public as well as the private sector, will continue to merit our confidence and the place which is theirs in the nation first, and then in Africa and in the world.

The task which awaits the Cameroonian youth, that of creating a new Cameroon, is an exalting task no doubt, but difficult and long which demands sacrifices. That is why I tell you without ambiguity, my young and dear compatriots: If, in participating in this great task, you seek first of all sure material and immediate satisfaction; if you cannot persevere a hard struggle that lasts for years, perhaps decades, with the reverse, and most of the time without certain compensation; if you doubt for having as the only certitude that the cause to which you are attached to the nation will triumph one day: you are not worthy of this country.

But if you are among those who know how to devote themselves for great causes; who know that a part of the national destiny is always offered to the creative initiative and the courage of the youth; if you have the desire for patient work and tenacity for a faith and for an action which will impart on the future, then without doubt, this country needs you.

It is on this note of hope, convinced that our good and dynamic youth will always give their best for the triumph of the national revolution that I wish, from the bottom of my heart, to all the young boys and girls of Cameroon, with the entire nation, a happy Youth Day.

Long live the Cameroonian Youth,
Long live Cameroon

5.12: Address by the President of the Republic to the Youths of Cameroon on the Occasion of the 12th National Youth Day, Yaounde, 10 February 1978

Theme: "Participation of the Youths in the Green Revolution"
Young People of Cameroon,
My Young and Beloved Countrymen,
Here we are once more on the eve of the public holiday which the Nation has dedicated to you as proof of its steadfast sentiments of affection, attachment and patriotic devotion.

I would like to take this opportunity not only to wish you good health, happiness and success in all your endeavours, but also and above all to say how comforted the nation as a whole feels because of your real and effective participation in the task of nation building. These sentiments are at the origin of the great hopes which the nation continues to have in you for the building of a new Cameroon.

For, the distance covered during the last decades was the result of a struggle in which the Cameroonian youths took an active part and which enables the Nation to evermore strengthen its unity, advance its progress and development in peace, assert its cultural identity while conveying to the world, through its indisputable influence, its message of fraternal solidarity in friendship and cooperation with all nations of good will.

What we have achieved so far is proof that development is the reward that comes to a people united at all levels, a people prepared to make the necessary sacrifices and a people who are creative, show a desire for progress and are persevering. We can, in this context, say that the Cameroonian people, and particularly our youth, have always lived up to our noble and legitimate aspiration.

This means that today and tomorrow, you should, with more determination, devotion and acumen, work hand in hand in close collaboration with all the other vital forces of the nation, so as to make Cameroon an entity in which all citizens can find the means by which they can personally enhance their social progress in the context of a common destiny.

This means above all that the ever enthusiastic, dynamic and enterprising Cameroonian youth are called upon, more than ever before, to transform their country into a vast development site where they will put their creative genius and technical know-how into practice in a spirit of solidarity, patriotic devotion, and with a high sense of duty, honour and discipline.

Fellow Countrymen,

Even though the satisfactory results of the past twenty years in all sectors of national activity which enabled our country to pursue its development in peace give us cause for rejoicing, we must however recognize the fact the rapid development of our country, its transformation into a modern nation, cannot be effected without the advancement and modernization of our agriculture.

I have that this feeling of satisfaction, hope and pride in the great venture of building a New Cameroon depends on our awareness of the strategy of national progress, based on self-reliant development which our Great National Party had defined as development of the people by the people, and for the people. At the economic level, the Green Revolution stands out as one of the decisive factors of that self-reliant development.

In this context, our legitimate feeling of satisfaction, hope and pride as regards the triumph of our National Revolution rests on the will and determination with which our people and particularly our youth are working towards the success of the Green Revolution.

The diverse and spontaneous forms of demonstration of this will and determination are beginning to breathe life and dynamism into our countryside and correspond to this decisive impetus which we mentioned during the Bafoussam agricultural show and which should drive on the Nation in order to make agriculture and stockbreeding their best life's activity.

It is in this direction that the Party and Government are trying to translate into reality the priority which is given to the promotion and development of this sector.

This interest is shown not only in the facilities which exist in the form of guidance, support and animation structures for rural areas but over and above all in the increasing public investment in this field.

It is in this context that we should situate the measures which are recently taken by the Government to give our youth the necessary facilities for their settlement, as efficient and responsible model economic partners, in our countryside and villages in order to ensure their own progress and help to increase national production.

The progressive, rational and harmonious settlement of these pioneers foe progress in our villages will not only contribute to the regeneration of our countryside but also to stamp out the evil known as the rural exodus and its effects in the urban centres, namely juvenile delinquency and pests to family members.

But the settlement of these young farmers in our villages and countryside can only produce the expected results if it is based on an organization of work which itself requires the continuous guidance, initiation and training of the young people concerned in cultivation and stock farming methods.

In this context, the agricultural and stock farming services providing technical advice should more than ever before follow up the settlement of young farmers in our countryside so as to offer them advice and the benefit of their experience in order to permit them overcome the difficulties involved in their integration and development.

Young People of Cameroon,

My Young and Beloved Countrymen,

We can never overemphasize the fact that the Green Revolution is a global action for the radical transformation of our society into a modern entity, an action which is meant to provide each one real possibilities of development and advancement, an action which requires the mobilization of all energies of all the vital forces of the Nation and more particularly our healthy and dynamic youth.

As this turning point in the history of our country, when the whole nation is seeking to assert itself through its own resources and in fraternal and friendly cooperation with other peoples in a world in search of new balances, we must make good use of our time in order to consolidate and expand our possibilities of development.

I am once more making an urgent appeal to our youth who in all circumstances have always proof of courage, dynamism, responsibility and enthusiasm, to join the ranks of other men and women of Cameroon in this exciting enterprise of the rehabilitation of farming, the revitalization and promotion of our agricultural sector in order to reinforce the bedrock of our National Revolution which will certainly lead our country towards a better future.

In this direction, our Great National Party will continue its action of civic training and awakening the youth to the Green Revolution, within the YCNU. The provincial conference of the YCNU and its national search for the ways and means of effectively sensitizing and mobilizing the various strata of our youth towards the task of nation building within which we situate the promotion of our agriculture.

Hence, the great hopes which the country has in our youths will not only be a wish but a real guarantee of the success of this march forward which the Nation has undoubtedly embarked upon in all fields so as to improve the welfare of all Cameroonians.

With the firm conviction that you will increasingly demonstrate your abilities, your availability and dynamism for the success of our National Revolution behind which all the people of Cameroon have mustered their forces, I wish you, YOUNG PEOPLE OF CAMEROON, a happy youth day.

LONG LIVE THE CAMEROONIAN YOUTH!
LONG LIVE CAMEROON!

5.13: Address by the President of the Republic to the Youths of Cameroon on the Occasion of the 13th National Youth Day, Yaounde, 10 February 1979

Theme: "Commitment of the Youths to the National Political Life"
Young Girls and Boys of Cameroon,
My young and dear compatriots,
On the occasion of the 13th Youth Day, it gives me particular pleasure to address to you my warm wishes as well as those of the entire nation. In so doing, I will like first of all to reaffirm the confidence that the entire Cameroonian has bestowed on the youth, which by its capacity to serve the great causes should be the catalyst of the future, our most sure hope.

This confidence and hope I must say, the Cameroonian youths deserve it through the brilliant victory which it brought in various areas in the past year, especially in the cultural, sports, and political domains. It is in this context that last December, the Cameroonian youths through their different representatives participated enthusiastically and proudly in the first national conference of the YCNU. It was for it to demonstrate a spirit of responsibility and ardent patriotism, a decisive stage in the road of its progressive and irreversible integration in the ranks of the Cameroon National Union as a guarantor of the success of the peaceful revolution that our people are pursuing with determination and sacrifice with a view to making Cameroon a modern nation which every day consolidates its unity, ensures its progress in peace and justice, fashions and radiates its personality and its identity in the world.

The eloquent results registered during these national meetings as well as the seriousness and the sense of devotion and honour which reigned during this national youth conference enabled our people to realize the maturity and dynamism of our youth within the frame of the maturity of our great national party.

In this connection, the task of assembling and of concerted mobilization that our great national party could not leave the Cameroonian youth indifferent to which the entire people make immense sacrifices through education with a view to making it more apt to assume the historic responsibilities within the nation.

It means that the Cameroonian youth should react with enthusiasm to the call of the Cameroon National Union through its capacity to dedication to the ideal as well as through its potential energy and enthusiasm to the work of solidifying national unity and mobilization of everyone for progress and radiance of our nation in the world.

My young and dear compatriots,

The special place that our country occupies at the top of the list of emerging countries demands that our youth should become more conscious of the exemplary role they should play and which should correspond to the situation of our country in a changing world.

Like I said during the Congress of Maturity in Douala in 1975 "We are in effect witnessing a crisis of civilization. It is important in knowing if humanity on the basis of its immense scientific and technological advancement, could build a world void of the imperialism of great powers, ideological interests, could construct a world equally beneficial to carter for the world being of everyone, in short, if humanity could be capable to promote an authentic and universal civilization.

Such an international order creates three objectives for the youth.

First , a cultural objective for because of the immense resources that the state allocates every year in education, the youth at all levels should react positively to the sacrifices of the people by taking its work more seriously and by consecrating efforts for the acquisition of knowledge susceptible to accelerate the movement of the progress of the nation and ensure a national culture which permits our people to come fully armed to this give and take rendezvous, which constitutes a universal civilization.

Then is an objective of development, because it involves for our country, to rely first of all on its own strength and based on the potentials of physical and intellectual energy which are in our youths and which constitute the driving force of our policy of self-reliant development of the people, by the people, and for the people. In a world in search of new balances and in an international conjecture dominated by a persistent economic crisis, the Cameroonian Youth should know that the period of laxity is definitely over, and that "We cannot build a new international order which brings to the world the proves of our capacity to always master our development problems better through this message which speaks for the entire Africa, and which prolongs the voice of our ancestors in the lapse of time, reminds us of solidarity as the foundation of all authentic human community".

That is why solidarity constitutes the supreme objective and the determining force, without which neither the nations, nor the international community could accomplish their vocations of emancipation of the individuals and collective civilizations with a view to creating a new world, more just, more balanced, and more human.

It is in this context that the Cameroonian youth should prepare to participate actively in the struggle waged by the entire humanity for progress, freedom, and human dignity, which in the African context is less respected by the policy of apartheid in Azania, Namibia, and in Zimbabwe. In this connection, the mission of the youth should in fact be neither that of loud and empty ideology, nor the crude speeches of those who to develop a country and humanity without working, and the creative effort of a new world, for as I said in the past, "The royal effort is the only way which permits a conscientious people in their responsibilities before history to bring in their movement for progress the more outstanding victories and put in the highest rungs of the ladder".

Young Girls and Boys of Cameroon,

The great victories that await us are above the forces of inertia, apathy, and divisions, we are mobilized in solidarity like one man around an ideal of unity of our people and of our great national party with a view to triumph in this peaceful revolution in which we are engaged.

These victories which will be the fruits of a task of a long duration should start with an active and concerted militantism and supported by a personal engagement and determined to give the best of oneself in the accomplishment of its tasks in view of the pursuit of the high destiny of the nation. You should express such commitment in actions in your daily life, in schools, in farms, workshops, and factories, in offices by executing your duties with honesty, rigour, and discipline which requires the full conscience of your responsibilities in the nation and which requires that you should refrain yourself from a carefree attitude or hurry in finding fixed easy solutions. You should henceforth translate such commitment through your massive and responsible participation in the activities of our great national party within the YCNU with a view to promoting and reinforcing the concord and unity of our people and to make the Cameroonian nation a model society which ensures to every one of its children, peace, dignity and happiness.

If this is the determination and commitment of our youth to serve Cameroon with faith, dedication, and patriotism under the aegis of our great national party, then we can hope that the national revolution in its triple political, economic, and cultural dimension, will have a bright future which will permit our country to always deserve the confidence, consideration, and respect of other people of the world.

Long Live the Cameroonian Youth,
Long Live the United Republic of Cameroon.

5.14: Address by the President of the Republic to the Youths of Cameroon on the Occasion of the 14th National Youth Day, Yaounde, 10 February 1980

Theme: "Commitment of the Youths to the National Political Life"
Young Girls and Boys of Cameroon,
My Dear Compatriots,

The Youth Day gives me an agreeable opportunity every year, in the month of February, to address my warmest wishes as well as those of the entire nation. Only institutions that respond to a necessity like your Youth Day, can become a consecrated tradition. In this way, the Cameroon Nation, in line with the dynamics of its historic unity comes together twice a year: 20 May, the adult people, builders of the present, remind themselves and reinforce their will; on 11 February, the youth, guarantors of the future, project and commit themselves.

This year's Youth Day coincides, at the same time with the 20th anniversary of the independence of the Republic of Cameroon and the beginning of the 3rd decade, which itself announces the end of a century marked by a double crisis of growth and civilization, which calls on humanity to seek and find not only new balances but also new reasons to act and exist. Cameroon, like her youth, cannot be indifferent to this our interdependent world. But before and beyond this crisis of our time, whose gravity is evident and which affects all the states, our country is engaged in the process of its own revolution, albeit peaceful but demanding, which should make it a country that masters its destiny, forging its unity, assuming its development, fashioning its personality, elaborating its own culture, radiating in the world.

And the Cameroonian youth has the exalting privilege to belong not to an old nation, decadent, in desperate quest for an ideal and renaissance, but to young nation, in full emergence, rich in its creativity, nourished in its cultural pluralism and its bilingualism. It could therefore not be left behind in this vast and profound movement of collective promotion which principally concerns it because it is the main beneficiary, because it is already an actor.

I have also said it many times that the Cameroonian Youth is the future of the nation. But I have also iterated, completing the definition of its place and role in the enterprise of nation building, that the Youth is already the nation of today. This was to show you the confidence bestowed upon you. It was at the same time to invite you, in a formal manner, to commit yourself in the great common task of national construction.

My young and dear compatriots,

I must say, out of pleasure and to congratulate you, that the call for mobilization and participation of the youth has been largely favourable among the youth and the nation. Last year , more than the previous years' produced better and more assuring results in some of the essential areas of national activities meant for the preparation of youth to active life, especially in the political, economic, and sporting fields.

At the political level, the first CNU national youth conference brought together youth representatives for a serious and constructive dialogue aimed at situating their legitimate aspirations in the general efforts of an emerging nation.

It is therefore at the present stage of national development to bring the youth, better equipped with objectives defined by the party, and actions undertaken by the government, to integrate themselves in the ranks of the CNU, the guarantor and authority of the success of the peaceful revolution which our people are resolutely engaged in.

These first national youth meetings of the CNU, through the desire for patriotism and the interest demonstrated have revealed the growing awareness by our youths of the imperatives of national construction. Henceforth, it is necessary to pursue this political maturity under the auspices of our great national party, whose noble objectives and the results of its actions should nourish the sense of the youth ideals and stimulate their predisposition for commitment and duty.

At the economic level, the remarkable fact, source of the new and promising times, is the introduction of more youths into creative activities. I am referring to material goods as well as those of spiritual value. Thus, the availability towards the activities of the National Civic Service for Participation in Development, whose objective for civic, moral, and professional training with a view to integrating them in the production cycle constitute a significant programme, concretizes your determination to prepare yourself for future arduous tasks.

Moreover, your practice of increasingly appreciating manual work in all the schools show that beyond the gesticulations, you have understood that manual work is nothing degrading. On the contrary, the exploitation of the earth which valorises man is as much physical exercise as gymnastics of the spirit.

In a country where the mind, the creative force and the traditions have their roots in the rural world, where the national wealth comes from, for a large part, the resources of the earth, the green revolution constitutes, for the entire nation as well as for the youth, a major option which tends to give back the honour of rural activities in the development of the rural world and halt rural exodus.

With regard to sports, which this year, more than the previous year showed the penchant of the youth for success, accomplishment, and glory, it responded to its multiple vocation of training the body and spirit, consolidating national unity, putting her mobilization capacity to the service of this great national ambition: development.

My young and dear compatriots,

For the recent sporting victories and at this exceptional occasion of her annual festival, I address again the very lively and warm congratulations and in a solemn manner all the Cameroonian youth who shook Cameroon and Africa into an exalting rhythm of success.

Young Cameroonians, those in the villages, the cities, the schools, the offices, and the farms, you have arrived at this stage where one can only reach through discipline and the will of improvement. That is the ambition which you should henceforth have, not only in the stadia, but also in the vast theatres of national construction. I know you are capable of such ambition. I give it to you and I encourage you.

My young and Dear Compatriots,

Because the nation makes enormous sacrifices to ensure your education in schools and socio-professional training in the field, because it attaches a premium which comes to the vast enterprise of restoring our personality and our identity, in a word, because it expects to prepare fully apt Cameroonians in the participation today and in the succession tomorrow, you should demonstrate exemplary conscience and correctness in your daily behaviour.

No doubt, parents like nations have the children they deserve. It shows their irreplaceable role, they who, from the origin, before and during school, in short from infancy to adolescence, should inculcate to children the social physical and moral virtues which make men of value, growing at the same time in age, experience, and wisdom: the will to work, the sense of duty, sacrifice, and solidarity, the attachment to noble causes, the attachment to the fatherland.

It is therefore the place of the Cameroonian people, that is the parents, educators, and moral authorities, defying all fatalism and all artificial transposition of foreign situations to our context and to our higher goals, to give to Cameroon the wise and worthy youth who warrant the accomplishment of her great destiny in Africa and the world. The CNU on its part will continue unfailingly in this regard, for it is the condition for success and the survival of the work of national construction, which it remains accountable at present and in the future.

But if the imperious mission of parents and educators, like that of the state is to help you to forge your personality in the grill of aptitude and rectitude, it is your responsibility to acquire and maintain a high and lively conscience of the historic stakes which is the integration of the youth in the process of the gestation and maturation of the Cameroon nation. This involves commitment, discernment, and responsibility.

Young Girls and Boys of Cameroon,

My young and dear compatriots,

You can see, our peaceful revolution, like all revolutions worthy of the name is a great bet. A bet in the quest of verifying the finality of the action which remains internally, the promotion of material and moral wellbeing of everyone, in a frame of a nation made solid and healthy through unity and peace; in Africa and in the world the active participation in all the efforts leading to the liberation of the continent from the colonialist and racist domination, and the promotion of a cooperation which tends to institute a new order based on justice, solidarity, and peace. A bet also in the quality of the means put at the disposals and the results obtained which give to the pursued objectives the plenitude of their value.

This bet, at the same time demanding and exalting which is a call to the youth, the first builders of our nation who you are your ancestors has started to bear fruits; it remains to be won for the building of a young nation is a rude daily conquest. It remains above all, that from now on, the Cameroonian Youth, inheritors of the Cameroon of tomorrow follow one of the sacred lessons of popular wisdom. It remains, I say that the Cameroonian Youth should jealously preserve and sanctify the patrimony, without forgetting to adapt it.

In that way, our sacrifices would not be in vain, our hopes will be met with. Thus the individual and collective obligations, which, day after day is forged in the minds and consciences of men like on the grounds of this country will prepare and guarantee the future, an ideal that we will like to be sure and radiant.

And since this year your Day, like a prelude, announces the grand rendezvous of the 3rd Congress of the CNU in Bafoussam, a rendezvous of the Cameroonian people with itself and with history, it is my wish that this Youth Day serve as the opening of the triumphal symphony of our national unity.

5.15: Address by the President of the Republic to the Youths of Cameroon on the Occasion of the 15th National Youth Day, Yaounde, 10 February 1981

Theme: "Civic Responsibility and Discipline"

Young Men and Women of Cameroon

My young and beloved fellow countrymen,

In keeping with our traditional get-together of 11 February, I am here again this year to extend to you my most fervent wishes of good health, happiness and prosperity and, on the threshold of the new decade, to reiterate the attention and interest of the nation.

One year after the Congress of the Mastery of our Development in Bafoussam, in the wake of the Bertoua Agricultural and Cattle Show, which together constitute salient milestones on the path of the relentless effort we are making to ensure the total fulfilment of the Cameroonian men, I am pleased to congratulate you on your contribution to the development of our beloved country.

As a matter of fact, you have already, over the last two decades, carried out activities that have no doubt contributes to the progress of the nation and to the strengthening of our policy of unity, social justice and peaceful development.

Faced with the upheavals of a crisis-ridden world that inhibit the development efforts of young nations, you have continued to distinguish yourself by your dynamism, your exuberant patriotism and your determination within the specific role that you have been called upon to play in the development process.

Thanks to the well-understood attempts at the sensitization and guidance carried out by the supervisory structures which have been put at your disposal, you have, where and when possible, endeavoured to resist the temptation of such social ills as laziness, rural exodus, irresponsibility and juvenile delinquency.

May I enjoin you adhere to this worthy behaviour which reflects both your awareness of your responsibilities and an assertion of your maturity, and line with our desire to effect a drastic change in attitudes and rid our society of negativist tendencies, retrograde practices and harmful imitation.

This is the time and place to again stress the importance and delicate nature of the role of the educator in these days of cultural mélange, universal dissemination of information, rapid growth and modernization of living conditions. This means that we all, parents, administrative, traditional, religious and political authorities, adults and senior citizens who are custodians of our traditions must redouble our efforts in guiding the youths who are living in a changing world by imbuing them with a high sense of responsibility as citizens, in other words, by making them true catalysts of the development that will shape their future.

For the youths to participate actively in nation-building, "they must feel involved, and this can only be so if they are organized and have received proper ideological training; in short if they are politically committed".

We must emphasize the specific role of the YCNU in this respect. The YCNU is a pre-eminent forum within which the youths as a whole could be imbued with the feeling of the confidence and made fully aware of their responsibilities. Thus fully representing the Cameroonian youths, the YCNU could effectively develop its programme for the political education of the youths, their organization and mobilization in harmony and cohesion, familiarization with national realities and promotion of development projects.

In this connection, there will be reforms in school and university education and in the extra-curricular activities of the youths, with a view to further adapting our educational system to national realities and adjusting it to our aspirations. All these reforms will aim at reinforcing the creative, concrete, dynamic and motivating dimension of education and at asserting the cultural identity of our country.

My Young and Beloved Fellow Countrymen,

During the Third Congress of our Great Party at Bafoussam, I had the opportunity to talk about the renewal and revitalization of the rural unit, namely, the Village community in its physical reality as well as in its social and spiritual originality. Indeed, we are convinced that the entire rural world, if better developed and more carefully "urbanized", could then be better equipped to fulfil its primary vocation of constituting a basic nucleus of the national economy, hence providing the groundwork for industrialization, contributing to self-sufficiency in food, regulating life and activities between the towns and villages, and providing stability through housing and the stamping out of unemployment. The rural world could, in short, become a dynamic centre for cultural renewal and human rehabilitation.

With the massive support of the youths, who spearhead our clearly stated determination to be masters of our development, it will, in the final analysis, be a question of transforming the concept of self-reliant development into a programme of action rigorously programmed in time and space, drawing on the enthusiastic and committed participation of all the forces of the country.

I other words, you, the youths of this country, who are full of energy, open to and capable of generating change in the rural world, must be prepared to participate actively in the experiments which will be carried out with a view to gradually fostering the revitalization of village communities.

I am therefore appealing to the Cameroonian youths of all social strata to become the eager and resolute pioneers of this exciting and humanistic venture which will enable us to meet the multi-faceted challenges thrown at us by a harsh world and a difficult economic situation.

My Young and Beloved Fellow Countrymen,

You have, on several occasions, exhibited your preparedness and ability to participate actively in nation-building. You have thus, within the National Civic Service for Participation in Development, among other normal activities of the programme, participated massively and in a collective show of solidarity and humanity, in the "GREEN SAHEL OPERATION", which enabled more than a million trees to be planted in the Sahel belt of our country.

In the same move, and with the same enthusiasm, you participated in various projects requiring communal efforts, for instance, in the building of youth hostels in Yaoundé and in other parts of the country.

In the field of sports, you have brought home to the Cameroonian nation, united in the perfect ones of thought and feeling symbolizing its enthusiasm, significant victories won after a difficult struggle but in an atmosphere of discipline, courage, and brotherhood. These exploits, while clearly illustrating as I have said before, the spirit of sportsmanship and valour of the Cameroonian youths, are proof of the vitality and radiant energy of our people in their drive to build a strong, united, responsible, and proud nation.

Through all these exploits, you have shown that you are worthy of the nation and the fatherland. I again seize this opportunity to congratulate you, and to encourage you to continue your march forward. For, as I have stated on several occasions, sports are a precious medium for national integration and the development of the physical, civic, and moral virtues of the citizen. They are also a vital factor in promoting a world of peace, friendship and brotherhood when practised in an attempt to attain perfection or in an atmosphere of healthy competition.

My young and Beloved Fellow Countrymen,

Cameroon, like all other African countries, is attempting to build its future in a turbulent international framework fraught with serious tensions that are ruthless towards fragile communities. It is our burden duty in this situation to mobilize all our human and material resources, affirm our belief in our ability while being open to all types of exchanges with the rest of the world, rehabilitate our traditions by injecting the dynamics of the modern world into them and promote scientific and technological progress for the well-being of our people.

This is what we have called mastery, which henceforth will be the philosophy guiding our action and which should inspire and orientate the efforts to be made in the field which contribute to self-sustained development, subject only to own system of values, and involving all facets of national activity in a harmonious and rational manner.

Viewed from this angle, the role you have to play is of primary importance and your responsibilities before history are heavy.

It goes without saying, however, that you can effectively play this role only as long as you do not, under the pretext of untimely claims, engage in useless agitation and futile wrangling which could be exploited by the enemies of the nation who are always ready to attempt to destroy this beautiful structure of unity, stability, national concord and progress.

This is the time and place to refer, with indignation to the situation that has been existing at the Yaoundé University since February 2. Some students are masterminding continuing agitation within the University campus and preventing their colleagues who wish to attend classes as usual from doing so.

Everyone knows that the state has never backed away from any sacrifices nor left any stone unturned to develop education in general and them university in particular.

From year to year, and often to the detriment of other sectors which also require urgent state attention, increasingly huge financial sacrifices have been made on behalf of the University so as to keep pace with its growth.

Consequently, it is out of the question for the University to be transformed into a hotbed of political subversion or of disorder and agitation. The University, as I have said before, must be the "focus of intellectual activity, pride and national solidarity contributing to the consolidation of our young nation".

Faced with this situation and convinced that I am reflecting the feelings of the overwhelming majority of the country as a whole, I declare that the Government will not allow the normal functioning of a set-up like the University that is so important to the development of the nation to be perturbed by the speculative claims and provocative actions of a few citizens who are unaware of their responsibilities and are instead solely concerned with claiming rights that are not commensurate with their real duties as the elites of the nation.

Order will, by all means, reign at the University.

I will call on the lecturers to be fully conscious, more than ever before, of the civic dimension of their task of education. They must, by their behaviour and their teachings, clearly show that they are not only masters of civic responsibility but also educators, in other words, that they groom men and provide responsible guidance so that the University will become "a school of moral rectitude, justice and adult responsibility and not an escape from imperious duty, from the exigencies of society and the state".

There is cause to be pleased with the fact that most of our lecturers are aware of their task as educators and do behave as citizens who are committed and determined to raise the children in their custody to a standard that is commensurate with their historic responsibilities within then Nation by staying faithful to the values of our constantly changing society.

Ultimately, and this is reassuring, we know, that we can rely on the commitment of the overwhelming majority of our youths to effort and discipline and on their patriotism, dedication and support for the efforts undertaken to build a stable, strong, and prosperous nation.

While turning to the future with optimism, therefore, I would like this fifteenth anniversary of the Youth Day to give to all the young men and women of Cameroon not only an opportunity to be pleased with the tasks accomplished and the victories won but also time for reflection. May it also give them greater determination to stay in the forefront of the struggle of the people to build a glorious destiny in dignity and justice for the growth of our beautiful country.

LONG LIVE THE CAMEROONIAN YOUTHS!
LONG LIVE CAMEROON!

5.16: Address by the President of the Republic to the Youths of Cameroon on the Occasion of the 16th National Youth Day, Yaounde, 10 February 1982

Theme: "Youth and Mastery of Development"

Young Men and Women of Cameroon,

My young and beloved Fellow Countrymen,

Each year, I feel renewed pleasure when I speak to you on the occasion of the Day which the nation has dedicated to you in testimony of our affection and confident interest in the youth of this country.

It is also with pride which the entire nation earned from the great exploits which you accomplished not only in the field of sports but also in your efforts at increased and effective participation in the noble task of building a new Cameroon, that I extend to you my fervent wishes of good health, happiness, and development.

I am particularly happy to speak to you today on the eve of this National Day which coincides this year with two significant events: the launching of our Fifth Five-Year Economic, Social, and Cultural Development Plan, and the Tenth Anniversary of the Peaceful Revolution of 20 May 1972.

This is undoubtedly a suitable moment for reflection and meditation as the responsibilities we have already assumed and those still more ardently awaiting us in the future for the attainment of our objectives of National Revolution, and especially for the successful accomplishment of programmes contained in the Fifth Five-Year Plan and which must lead to a tightening of our grip on self-reliant, endogenous and self-sustained development in order to meet the aspiration s of our people.

This Day should also enable you to show meaningful proof of your commitment and desire to serve your Fatherland with devotion, dynamism and loyalty and to remain faithful to the ideals of our Great National Party, the Cameroon National Union, for triumph of our National Revolution.

This means that Cameroonian youth who are the most dynamic of the active forces of the nation because they are better prepared to undertake development activities, must assert themselves as a driving force behind our ambition to master our destiny.

As you are aware, the mastery of development lies mainly in the active, lucid and voluntary role which all the active forces of the nation play in the loft task of building our country.

And because they constitute the centre of gravity of national progress, Cameroonian Youth must resolutely rally behind this call and participate in this mobilization of mind and body aimed at making Cameroon a modern and prosperous nation.

That is why the Cameroonian Youth must, more than ever before, be imbued with the dual sense of responsibility and participation.

Participation is a requisite because authentic development, that is, for the people and by the people, can be ushered in by the untiring efforts of the people, who are the architects of their own development.

This also means that each and everyone must be committed to our relentless struggle for progress.

But participation requires a sense of responsibility in order to be effective, and thanks to that responsibility, each and every one of us has become very conscious of the need for the people, for all groups of people, to take fully in their own hands their destiny in the economic, social, and cultural areas.

For its part, the Government has left no stone unturned in a bid to ensure that the Youth have ample opportunity for the actual exercise of these responsibilities, and that there are facilities capable of successfully integrating the Youth more fully in the development process. The substantial resources set aside for the education, training, health and leisure of the Youth testify to this.

These efforts and sacrifices are natural consequences of our recognition of your entitlement to a more dignified life with prospects for full individual developments.

However, these efforts and sacrifices would have been wasted if the Youth themselves do not respond to them with effective contribution characterized by responsibility, readiness to serve, patriotism, discipline, a sense of the general interest, devotion, civic duty, good moral values and hard work.

You are the embodiment of the well-being of our society today and, at the same time, you are the rich reservoir of our hopes for the emergence of a nation which is more responsible, more just and more human. Your attitude today which is characterized by solidarity, and voluntary and committed participation in national programmes, will determine our ability to conquer the present and withstand the future.

In this context, the cultivation of the soil and the revitalization of the rural areas depend more particularly on the Youth, who are the most dynamic group of the population, and who are quantitatively and qualitatively endowed with enormous physical, moral, and intellectual potentials.

Young people should understand that the Green Revolution is not to be considered as a substitute or a solution rushed into out of despair, and which is not adopted until all other chances have been exhausted. The Green Revolution implies an ever increasing mastery of the techniques of modern farming which are necessary if we are to boost output and increased production. As I have often said, Young People should be aware of the dignity of cultivating the soil, which is the origin of all forms of wealth and the starting point of all civilizations; they should be aware that when it is practiced with love, conscientiousness and efficiency, agriculture like the other areas of national activity, can provide great personal satisfaction while unmistakably leading to social progress.

In the daily struggle to become masters of our development, the Young People, nurtured and raised in our educational system from the nursery school to the University, should fall with national awareness for progress.

This means that the Youth must stave off a number of challenges with similar number of challenges: ignorance for example, must be met with a real yearning for knowledge; deficiencies in the technology of industry, agriculture, stockbreeding, and trade without which there can be no tangible and long lasting development and deficiencies in the techniques of private and public administrative organization must all be made up for; finally, challenges of a cultural nature must be met with creativity so that we can rehabilitate and redeem authentically Cameroonian values.

The responsibility of our Young People in schools and universities is therefore decisive. They can meet these challenges only if, after acquiring a mastery of science and knowledge, they identify with national realities and divest themselves of such ills and laziness, dabbling, dispersion of efforts, baseless agitation, unreasonable demands, which tend to divert their attention from the training designed to meet the pressing needs of national development and realities of our country so as to make of our Young People useful and responsible citizens.

My Young and Beloved Countrymen,

We are going through a very exalting moment of our history. It is a decade during which Cameroonians have to accelerate national progress by becoming real catalysts of a development that is geared towards the total advancement of the masses.

Such development requires that Cameroonians, and particularly the youth, like the rest of the nation, participate fully in the nation building effort.

Obviously in so doing, the Youths are each day confronted with the corrosive influence of the consumer society and the avalanche of information beamed to the masses by the media of the industrialized society which quite often distort their view of the world by shunning the cultural message which we carry and instead disseminating information that reproduce stereotypes that are foreign to our culture.

Faced with such a situation, it is of absolute necessity that we carry out a systematic analysis of the disinformation to which our cultural heritage be subjected and the historical, cultural, or ideological factors that underlie such action and then deploy a continuous and multi-purpose effort to counter them by identifying with and bolstering our national reality and participating more resolutely in the nation building effort.

However, in order to contribute to the advent of a civilization that identifies with progress, brotherhood, and peace, Cameroonian youth must also overcome their own contradictions and together commit themselves to the grandiose task of eliminating those scourges like tribalism, clannish attitudes, nepotism and subversive propaganda, social ills such as delinquency, banditry, crime and lack of duty consciousness which might ruin our beautiful task of nation building. Our youth should instead promote the profound aspirations of the masses.

You are being asked, in other words, to develop yourself-confidence as to foster an amalgam of creative thinking that will enable you to imagine original ways and means of pursuing our development and achieving new heights for Cameroon and Africa.

In this Africa where some people are still under the yoke of racial oppression, Cameroon will always be ready to play its role.

In this Africa where there is a feverish search for ways of pursuing a type of development that will usher in well-being without destroying the soul of the Africans,

Cameroon will be able to initiate original approaches which will serve to anchor the hopes of today in ageless values.

In this world where there is growing inequality between nations, between groups in society and between individuals, Cameroon may help to open avenues of equity and social justice.

In this world where the flame of discontent are being formed by injustice and selfishness and activated by distrust, and wherein Africa in particular stands out as a theatre for the proliferation of hotbeds of tension, division internal upheavals which compromise unity and inhibit development, Cameroon can strive to ensure that the spirit of peace and unity triumphs, and that of tolerance and awareness of the stimulating diversity of cultures and ideas prevails.

This is the objective towards which the combined efforts of all Cameroonians must therefore be directed in an outburst of enthusiasm that would move them from the very origins of their beliefs to the diverse horizons of progress that they would have mastered and enable them to unite among themselves and to be receptive to others.

This is why I believe Cameroonian youth will, in future, be able to continue with the work that has started and stay at the forefront in Africa and the world. To achieve this objective, our youth will rely and the mastered structures of national development adapted to the realities of our time and serve as the harbinger of progress for the nation which they intend to serve.

Consequently, while looking forward to the future with confidence and serenity, my wish is that this 16th National Youth Day Celebration be, for all the girls and boys of Cameroon, an occasion, no doubt, to be pleased with what has been achieved but more specially an opportunity to reflect on and commit themselves to preserving such assets, promote our growth and stay in the forefront of the nation building effort in peace and concord.

LONG LIVE CAMEROONIAN YOUTH!
LONG LIVE CAMEROON!

6

President Biya's New Deal Messages to the Youth: 1983-1991

6.1: Address by the President of the Republic to the Youths of Cameroon on the Occasion of the 17th National Youth Day, Yaounde, 10 February 1983

Theme: "Rigour and Moralization of the Cameroonian Society"

Young People of Cameroon,

My young and Beloved Fellow Countrymen,

On this eve of 11 February, the date set aside for the Youths by the Cameroonian people and the Nation as a whole, it is a great pleasure for me to address you for the first time as Head of State. In doing so, I am both respecting a tradition and, above all bearing testimony to the unwavering care and affection which this Nation has for the Youths.

I would like to seize this golden opportunity to once again extend to you my wishes of good health, happiness and success, and express the legitimate pride which the Cameroonian people are feeling each day with increasing conviction about your effective contribution and patriotic devotion to the great task of nation building.

My young and beloved Fellow Countrymen,

Cameroon has just smoothly gone through a period of great historical importance. I am referring to what the National President of the CNU termed during his meeting with the Bafoussam militants last 17 January 1983 as a "New Peaceful Revolution".

It is a pleasure for me to note that, on that occasion the Cameroonian Youths manifested their remarkable patriotism by taking the historic event with such devotion and dignity as is commensurate with the maturity of the Cameroonian people as a whole.

You did not listen to the demons of destabilization, demoralization, and demobilization. You have discouraged the diverse manoeuvres, false propaganda and the campaigns to instigate sectarism. By so doing, you have not only shown proof of your lucidity and unswerving attachment to our institutions, but have also satisfied the expectations and hopes of the nation as far as the hopes as concerned.

While thanking you from the bottom of my heart for all the events organized to illustrate your support as militants, while congratulating you for your high sense of responsibility towards the nation, I would like to tell you once more that I expect from you ever increasing and responsible commitment to mobilization.

These two attitudes, called for at the Congress of Bafoussam, and based on the policy of political, economic, social, and cultural mastery are inextricably rooted in the need for rigour and the concern for ethical behaviour forcefully underscored at the Fifth National Council of the Cameroon National Union.

In a tumultuous world where the spectre of crisis looms and which is dominated by conflicts, divisions, violence, economic inequalities, selfish interests and misery, Cameroon has succeeded in offering Africa and the world a reassuring image of peace, stability, and I will say, prosperity.

We owe this great achievement to the enduring action carried out to consolidate national unity and to our policies of planned liberalism, self-reliant, balanced development which exalt the participation of all the vital forces of the nation, mobilize and rationally exploit all our human and material resources.

Hence, we are pleased and proud of these precious achievements made at the cost of the untiring sacrifices made by everybody, thus, proving, if it were necessary, that the development that we are pursuing with all our energy and determination is the work and reward of a United, industrious and committed people capable of assuming their own destiny.

Yes, my Dear Young Fellow Countrymen, the many achievements that we made during these past years were the result of a fierce and sustained struggle waged closely together with the Cameroonian youths, the vital force and precious wealth of our country, the leaven and driving force, and the most dynamic, healthiest and most available of the nation's vital forces.

But as I stated in my end-of-year message, "We should not passively take pleasure in contemplative and static self-complacency for the enemies and the detractors of our institutions have not laid down their arms" . In this prospect, "Our major concern will be to maintain the pace of our development and revitalize and boost its quality while remaining loyal to our objective of self-reliant development".

Consequently, I am glad that by a fortunate coincidence which is significant in many respects, the theme of your day this year is "Rigour and Moralization of the Cameroonian Society".

It is thus incumbent on you, Dear and young fellow countrymen, to be the vanguard corps of the struggle waged by the party and Government to moralise the Cameroonian society. It is your duty, more than ever before, to be the unadulterated leaven of moral rectitude, self-abnegation, integrity, honesty, and probity, and also of generosity, commitment to effort, and creative initiative.

You should remember that nothing great and sublime can be achieved without sacrifice, self-discipline, and a certain amount of self-control.

But alas! There has been, among the youths, a fresh outbreak of evil practices characterized by a staggering increase in banditry, a propensity for unbridled quest for wealth and various forms of trafficking.

Also, there are numerous cases of laisser-faire, apathy or agitation, indifference or rebellion among youths.

If we want to condemn and combat energetically these evils which bear the seeds of the decline of a society that we would like to be sound and dynamic, we must also pursue, with more determination than ever, our policy of youth guidance, in particular the organization of extra-curricular activities which will enhance their interest and ambition in development.

It is in this light that studies will be carried out with a view to promoting or developing extra-curricular activities which, on the one hand, will be capable of offering the youths the opportunity of undergoing or completing their vocational, cultural, civic and social training in mutual co-operation with adults and, on the other hand, helping the youths, as it is already the case at the National Civic Service for Participation in Development, to carry out the tasks required of them by development programmes, irrespective of their social environment.

Our Great National Party could play a crucial role in this respect.

Thus, the overwhelming majority of youths will be ready to assume their well-known enthusiasm and reserves of energy their share responsibility in the task of nation building.

As my distinguished predecessor rightly stated, it is only at this price that you will succeed in the exalting task of building your country; you will first have to give it life in your minds before it form in the world.

My Dear and young Fellow Countrymen, as you are aware, the government has never spared any effort nor overlooked any opportunity to reassert and convince you that the Cameroonian youth is its hope, its most valuable hope.

These efforts and this care of public authorities will be relentlessly continued because, as a matter of fact, to our mind the term "youth" means – in addition to age - a psychological state that comprises the ability to be receptive, an open mind, a drive and availability. In this respect, our ambition is to make of every Cameroonian citizen, a citizen who is aware of his duties and responsibilities.

I am convinced, as you have on several occasions shown in the field of sports, studies, art and many others, that you will be able, through your ability to meet the challenges of history and to serve great causes, to meet the lofty aspirations and expectations of the entire Cameroonian people.

Dear and Young Fellow Countrymen, I can assure you that the Cameroonian nation as a whole is keenly following and appreciates your successes and glorious performances that have earned for our beloved and beautiful country, influence, esteem and admiration.

Consequently, I repose in you all my confidence and urge you to continue in this manner so that, more than ever before, you will be the symbol of this youth which knows how to study the world from a new point of view and with an innovative mind. Such a study is possible because you will have been committed to the most exalting adventure – that of nation building, for the improvement of the living conditions and the development of all Cameroonians who yearn to live in peace, brotherhood and freedom in a modern and prosperous country.

LONG LIVE THE CAMEROONIAN YOUTH!
LONG LIVE CAMEROON!

6.2: Address by the President of Republic to the Youths of Cameroon on the Occasion of the 18th National Youth Day, Yaounde, 10 February 1984

Theme: "Youth and Rigour at Work"

Young Fellow Countrymen,

The feliticious tradition which, every year, leads the Head of State to address the Cameroonian youth gives me the pleasure today, once more, to address you officially for the first time as the elected President of the Republic of Cameroon. To me, this opportunity is more than mere coincidence; in fact it seems to have been marked out by destiny.

Consequently on this eighteenth anniversary of the National Youth Day, it is special warmth and pride that I am conveying to you wishes of happiness, prosperity and success as Head of State. I would also like to bear witness to the concern, love, and confidence that the entire Nation is showing towards you as representatives of the most dynamic component of our people and the most invaluable asset of our country.

I have always underscored the very special role that must be played by the Cameroonian Youth in building of our young nation. At the dawn of this era of the New Deal, this role takes on a more dynamic significance which demands from you renewed commitment and the assumption of more responsibility. The New Deal which, in fact, is the keynote of my present term of office as PRESIDENT OF THE Republic, must quicken the pace of development in our country, thus maximizing the opportunities for it to assert itself as a nation that is solidly united with the same destiny and aspirations.

We should remember that the New Deal is proposing a society whose main options were thrown to the whole country and approved during the Presidential elections of 14 January 1984. Therefore, what is left now, as I have said, is to implement those options by jointly pursuing a policy the watch words of which will be rigour and moralization, liberalization and democratization; a new style is required in State and Party activities and need new dynamism aimed at mobilizing the Cameroonian society as a whole.

This policy, which generally presupposes a change in attitudes, implies specific responsibilities for each category of citizens. As concerns young people in particular, the implantation of the New Deal requires of you, with regard to your obligations, a new awareness commensurate with the challenges we are facing at this decisive turning-point in our long and irreversible march forward.

It is evident that the New Deal, the ambition of which is to make Cameroon an integrated society, founded on the unity of ideas, the quest for efficiency and sound values – a society which fosters the full development of the Cameroonian and which is the centre of cultural advancement in Africa – the New Deal policy, I repeat, cannot succeed unless the young people effectively become its essential driving force. For who, indeed, more than the youths who are less exposed to the ineptitudes of the past and less prone to selfishness, who are more responsive to the calls of the future and to generosity – who, more than they can more effectively promote the profound changes in attitude, behaviour and structures which this policy implies?

This means that through your constructive criticism, sense of analysis, quest for perfection, sense of duty, in short, your creative dynamism, you will transform Cameroon, our beautiful country into a real and great model of development.

It also means that in addition to your acknowledged qualities of determination, perseverance, faith in effort and sense of generosity and creative genius, you have to display a sense of rectitude, honesty and intellectual probity so that our society can be built on a more propitious foundation.

Again, this means that more than in the past, national unity which remains an indispensable bedrock of the New Deal, has ceased been for you an unattainable ideal, and an abstract notion, but is now part and parcel of your daily activities, and that by overcoming particularisms and all sorts of indifferences, you are ready to move to the highest phase of national integration.

Lastly it means that you are determined to assume your responsibilities with enthusiasms and all your responsibilities which you are expected to assume resourcefulness in the effort being made every day by the Nation to become master of its destiny.

The eighteenth Youth Day anniversary should not only be time of rejoicing, but also a good opportunity to reflect on the efforts you still have to make and on the within the framework of the New Deal. In other words, it should be an illustrious manifestation of your firm and unshakable determination to ensure the continuous progress of our development in all areas.

That is why, being conscious of your ability to take up the challenges of history and meet the expectations of the Nation, in short, your ability to support great causes, I am happy that the theme of this Youth Day anniversary is "Youth and Rigour at Work".

Indeed, as I stated in last year's message, "at the individual and collective levels, nothing great and sublime can be achieved without sacrifice, self-discipline and a certain amount of self-control".

Without these cardinal values which constitute the strength of men and peoples, the nation and firstly its Youth might be involved in the fresh outbreak of evil practices such as banditry, the bent for corruption, and the unbridled quest for wealth, and various forms of trafficking, laxity, idleness, indifference, and gratuitous and nefarious rebellion.

This means that these virtues are essential for the building of this progressive and balanced society conducive to the advancement of each and everyone in equality, freedom and justice which we all hope for, since we all know that there can be true freedom only if it is exercised in a responsible way and with respect for public order; and that our common duty will be to continuously reduce with the utmost patience, all aspects of injustice in our society and in a similar manner, intensify your efforts towards the attainment of a level of social justice commensurate with the expectations of our people.

You have certainly understood my Dear Young countrymen, that the task awaiting us all at this stage of our destiny is immense, exalting and difficult, because development is the gradual result of the hard work of the nation as a whole and the type of society I have proposed to Cameroonians can be achieved and made to last only with the active participation of all the people, and particularly the youth.

I am therefore pleased to seize this singular opportunity to renew my most sincere thanks to each and every one of you for the spontaneous, committed, massive, enthusiastic and unreserved support you have always given me on important occasions which have marked the life of the nation since 6 November 1982. This total support and resolutely positive attitude undoubtedly show the sincere patriotism and fervent militancy which stimulate you; indeed I fully appreciate this.

The road we have covered together since 6 November 1982 and the significant victories we have won are for me the assurance of the determination and enthusiasms you all have to unflinchingly support our great struggle to build a new Cameroon.

LONG LIVE THE CAMEROON YOUTH!
LONG LIVE CAMEROON!

6.3: Address by the President of the Republic to the Youths of Cameroon on the Occasion of the 19th National Youth Day, Yaounde, 10 February 1985

Theme: "Participation, Development, Peace"
My Young and Fellow Countrymen,
Here, once again, is the eve of that day set aside for you by the Nation as a token of its deep feelings of affection, concern, and attachment.

I therefore seize this opportunity offered me on the 19th Youth Day to convey to you my special wishes of health, prosperity, and long life; I hope that 1985 will be for you and the entire nation a year of development and peace.

I am pleased with the theme of this year's Youth Day, which is "Youth, Peace, and Development". For, without peace, by which I mean the peace in your minds and hearts, the peace in our society, there cannot be real development.

Indeed, the results we have attained so far show that development comes from peace. It goes only to an interdependent people, to a creative people, desirous of progress, to a perseverant and generous people. This means that now and in future, you must more than ever before work with determination, dedication and abnegation, hand in hand with all the nation so as to make Cameroon a society in which there is tolerance, concord and justice. Above all, the youth of Cameroon, ever enthusiastic, dynamic, and enterprising, are more than ever before called upon to transform our country into a vast worksite for development where our people can demonstrate their creative genius.

My Young and Fellow Countrymen,

It pleases me to recall that the nineteenth National Youth Day is taking place after the two provincial and National Youth Conferences of the Great Unified Party.

Please accept my warm congratulations for your precious contribution to the success of these conferences. By your positive participation in the deliberations, your constructive proposals and your dignifying and impressive behaviour during the two conferences, you proved that you are resolutely committed to the great task of nation building.

Because they are the symbol of innovation and change, youths constitute the spearhead of the National New Deal policy which I instituted since 6 November 1982 and which the Cameroonian people overwhelmingly approved on 14 January 1984. This progressive, national and harmonious change requires the contribution of all Cameroonian. The Nation therefore anxiously expects your positive suggestions for an active participation in the acceleration of the development of the Nation.

This is why I am calling on our youths to be at the forefront of the struggle for the methodical transformation of Cameroon into a land of plenty and prosperity.

My Young and Fellow Countrymen,

On the eve of the Bamenda Congress, which is a Congress of the New Deal, I am calling on you to work harder and to be ready to assume your responsibilities so as to cope with the call of history. This Congress is one that will reaffirm Cameroon's identity and consolidate the new dynamic machinery.

On the morrow of the Second Extraordinary Congress of 14 September 1983, and the extensive campaign to revitalize Party activities, the CNU can, and must become, the crucible of our authentic emancipation, the catalyst of our political, economic, social, and cultural development – a party open to all political leanings and to all men of goodwill, determined to build in national concord, a new and balanced Cameroon Nation extricated from the sequels of the positive achievements of the Nation.

Through the constant increase of budgetary appropriations earmarked for National Education, Youth and Sports and other ministries and bodies directly or indirectly responsible for the youths, the state is enhancing the full development of young Cameroonians in the towns and rural areas. The laudable results recorded in such diverse areas as agriculture, animal breeding, culture and sports are proof that the sacrifices made by the state are not in vain.

Aware of your patriotism, I have no doubts that you will, like in the past, be worthy of the trust that the Cameroonian people have in you for the growth of our nation. I request you to work relentlessly and with abnegation so as to be always deserving of the fatherland and build in peace a state which is not a mere juxtaposition of ethnic, religious or language groupings, but a real national community founded on common ideas and a common destiny.

In a world situation characterized by a lingering economic crisis, national selfishness, struggles for supremacy, ideological conflicts and self-interest, we have to be vigilant and ambitious in order to continue to progress. This is why the

Nineteenth Youth Day should be seen just as a critical moment of profound meditation on the activities that we still have to undertake so as to boost and sustain our development in unity and peace.

Such is the appeal of history to the Cameroonian youth. It is your duty to answer it by pooling the efforts that will enable you and the generations to come to ever strengthen our solidarity, development and peace.

LONG LIVE THE CAMEROONIAN YOUTH!
LONG LIVE THE REPUBLIC OF CAMEROON!

6.4: Address by the President of the Republic to the Youths of Cameroon on the Occasion of the 20th National Youth Day, Yaounde, 10 February 1986

Theme: "Youth, Peace, and Development"

My Dear Young Compatriots,

I am pleased to address you today.

On the eve of the 20th Youth Day placed under the theme "Participation, Development, Peace". I want to show you the important place I reserve in my heart to the youth of Cameroon.

In my capacity as the Head of State and in my own name, I sincerely wish you good health, success, and happiness. You are the future of the country. I count on you. You can count on me. The Cameroon of the New Deal is keeping its promises.

At the University level:

In Buea, opening of the University Centre and its Advanced School of Translators and Interpreters.

In Yaoundé, start the building of five amphitheatres at the University; restoration of the University restaurant; completion of the expansion of the National Higher School of Polytechnics; granting more than 1,000 additional scholarship; commencement of studies to improve student housing; commencement of studies for the expansion of ASMAC.

More generally, substantial financial assistance has been granted to our students abroad and in Cameroon; financial support has been given to the Ngaoundere, Dshang, and Douala University Centres; 1,700 university graduates have been recently recruited.

At the school level, continued building of schools, colleges, high schools and other training centres in the ten provinces of our country.

For the unemployed youth, the creation of the national labour market is open to all young people. For the rural youth, bonuses for the settlement of young farmers; bonuses for plantation regeneration; bonuses for the opening of new plantations; revitalization of the National Civic Service for Participation in Development.

In addition, we intend to encourage and develop still further the practice of sport. Finally a real youth and animation policy was defined during the National Youth and Mass education Committee meeting.

Thus a lot has been achieved in a short time, but a lot still remains to be done ... and for that, I need you!!1

I expect you to be responsible men and women.

I expect you to be efficient in all your actions.

I expect all your actions to be of high quality.

I ask you to participate ever more actively in our joint venture of building and developing our country.

I ask you to be at the service of your country so that together we can build the Cameroon of tomorrow – your Cameroon.

I ask you for your help in my fight for moral rectitude.

I ask for your help in my on-going fight against the ills which plague our society:

- Delinquency;
- Unscrupulous business;
- Wait-and-see policy;
- Laxity; and
- Idleness.

We shall win this war which we are making before history and before men! At the dawn of this new my best wishes go with you to the examination halls, to the stadia, to the fields, to the workshops, to the offices and to the factories.

By my voice the Cameroon of our forefathers is bring to you, in love and pride, its resounding message of encouragement.

You are the Cameroon of the future, prepare right from today the future of Cameroon.

LONG LIVE THE YOUTH OF CAMEROON!
LONG LIVE CAMEROON!

6.5: Address by the President of the Republic to the Youths of Cameroon on the Occasion of the 21st National Youth Day, Yaounde, 10 February 1987

Theme: "What Youth for the New Deal?"

My Young Fellow Countrymen,

On the occasion of your day this year, it is a pleasant duty for me to convey to you this message, a message of hope and encouragement. Hope to see you more committed than ever in the struggle we are engaged in to build the New Deal Cameroon. Hope to be able to count on youthful vitality, on your creative genius and the generosity of your hearts, to accelerate the economic, social, and cultural development of our country. Encouragement to work tirelessly and strive to surpass yourselves not only for your own satisfaction but also for the benefit of the entire Nation.

To this end, you must combat, indeed, all of us must combat, those ills which you could easily fall prey, especially delinquency, banditry, and lack of patriotism. You must cultivate a sense of hard work, moral rectitude, efficiency, honour and dignity. Yes, you must cultivate all the qualities which are the bedrock of the grandeur of individuals, peoples and nations.

In a word, your constant preoccupation should be to build, in concord and unity, a strong and prosperous Cameroon. In fact, that is the subject of reflection for this anniversary of the Youth Day.

Young Fellow Countrymen,

Last Year much was done for your training and social advancement. A National Bureau of the Youth wing of our Great Party, the CPDM, was created at the Bamenda Congress and went into activity after the democratic election of its members; this shows the importance henceforth given to the youth in the nation's political life.

As for education, many sacrifices were made at all levels to enable the greatest possible number of young people to acquire knowledge. These included:

- The construction of 847 classrooms at the primary and nursery school level;
- The construction of 188 classrooms at the general, secondary, technical, and vocational education level;
- The construction of five lecture-halls and multi-sports complex of the University of Yaoundé;
- The completion of the first phase of the Ngoundere University Centre;
- The award of thousands of scholarships and many grants to students undergoing training in Cameroon and abroad; and
- A substantial increase in the State's contribution to the running of private educational establishments.

With regard to young people in rural areas in particular, the National Office for Participation in Development was recognized to enable it intervene throughout the country and better ensure the guidance and follow-up of young people who have been trained.

As regards employment, the State has made considerable efforts. Adjustments to the special programme for the recruitment of University graduates made it possible to employ a great number of young people in the public sector.

As for sports, many victories and trophies were won on the international scene, thus demonstrating the vitality and combativeness of the Cameroonian youth.

Young Fellow Cameroonians,

All the achievements I have just mentioned show that the people and Government of Cameroon are concerned about you and have confidence in you. I urge you to continue deserving this concern and confidence through your untiring efforts, hard work and efficiency; a high sense of patriotism, good citizenship, duty consciousness, and responsibility.

I count on you for the consolidation of all we have achieved in every field of our national life. I count on you to satisfactorily pursue our national New Deal Policy, the success of which requires well-educated youths with healthy minds and bodies, youth who are committed and hardworking.

You are not only our country's hope but also its present source of vitality. In other words, you are the guarantors of its present and future triumphs. We need you, we need your vitality, your devotedness and your creativity to continue, without respite, in discipline, harmony and fraternity, the building of a great and beautiful country. I sincerely wish you success and happiness throughout 1987.

LONG LIVE THE CAMEROONIAN YOUTH
LONG LIVE CAMEROON

6.6: Address by the President of the Republic to the Youths of Cameroon on the Occasion of the 22nd National Youth Day, Yaounde, 10 February 1988

Theme: "The Youth Facing Their Responsibilities"

My young fellow countrymen,

I am pleased to be with you all here, on the occasion of this twenty-second National Youth Day – your feast day.

We are now on the morrow of the Maroua Agro-pastoral show which was a testimony to our determination to work and to our food self-sufficiency.

We are on the eve of legislative elections, which is proof of our determination towards democratization. Cameroon, your country, is therefore pursuing its national New Deal drive and counts on all youths to give it a new impetus.

You are very many. In fact, 55% of Cameroon's population is made up of citizens less than 20 years old.

You know to be dynamic,

You know how to participate actively in the national effort, and you have proved it!

Young workers, young farmers, young students, … you are the future of Cameroon!

Our country is facing economic difficulties at the moment due to the world crisis. The initial solutions will be found in the strong determination to preserve our achievements and in hard work by us all.

In Maroua, I exhorted farmers and stockbreeders to maintain our food self-sufficiency. I am requesting you all now to be conscious of your capital role in building tomorrow's Cameroon.

Cameroon is developing to enable you develop:

For University and school infrastructure:

Between 1987 and 1988: 4000 new classrooms, new sports complexes, and many other extra-curricular facilities have been made available. In a space of five years, more than 100,000 million Francs has been invested in the building and equipment of government school; and more than 37,000 million has been granted as aid to private schools.

At present, there are 22,000 students in our universities: 70% of them have scholarships and nearly 30% have student aid. Out of the 12,000 students abroad, 7000 have scholarships and 2,700 are given student aid.

So far, we have taken concrete measures within our means to provide better guidance for you and increasingly enable you to achieve self-fulfilment.

At the level of rural production: over 20,000 youths have chosen rural production so as to put their energy at the service of their country. This movement will be intensified by the 12 young farmer's training centres, 12 rural training and further training centres, and 10 civic service for participation centres. They are an example of the goodwill of the Cameroonian youth.

And more generally, whatever your trade or occupation, you are all concerned:

As from today, you should work.

As from today, you should feel responsible.

As from today, you should take control of your future.

Your government will continue to support and encourage you.

I know you deserve it!

I have no doubt that you will do all in your power to become responsible citizens, deserving of the confidence that is placed in you by your elders.

You are the youth of the New Deal era.

You are the custodians of the nation's hopes.

The task of nation-building which keeps your parents busy on a daily basis will be your inheritance.

You have been brought up in the mould of peace, progress and social justice.

You cannot afford to disappoint those who have endowed you with these principles.

Never forget them.

For tomorrow will be your turn to imbue your own children with the same principles and with the love for their fatherland.

You should count first on yourselves as you work for the future of your country.

No to laziness

No to corruption

No to delinquency

No to vandalism

I count on you.

The country counts on you.

You like your country.

Cameroon has confidence in You.

6.7: Address by the President of the Republic to the Youths of Cameroon on the Occasion of the 23rd National Youth Day, Yaounde, 10 February 1989

Theme: "Youth and National Solidarity"

Youth of Cameroon,

My Dear Compatriots,

I am happy to join you once again in celebrating Youth Day. On this special day, I would like that we all remember some of your friends of the Monthe Institute who would have been here with us today.

Fortunately, the year 1988 will not go down in history as a year of tragedy only. I would like us to take stock of the year 1988.

You proved that you are responsible and trustworthy young people in the political, economic, cultural, and sporting arenas – four areas in which you must work constantly in order to achieve tangible results, four areas in which nothing is ever achieved for good.

In the political sphere, your sense of responsibility and commitment resulted in the brilliant success of the second National Council of the YCPDM; your growing presence within the Municipal Councils and the National Assembly further attests to that sense of responsibility.

In the economic sphere, we are witnessing the birth of a new generation of dynamic and honest businessmen. I am sure that this new generation of businessmen will put the interests of Cameroon before their own interests.

And a new generation of farmers is coming up in spite of the unfavourable economic situation. I am strongly encouraging them to continue to develop Cameroon.

In the area of culture, the youth appear geared to take over the baton. Several Cameroonian youth won prizes at international musical and literary competitions, and young talents were discovered at the Douala Festival of Arts and Culture.

The behaviour of our pupils and students has portrayed them as responsible and faithful to the ideals of the Party. This has been confirmed by reports about the seriousness of our students and by their examination results.

Moreover, the march in support of my policies organized by the students of the University of Yaoundé on 7 January this year is proof that they will have nothing to do with subversion, unrest and disorder. Our policy of moralization needs such sound-minded and serious youth who will show the example.

With respect to sports, several victories were recorded. The spirit prevailing everywhere is that of continuously improving performance in order to attain greater heights. I encourage all young people to adopt this spirit.

In order to participate effectively in the life and progress of your country, you need to behave like excellent sportsmen by:

- Improving your performance;
- Striving for greater heights;

- Respecting your fellow sportsmen;
- Developing a team spirit;
- Believing in victory.

For us to achieve a common victory, we must make sacrifices together we must tackle the problems due to the world economic crisis. In spite of this crisis, government, on account of the hopes it places in Cameroonian youth, is doing its best to train you and provide you with the means of ensuring your future and that of Cameroon.

It was deemed necessary to make special efforts in the agricultural sector. The rehabilitation of the National Office for participation in Development, currently underway, is aimed at improving the training of young farmers and the conditions of their settlement.

The number of young people opting for agriculture is, for us, a sign of good hope.

We count on all of you, young people in the rural areas, tom increase and improve production which is threatened by a drop in commodity prices, and the low competitiveness of your sector.

In fact, the aging population of the rural areas can no longer make significant efforts to extend and maintain existing farms. It is your duty to revitalize this sector and to provide the new impetus and force necessary for our agriculture to be maintained to an acceptable level. You will be the first beneficiaries of this endeavour. Government has clearly demonstrated its goodwill by maintaining the prices of staple products despite the persistent crisis, thereby asserting that it supports what you are doing.

In all sectors, I placed special emphasis on the training of youth as well as on measures designed to ease your entry into the work world. In that respect, activities have been undertaken for the promotion and development of training young workers has been reviewed to take into account the real needs of the modern sector, and, in particular, the rural sector. In addition, the Opportunities Industrialization Centre, commissioned in November 1988 at Buea, and set up with the assistance of the United States, is already producing the first encouraging results.

One of our priorities is to tailor training to employment, long-term activities are being geared towards the promotion of private training centres, which have first and foremost to take into account this requirement.

Education and employment are complementary. Consequently, it is necessary to train young people in the sectors that need them. The young people in schools and universities have not been forgotten. The number of primary schools, colleges, high schools, and universities we are opening or modernizing attest to the interest government is taking in matters that concern you.

You, also are forging the future of Cameroon. The studies you have started must be carried on to the end convincingly and relentlessly. I place my trust in you.

Young workers, young students ... I am prepared to listen to your problems. The policy I am advocated takes into account the needs of everybody, but certainly, only as far as possible.

Despite the difficulties caused by the crisis, government has made substantial financial sacrifices to maintain your level of education and training.

Endeavour to maintain the confidence I have in you.

Endeavour to prove yourselves worthy of your country.

Cameroon will be proud of you.

LONG LIVE CAMEROONIAN YOUTH!
LONG LIVE CAMEROON!

6.8: Address by the President of the Republic to the Youths of Cameroon on the Occasion of the 24th National Youth Day, Yaounde, 10 February 1990

Theme: "Sports, Faith, and Hope"
Young Cameroonians!

It is my pleasure to join you in celebrating this 24th Youth Day, your day.

Once again the entire nation demonstrates the confidence it has in you. On behalf of the Nation, I wish each and every one of you a happy Youth Day as well a prosperous 1990.

1990 , you will recall is placed under the sign of hope. Hope in seeing the crisis finally jugulated. Hope in seeing Cameroon achieve its economic recovery. Hope of achieving a growth curve that reflects the efforts being made by all Cameroonians. You, indeed all of us need to nurture these hopes.

In the social, cultural, and sports domains, the Youth of Cameroon has scored very many victories. The Youth of Cameroon have proved to be mature and responsible. Each of you is well aware not only of the difficulties our country is facing but also of the sacrifices being made for you, under difficult circumstances.

You have, on many occasions, shown your support for the New Deal policies and for Government action. The symbolic franc and the peaceful march by the Yaoundé University students can be cited as good examples of this support.

I congratulate you on your commitment.

Cameroon is doing very well in sports thanks to the brilliant performances of the youth. Here are some of the most laudable victories won:

- The African Nations' Volleyball Cup;
- The Volley Ball Champion Club's Cup;
- The Handball Champion's Club Cup;
- The very First Central Africa Table Tennis Cup;
- The last UDEAC Football Cup.

Cameroon is proud of these achievements. Discipline and perseverance have proved their worth, courage and endurance are the driving forces behind positive results. Let them be the sources of inspiration for all of you in the other areas of life.

In the cultural domain, the emergence of young talents in diverse areas augurs well for the future. They are helping to enrich our culture. Several successful festivals and exhibitions were organized in Cameroon, thus demonstrating the interest that our fellow citizens take in our cultural heritage.

Many are those who will be pleased with the opening of libraries throughout the country in a bid to encourage the public to read. They will also be pleased with the conversion of the former State House into a National Museum.

Your role in these social achievements deserves to be recognized. I am very pleased with the active participation of many young Cameroonians at:

- The 13th World Festival of Youth in Pyongyang;
- The Beijing International Forum; and
- The Dakar International Forum.

At each of these great cultural festivals, you fully exhibited your talents. I congratulate. I have cited brilliant examples, but there are many among you who hardly got to be mentioned. That does not mean that they are not important. Even though the majority of you may not boast of outstanding achievements, yet each of you, through your daily occupation, is contributing in shaping the image of your Youth.

It is up to you to shape a positive image. The quality of your achievements will depend solely on you, on your diligence, on your determination. Whether you are a student or a worker, whether you live in town or in the rural area, you all constitute the Cameroon of tomorrow and I expect you to give the best of yourselves at all levels. I know you are up to the task. For its part, Government is well aware of your needs in the realm or education, employment and vocational training.

Despite our current difficulties, I can assure you that no effort is being spared and no effort will be spared to enable you to succeed. Some concrete examples in 1989 alone:

- A total of 800 classrooms were built with a priority being given to rural areas and areas with concentration of the school population;
- 11 General Secondary Education colleges were opened throughout the Nation;
- Under the programme of construction of six technical high schools in six provinces, work has been completed on the Sangmelima Technical School and work on that of Nkolbisson is in progress;
- The Advanced Teachers Training College (ENS) now has a science building which should contribute to enhancing teacher training;
- Closed circuit television was installed at the University and will soon be operational;
- Tutorial rooms and academic staff offices were built at the Faculty of Law and Economics;
- More than 15,000 scholarships, including 3,000 new awards, were granted to students of Yaoundé University; 480 scholarships were granted for studies abroad.

The Government has just signed an agreement for the building of a new university campus so as to increase the intake of students. The new campus will include:

- Halls of residence with a total of 1,280 beds;
- 11 auditoriums;
- 112 halls for tutorials and practicals;
- 151 offices and 3 libraries;
- 2 restaurants;
- Sports facilities as well as medical and social welfare centre. Under the agreement mentioned earlier, the Faculty of Science will be expanded and equipment will be supplied to the science building of the Advanced Teachers Training College.

Negotiations will be concluded soon on the building of other halls of residence with a capacity of 3500 beds.

- The administrative reorganization of the University was carried out. This will ensure better management of university welfare services and student guidance;
- Government grants to private education have been maintained at six thousand million CFA francs.

As you can see, everything is being done, in the best possible way, to ease you access to working life. But entry into working life is not always very easy. The employment of youths remains a major concern. The National Employment Fund which is being set up will pool job supply and demand for your problems is to be addressed. The Fund will have several missions:

- Informing and counselling young job seekers with a view to employing and redeploying them;
- Developing or setting up small enterprises, especially in the rural area; and
- Identifying labour-intensive sectors, in order to channel the youth towards them.

Vocational training, which is a top priority, will be given a new impetus by closely involving labour and management in any action taken. The Government has also taken steps to render higher education more professional. All these efforts should lead to a revival of the economy within which you will be able to apply your various skills whether you are degree-holders or not, cadres or ordinary employees.

All sectors, at all levels, need to be strengthened and injected with new blood.

Young Cameroonians,

You are part and parcel of an economic system. It is up to us, together, to make it more viable. Your participation is essential. Our country tomorrow will be what you make it. Avoid the easy way out. Do not cheat! Show the right example. At the dawn of this year, all youthful resources must be mobilized. You are the future of Cameroon and all our hopes lie in you. Let us remain faithful to our contract of confidence. I know I can count on you. All that we are doing today is being do for you. Ask yourselves also what you too can do for your country.

LONG LIVE THE 24TH YOUTH DAY
LONG LIVE CAMEROON

7

President Biya's Democratic Cameroon's Youth Day Messages: 1991-2008

7.1: Address by the President of the Republic to the Youths of Cameroon on the Occasion of the 25th National Youth Day, Yaounde, 10 February 1991

Theme: "Freedom, Democracy, and Discipline"

Young Cameroonians,

As has been the case over the past twenty-five years, Cameroon has once more honoured its tradition. As is the case each year, Cameroonians is getting ready to celebrate its Youth day. On behalf of all Cameroonians, on behalf of the Government, and on my own behalf I wish you all a happy Youth Day and renew my wishes of success in 1991. Sons and daughters of Cameroon, you are the future, you are the hope of an entire Nation. Learn to put your strength and skills, no matter what they are, to good use. That is what I am asking of you. You all know that we are pursuing our courageous fight against the economic crisis. We are making every effort to enable Cameroon to recover a healthy economy that will be profitable to everyone. These efforts are beginning to bear fruit but we must still make sacrifices and, above all, preserve.

In the face of our difficulties, many of you have shown great maturity. Thank you for your support, thank you for your patriotism, thank you for your understanding. As you well know, the welfare of the Cameroon Youth is still one of my major preoccupations. Your numbers in primary schools, secondary and high schools and the faculties are ever increasing.

About 2 million of you are in primary schools, more than 500.000 in secondary and high schools and more than 34 in higher institutions of learning. This figure is increasing at a rate of about 25% per annum. The State is monitoring this development very closely and in spite of the crisis, is adapting to the rising numbers as can be seen from many measures that have been taken, for example last year, at the primary and secondary levels, 350 government schools were opened while 305 private ones were approved.

At university level we are still making great sacrifices for students-more than 5,000 million in the form of scholarships, aids and limited assistance to those studying abroad. Many efforts are also being made to improve the quality of education, adapt it to professional life and to provide new infrastructure. In this connection, highly qualified staff have been recruited; new and more appropriate teaching methods are being applied, and-professional post-graduate courses have been introduced in the faculties.

On a more practical level, a new science block has been commissioned at the Advanced Teachers' Training College (ENS),- an agreement to the tune of 11 thousand million CFA francs has just been signed with the Spanish government to equip the laboratories of this institution, and to extend and equip the laboratories of the Faculty of Science; and- a new campus is under construction at the Dshang University Centre. But we do not devote our efforts to the education and housing of students only. All young Cameroonians are taken into account, whether they are students or not. All sooner or later whether you are students or potential workers you will face the problem of employment. I am aware of this. So too, are you. This is why the measures taken by the government are intended to facilitate your entry into professional life.

Here are some examples: The National Employment Fund will soon become operational; The privatization of public enterprises has started and the initial results indicate that several thousand jobs will be created in the near future; The Aid and Loan Guarantee Fund for Small and Medium-sized Enterprises (FOGAPE) and the Agricultural Credit Bank encourage self-employment and the setting up of small and medium-sized enterprises and industries in both urban and rural areas. In this connection, the "Young Promoters" project- a joint initiative of the International Labour Office and the Aid and Loan Guarantee Fund for Small-and Medium-sized Enterprises to set up forty businesses is progressing steadily.

Furthermore, promotion of Adapted Farming Systems based on animal Traction (PAFSAT), in the North-West Province, an example of co-operation between Germany and Cameroon, provides our rural youths with an alternative to train in animal traction. Rural electrification projects, like the one in the North – West Province which was accomplished with the much valued assistance of Great Britain, and the "Noun Road" project, designed to help rural youth settle in their villages and develop their potentials. Promising activities carried out by the Centre de Creation d' Enterprises" (business promotion centre) in Yaoundé, which is the fruit of co-operation between Canada and Cameroon. Initiatives by social centres, women's centres in creating employment for young girls, are equally social assets as well as mature and responsible endeavours. Cameroon does not want to leave out any one out, our youth constitute the group that is least mentioned. They are the ones who have to be shepherded.

The "institution Camerounaise de l'Enfance" at Betamba and the Burstal Institute at Buea have been equipped or refurbished. And public day nurseries as well as a home for abandoned children have been built in Yaoundé. It is normal for a country to be closely interested in its youth. It is normal for government to take all possible steps to assist the youth to grow to mature. And to bloom. It is normal for a Cameroon to do its best for you. But, you know as well as I do, that no State can take charge of responsible citizens, who let themselves being carried away by events and who exist rather than live.

In such times of crisis such as the one we are experiencing today, the community and, indeed, the whole country, count on resourceful, imaginative, daring and responsible men and women to survive and face the challenges ahead. Persevere!

Continue to believe in your ideals! Cameroon strongly encourages private initiatives that tend towards our policy of liberalization of the economy. All our initiatives will be encouraged if they are targeted towards progress and development. You are lucky to be living witnesses of a turning point in the history of Cameroon. You are lucky to be fanned by the wind of Liberty and Democracy. Democracy, which is the outcome of a resolute policy of liberalization chosen by your parents, is one of the most handsome gifts we can offer you. You are lucky to be living in a free country; do not jeopardize your luck by following tantalizing mirages.

Make good use of this freedom. People can fully express themselves without taking to the street, without causing destruction and without looting. Expression through acts of vandalism, illegal demonstrations, excessive demands, rowdiness and disorder is not worthy of responsible youth. Say no to confrontation. Accept nothing else but dialogue and frankness. I exhort you to be vigilant in the face of manoeuvres aimed at exploiting you for unavowed ends, which place your future and life in jeopardy.

Schools, and the University in particular, should not diverted from their fundamental goals. The school should remain a place where people are prepared for individual collective, social and national responsibilities. No one should use the school for goals than those of instruction, education and training. Think of you future, of yourself ad also of those who will come after you. Like you, they will need structures and facilities for their education and training.

Our priority and common concern is overcoming the economic crisis and ensuring better living standards in Cameroon, rather than tiring out ourselves in baseless wrangling. Be constructive! Draw a positive conclusion from each lesson in life. Make use of the education given you and assert your personality. In short, live up to the expectation of your elders. Make your country progress. Forward ever.

The whole world is undergoing change. The 21st century is already around the corner! Cameroon will be able to survive only with youth that master the use of reliable economic, scientific and technical weapons. Cameroon counts on you to consolidate its achievements in order to become a more prosperous and stronger nation. I know that you are deserving of our total confidence.

Long live the Cameroonian Youth

7.2: Address by the President of the Republic to the Youths of Cameroon on the Occasion of the 26th National Youth Day, Yaounde, 10 February 1992

Theme: "Patriotism, Responsibility, and Commitment"

Young Cameroonians,

Thank you for having honoured our great annual come together. Like you, I am looking forward to celebrating this Youth Day, your feast day. The youths symbolize hope- hope for our country and hope for the future. The year that has just ended will be a landmark in our history. As a turning point at the political level, it will be remembered as the year of democracy.

For, the democratization process we started since I took office as President is now bearing fruit after several years of effort and reflection. The social climate and the life of the nation are a true reflection of this profound change. The resulting exhilaration has caused a change in attitudes and comportment, which are sometimes, devoid of commonsense. And you are better placed to know this.... But you also know that democracy is a difficult conquest. Cameroon has chosen its path and is considered a pioneer on the Africa continent in this domain. It therefore distinguishes itself from a good number of countries where freedom and tolerance do not always exist..... Although we are still facing some unrest, the social climate should soon reflect a more real and truer picture of the situation. A more real and truer picture of the situation.

A more responsible behaviour from Cameroonians, the youths included, would be for them to go out in great numbers to the polls during the forthcoming early Legislative Elections. Now is the time or never to make your voices heard and to contribute fully to the political life of our country. I exhort all those of you who are of voting age to go to the polls. It is your legitimate right and over and above all, your civic responsibility. I have faith in the youths of Cameroon and trust in the future. We are convinced of having charted the right course. In our forward march we have had to encounter difficulties but have never given up because our goals have always been clear.

Our main goal is undoubtedly to give Cameroon a brighter future, and a brighter future is dependent upon the well-being of each and everyone at all levels. To obtain this goal, we have worked and are working relentlessly to build a prosperous Cameroonian Nation despite the recession, and to endow it with a strong democracy which guarantees respect of the individual. Like all Cameroonians, you are concerned.

Because your elders have built and are continuing to build this country day by day, and you, all of you together, will consolidate it. What we have done is not necessarily perfect, but we have done it whole heartedly, thinking of you and your future. You must bear in mind that your role is primordial to the future of Cameroon, and the future of Cameroon lies in its unity. You are children of one Nation. Put your energy and know- how to serve it. Some of you have understood this and are already serving the Nation through Youth Association and groups in which you display creativity and engage in reflection.

124

This is a worthy example. The youths are the mirror of the Nation. You are the mirror of Cameroon. Your parents have been able to provide you with an education which they themselves did not have. Cameroon is proud of its youths. You have learnt to think for yourselves and we will never stop you from doing so. Do this responsible, dispassionately and without hatred. We respect your rights; you should honour your obligations. We respect your rights; you should honour your obligations.

Cameroon cannot move forward without you, that is true. But for your part, you cannot develop in a country weakened by division and misunderstanding. You are all aware that great efforts have been put for you at the educational, social and economic levels. We know that more efforts must be made to help you and make you enterprising and dynamic Cameroonians. The educational system, no matter how efficient it may be, must take into account economic imperatives and permit you to have an easy access to employment under optimum conditions. The system must be improved so as to better accept training to the needs of the job market.

Today, I call on each and every one of you to strive to be worthy of the hopes we place in you. To you, young Cameroonians in rural areas, exhort you to muster all your energy to support and complement the efforts of your elders. The baton will soon be handed to you. To you, young students, I request you to give absolute priority to your studies. You must be prepared to take up your future responsibilities.

Cameroon will need efficient and reliable leaders, managers, civil servants, farmers and workers. In short, Cameroon will need responsible citizens. You know perfectly well that the interests of the Nation do not in any way contradict yours. Be ready to serve your nation with all your heart. Cameroon will only become what you make it. Always bear in mind that your parents will forever be proud of you having made you Cameroonian citizens capable of shaping their own future.

Long Live the Youths of Cameroon!
Long live Cameroon!

7.3: Address by the President of the Republic to the Youths of Cameroon on the Occasion of the 27th National Youth Day, Yaounde, 10 February 1993

Theme: "Youth, Peace, Unity, and the Future of Cameroon"

My Young Fellow Countrymen,

Youths of the cities and of the countryside, youths of factories and construction sites, youths of primary schools, colleges and high schools, youths of university faculties and professional institutions, and you too, young job-seekers, the deprived and the handicapped, I wish you all a Happy Youth Day and renew to you best wishes for the Year 1993. The youths are the future of our country. They are the ones who will inherit all that we would have achieved. You therefore have an essential role to play in the attainment of our country's objectives.

One of our basic objectives is to achieve our national unity which is the precondition for peace and is the key to our common destiny. Cameroon, as you know, is medley of tribes, languages, religious and culture and we are always confronted with obstacles such as tribalism, linguistic differences, nepotism, fanaticism and selfish interests. Your duty is to help us overcome these obstacles. The Cameroon of tomorrow belongs to you and its unity will depend on the efforts all of us put in today. Another fundamental objectives is the consolidation of our democracy. Here again, the youths who are receptive to change have an important role to play.

Last year, the lowering of the voting age made it possible for many of you to cast your votes during the legislative and presidential elections. You fulfilled your civic duty as responsible citizens and contributed to the advancement of the democratization process in our country. The learning process of democracy, just like the quest for knowledge, is a school of freedom, tolerance, modesty and integrity.... You must never forget that. Schools and universities should not be used to destabilize the country, but rather build it! The purpose of the school is to train and educate you in order to prepare you to take charge of yourself and to assume your future responsibilities.

Our universities must remain par excellence, centres where science, knowledge and know-how are imparted and acquired. You must protect education from all those who want to divert schools and universities from their primary purpose. Schools and universities must be kept out of undue political demands. You must be vigilant. It is in your interest and that of the future generations. The Cameroon Nation is demanding and expects a lot from you. But, in return, your problems and when future are at the focus of its preoccupations.

Owing to the economic crisis, your training, employment and even your subsistence needs have been rendered more acute. I am fully aware of this, and despite a harsh economic context, we are doing all we can to solve them. Do not give in to discouragement in the face of difficulties. Do not despair. Face them with courage and determination. It is during trying times that one's patience, endurance and responsible men and women are seen.

Despite what some embittered minds may think, there is reason to hope, and I am asking you to have trust in the future. You are concerned with employment problems. They equally preoccupy us at the highest point. You are few thousand, graduates or not, who are seeking jobs. Economic recovery, resumption of investments, creation of jobs-such are our major objectives in the years ahead.

For the short term, sound programmes have been gradually put in place within the National Employment Fund like: -the young graduates employment programme; - induction courses within undertakings;- support programme for the creation of micro-enterprises. Over and above all, you must always bear in mind that our country is essential agricultural, and that while jobs are scarce in our towns, they abound in the rural areas. The land needs hands to till it. Similarly, to curb youth under-employment, we have just carried out a reform of Higher Education. This reform is intended to restructure, re-orientate and to give a new impetus to our university.

More emphasis will be put on professionalization and on the learning of trades so as to better adapt training to job market requirements. Students will enjoy the benefits decentralization and will have greater possibilities of training in areas that better correspond to our country's needs. The implementation of these reforms will require a considerable amount of resources and the contribution of all the interested parties, namely, public authorities, parents and, above all, teachers and students. Teachers must be fully aware of the importance of their role. They are guarantors of the equality of the courses given and therefore, of the worth and future of our educational system.

Our educational system is, and will remain what our teachers make it. Students, on their part understand that the university is neither a place for rest nor a retreat. The university is a place where people work, where people prepare for the future. With the liberalization of national life, we have stepped into the era of competition. The era of competition is one when pride of place is given to hard work, competence and merit.

Only the best, that is those who would have worked hardest and obtained outstanding results, will have the best jobs. You must all bear in mind that it is today that you have to prepare your future. You owe whatever you will become tomorrow to no one but yourself, and it is today that you have to work for it. Do not ruin your chances! Say no to the easy way out and to idleness. Learn , improve your minds, be observant and creative, and strive to do better than your elders. Study hard, and work untiringly. This is how you will be able to build your future on a solid foundation. Cameroon has confidence in you: You bear the hopes of our country. Continue to be deserving of this confidence. Follow the examples of our sportsmen who are winners and more especially that of our 'Junior Lions' to whom I extend very warm congratulations for their great performances in Mauritius.

Long live Cameroonian Youths
Long live Cameroon!

7.4: Address by the President of the Republic to the Youths of Cameroon on the Occasion of the 28th National Youth Day, Yaounde, 10 February 1994

Theme: "Youth, Sports and National Integration"
Young Cameroonians,
My Young Fellow Countrymen,
I am very happy to address you this evening as is the custom each year, on the eve of this feast day, your feast day. Before anything else, I would like on this occasion to tell you that issues bearing on your current situation and on your future have always been my prime concern. In other words, despite the prevailing difficulties, the future of our youths remains one of our main priorities.

Since the last time I addressed you, the fight against the economic crisis has harnesses all our efforts, making us take fresh drastic measures, notably, salary cuts in the Civil Services. While we fathom the security of the sacrifices so imposed on civil servants, and especially on those who are charged with the education of our children, it is unacceptable that these children are denied the right to education, thereby mortgaging their future. No matter how legitimate the claims in question are, refusing to teach has no justification. Where would we be heading for, where would society be headlong for if each professional group feeling itself unjustly treated, stops performing its duties? Let those who are privileged to have a job think of the thousands of young graduates who are legitimately aspiring for a job in the civil service.

The youths, because they are part of the society have undoubtedly been affected, directly or indirectly through their parents, by the constraining measures imposed by the crisis. As concerns university students, the State reviewed admission conditions into universities, as well as the policy of assistance to students at the same time as parents were also requires to make sacrifices. Faced with difficult situations, our students have, in general adopted a reasonable attitude. I congratulate them on this. The university reform which has been marked in particular by the opening of new universities was one of the major events of the past year.

This reform is aimed at improving the conditions of study of students and at broadening the base of training disciplines. As concerns secondary education, we have pursued our programme of opening, extending and equipping general and technical education schools despite a sharp drop in our budgetary resources. In a bid to render the organization of examinations more national, the GCE and Baccalaureate boards have been created. An educational system, no matter how perfect, would be losing its mark if it does not prepare the youths for trades and professions adapted to the needs of our society. This is why it has been decided that education in Cameroon should progressively become more professionally oriented. Unemployment in particular, is in fact one of our top concerns.

As you know, it is a global scourge which does not spare even the most advanced countries, and for which there is unfortunately no miracle drug. Each country, depending on its context, should seek its own solutions to the problem. In Cameroon, we have preferred, at the cost of drastic salary cuts, to preserve the jobs of thousands of civil servants among whom there are many youths, instead of retrenching. Public and private sector enterprises have also made that choice. National solidarity called for this. But, preserving jobs does not suffice. It is equally necessary to explore other sectors of our economy that are capable of opening new avenues to the youths who, each year join the labour market. Agriculture, for which our country definitely has special considerations, could become for our youths one of those 'mines' generating new jobs that we are seeking.

If , as we do expect, the recent devaluation of the CFA franc stimulates our basic commodity exports, it offers, in this respect, promising prospects. Coupled with better remuneration for our farmers, it should spur our youths to embrace farming activities which the government's new agricultural policy intends to promote. They could also turn to other crops, like food crops and off-season crops which are still in their early stage of promotion. It is Cameroon's right to expect specific assistance from its international partners in these areas. It goes without saying that fishing, animal husbandry, handicrafts and tourism, like agriculture, should attract our youths. It is clear that the evolution of the world economy ushers us little by little each day into a world of competition. The devaluation of the CFA franc which we all decided upon is one of such signals.

We shall have to rethink our habits and review our lifestyles. But above all, it would be necessary to work harder in order to make a success of this devaluation. Without being a panacea, this devaluation could turn out to be a real stimulant to our economy if we know how to make the best of it. All of us are concerned, especially you, young Cameroonians. Because you are the future of the Nation, because you are generous and tolerant, because your convictions are sincere, because you are full of youthful energy, am asking you to take up this new challenge with me, to make your contribution to the revival of our country, to remain faithful to your ideas by avoiding all forms of manipulation, to refuse all forms of cleavages that would drag us behind.

In this way, together, we will tread on the path of new sharing towards a more just and more humane society. Let us once more take the example from our Indomitable Lions who, despite meagre resources, have qualified for the final phase of the World Cup next June. Because they have talent, because they have faith, because they are spurred on by the hopes of an entire people, I am sure that this time again, they will do honour to their country.

Long Live Cameroonian youth!
Long live Cameroon!

7.5: Address by the President of the Republic to the Youths of Cameroon on the Occasion of the 29th National Youth Day, Yaounde, 10 February 1995

Theme: "Youth and the Mastery of the Democratic Process"

My Fellow Young Countrymen,

The entire Nation joins me, as it is the custom each year, in wishing all of you a happy Youth Day. We are particularly attached to the Youth day, and for nearly thirty years now we have been celebrating it with the same enthusiasm. This shows the prominent place you occupy in the Nation, the great interest we have in you, and all the confidence you enjoy. In seizing this opportunity to renew my best wishes to you at the dawn of this year, I would like more especially to say my satisfaction at the sense of responsibility you have shown throughout the past year. In fact, a great majority of you backed down from sterile agitation, although, like youths all over the world, have always been confronted with many difficulties. This simply means that you have chosen dialogue and sound judgment as the means of posing and seeking solutions to your problems.

This also means that in hard times you have resolved to devote yourselves to that which is essential, that is your work and your studies. This is what your parents expect of you; they who, in spite of these difficult times do not relent in making sacrifices to meet your needs, to provide for your education and to assume you an honourable place in society. This too, is what the Nation expects of you: a high sense of responsibility towards yourselves and towards the society. The State, for its part, has always borne your problems in mind, the extent and severity of which are essentially due to the lingering economic recession. Appreciable efforts are being made to cope with them. But, it is clear that it is by reviving our economy that we will be able to find more appropriate solutions.

And, in this respect, I am convinced that today, we have greater chances of success. With regard to employment problems in particular, we must show proof of greater creativity, and explore all opportunities offered by our country. And there are many of them, for example, Cameroonians have a long experience in farming, livestock breeding and fishing. Today, following the devaluation of the CFA franc, these sectors are profitable. I strongly urge our youths to show a greater interest in these areas especially now that the Public Service offers very few openings because of various financial constraints. It is true if your ideas have to materialize, and your projects realized, you need financial resources.

Bearing this aspect in mind, I have instructed the Government to urgently conduct a study aimed at renewing the credit policy of our financial institutions. Many recently organized promotional activities have brought to focus your many talents and your inventiveness in areas such as handicraft and industrial technology. The potentialities of our youths are real. I exhort you therefore, to persevere on the path of research and creativity which constitutes the real key to success in the face of present and future challenges. I know that things are hard. They are even harder for most of you. But that is how, in fact how, by going through trials, coping with everyday challenges and constraints, man is moulded, acquires experience, measures his capacities, and becomes a man in the true sense of the word- a responsible man. You must therefore arm yourselves with courage, put up a loyal fight and be hopeful.

My Young Fellow Countrymen,

This year, your feast day aptly invites you to reflect on your role in the democratic process taking place in our country. Obviously, you are involved in this process and it is important, at the stage in which we still ourselves, that the youths really understand the stakes involved and the rules of democracy. As the future of the Nation, the youths certainly have their say during this time of democracy which permits you to participate in the life of the State, to improve your talents and to express and assert yourselves. Observe, judge, express your feelings, and act. But do all of this within the ambit of the law, constructively, and in a spirit of democracy which supposes dialogue compromise and the quest for objectivity.

And above all, do not accept to be the instrument of obsolete ideologies, and illegitimate ambitions which constitute a threat to peace, national unity, and therefore, to the future of youths-youths who can also serve as an example to their elders. I am referring in particular to our Junior Indomitable Lions who have gratified and honoured us by lifting the Junior African Nations Cup trophy. Without huge means, but with mettle and talent, these youths have demonstrated that one should never lose hope in Cameroonians.

Once again, on behalf of the entire Nation, I congratulate them and wish that together Africa in the forthcoming Junior World Cup tournament. At the threshold of the Third Millennium which will undoubtedly witness unprecedented changes and breakthrough that will transform the world, Cameroon must hasten up on the path of modernity. In order to achieve this, the Nation counts on you; you, the youths of today. Always remain worthy therefore of our trust, and be the real architects of tomorrow's Cameroon.

Long Live Cameroonian Youths!
Long Live Cameroon!

7.6: Address by the President of the Republic to the Youths of Cameroon on the Occasion of the 30th National Youth Day, Yaounde, 10 February 1996

Theme: "Youth, National Unity, African Unity"

Tomorrow, Cameroon will be celebrating its Thirtieth National Youth Day. Thirty is the age of maturity and responsibility. But you all have always shown a great deal of maturity and high sense of responsibility. The most recent demonstrations of this was during the last elections. Like your elders, you chose your municipal councillors in calm and total freedom. Among the newly elected are many youth who are determined to put their skills and talents at the service of our people.

On behalf of the Nation, I congratulate you all, as well as the young councillors.

My young fellow Cameroonians,

This year the theme of the Youth Day is "Youth: National Unity and African Unity". It is a timely reminder that Cameroon will soon be hosting the 32nd Summit of the Organisation of African Unity. On that occasion, you must, through your exemplary conduct, boost the image of our country. In this regard, you must never forget that all the youths across Africa are facing the same adverse effects of the severe crisis hitting our countries.

My young fellow Countrymen,

You all know it. I have always paid keen attention to your major concerns. As much as possible we have always sought the appropriate solutions to them. And, the meagre resources of the State notwithstanding, we are determined to continue to explore all avenues open to us. I know that you are all aspiring for a freer and open society. You wish to be more involved in the running of the affairs of our nation. Thanks to the democratization of political life, you can now freely express your opinion and contribution in one way or the other to the running of our society. In this connection, the Constitution, which I have just enacted, is a major towards the consolidation of our participatory democracy.

You also wish to see an improvement in your living conditions in your living conditions be it to the urban or rural areas. The effective return to growth that we are witnessing during the current financial year will permit the State, with assistance from donors and friendly countries, to resolutely pursue its programme to revive public investments, create jobs and self-reliant employment. An emergency plan for youth employment has just been elaborated: 602 young people from rural areas have been trained at the Vocational Centre in Buea; 437 certificate holders have been trained in agriculture and stockbreeding techniques; 500 are learning office automation, computer science and data management, and 31 self-employment projects will soon be launched. The training programmes will certainly boost employment in agricultural, stock breeding and industrial sectors, thanks to the launching of major infrastructure projects. In this regard, the framework agreement recently signed on the Chad-Cameroon Pipeline has promising multiplier effects especially for young school leavers.

Another major concern you have is the quality of education imparted to the youth at school. Last year, the state enrolled 5000 student teachers, opened 263 primary schools, 11 rural Artisan Centres and 39 secondary education institutions, 38 government secondary schools were upgraded government High Schools and 27 Grade II Teacher Training Colleges to Grade I Teachers Training College. Furthermore, training branches were opened in technical institutions for medical professions and agriculture. Besides, control board for Government and private institutions have been set up and educational role of heads of school establishments redefined.

Lastly, you yearn for a society that is more just, more humane and has a stronger community feeling. I have prescribed a policy for the better sharing of the fruits of growth which will offer equal development opportunities to urban and rural youth. I know that the times are hard. Like all other Cameroonians, you make enormous sacrifices each passing day. Persevere. Let us have every hand on deck to build a more united and prosperous Cameroon.

Let us work for the advent of a united and economically sound Africa.

My Young Fellow Cameroonians,

Happy Youth Day to you all!

Long Live Cameroonian Youth!
Long Live Cameroon!

7.7: Address by the President of the Republic to the Youths of Cameroon on the Occasion of the 31st National Youth Day, Yaounde, 10 February 1997

Theme: "Youth and Solidarity"

My Countrymen,

I am happy to address you this evening, on the occasion of the Youth Day. On this happy event, the whole Nation joins me to share your joy and to wish you a happy Feast Day. You are the Cameroon of tomorrow. Prepare right now for tomorrow's Cameroon. The Nation in general, and the Government in particular, spare no effort in preparing the Cameroonian youth to assume their responsibilities of today and those of tomorrow.

Bearing this in mind, civic, intellectual and vocational education of youth has been put at the focus of national concerns. You know that the mastery of science and technology is indeed one of the main prerequisites for the building of a modern Nation, as shown to us today, by the developed countries.

You should therefore nurture this mastery in order to give an additional impetus to the modernization of our country. Despite the economic crisis situation, the Government has pursued the construction of new schools, new colleges, and new high schools. Many teachers have been recruited despite the freezing of recruitment into the public service. Our universities and higher institutions have been endowed with new facilities like the Library of the University of Buea, and soon, the Internet will be introduced in Higher Education.

In the same light, I have prescribed the creation of a Special Fund for Assistance of Young Girls in the science disciplines, and, the initiation of an aid programme for the less privileged students. All these efforts and many others, undoubtedly portray the great importance we attach to your training. But they are insufficient, given all the expectations of our youth today.

I am referring in particular to the problem of youth employment. Although in Cameroon, as it is the case elsewhere, the economic crisis has drastically reduced job opportunities, the State has pursued its efforts in this area, in particular through the National Employment Funds. An illustration:

- Between 1995 and 1996, about 700 young people were trained in government intensive vocational training centres, with a good member of them in industrial techniques;
- In the same vein, the programme devoted to inserting graduates of Higher Institutions in the mainstream of the economy has recorded real success with enterprises;
- Again, more than 13,000 job-seekers had placements on the job market through the National Employment Fund;
- More than 1,000 others received assistance from this Fund for self-employment in agriculture, stockbreeding, fishing and handicrafts.

These efforts will be pursued. Curbing unemployment remains a priority. But, it is clear that the most energetic solution to this lingering and serious problem resides in the overall re-launching of the national economy.

The Cameroonian youth must know that through hard work through sacrifices made by all, and through international cooperation, we can today, begin to contemplate the future with optimism. It is necessary therefore, that the whole Nation, the youth included, redouble their efforts at work, their sense of initiative, creativity and moral rectitude.

My Young Countrymen,
Cameroonians will soon be electing their Members of Parliament. I expect a massive and enthusiastic turn out from youth of voting age during the election whose importance for our young democracy is clear to all. Boost it with your fervour and patriotism. Do not ever forget: the Cameroon of tomorrow will be a reflection of its youth today.

It will be, to a large extent, what you make of it.

Happy Feast Day to all of you.

LONG LIVE THE CAMEROONIAN YOUTH!
LONG LIVE CAMEROON!

7.8: Address by the President of the Republic to the Youths of Cameroon on the Occasion of the 32nd National Youth Day, Yaounde, 10 February 1998

Theme: "Youth, Creativity, and Economic Recovery"

My Young Cameroonians,
This is the eve of the 32nd Youth Day. It is always with great joy, as you know that I address you on this occasion; you who form the majority of our nation; you who are its future.

My Young Fellow Cameroonians
Being young is not a virtues in itself. However, it means having all potentialities. And it is incumbent on those in charge of public affairs to kindle these potentialities. Accordingly, the state, despite the crisis has not relented in its efforts to provide our young people attending school with quality education accessible to the great majority.

Some figures are worth quoting: at the elementary level, 510 classrooms were built in 1997, 9 new grade 1 and II Teachers Training Colleges were opened. At the secondary level: 22 government secondary schools, 3 government secondary schools were upgraded to high schools, 8 government technical colleges were opened, 219 classrooms and 9 workshops were constructed. These figures are not exhaustive.

Moreover, a better application of texts and considerable financial efforts led to significant progress in various domains: the success rate in examinations has clearly improved, state subsidies to provide education have resumed, the recruitment, reclassification and absorption of thousands of teachers has been effected to offset a severe shortage of staff.

Obviously, international cooperation has provided substantial, and much appreciated assistance, but we have also had to draw from our own resources. You should be aware that these past few years budget appropriations for National Education have been increasing steadily despite an unfavourable economic situation. Considerable efforts have also been made in respect of Higher Education: new rules have been set that permit a certain resumption of assistance to students, measures have been taken to ease the integration of young girls in the scientific and technical branches in accordance to the priority given to the promotion of the Cameroonian woman, sustain the ongoing effort to increasing the number and improving the quality of student guidance facilities as well as providing them with new infrastructure and equipment, including hooking up to the internet.

This employment issue, I am aware of it, is your major concern. It remains, I can assure you our constant preoccupation. We are striving to make our educational system more professional both at school and university levels.

In addition, public and private vocational training centres have already permitted hundreds of young people to learn a trade and to qualify for a job in industry and in the tertiary sector. Many young artisans have also been able to improve on their skills with state assistance.

Through specialized bodies like the National Employment Fund, we have embarked on various activities aimed at placing the youth in the job market. Some 40,000 young people have been received and provided information on job opportunities. A vocational orientation programme in schools and a course programme for practice in industry have been instituted. More than 5,000 youth have obtained new qualifications under the training programme. Eighty percent of the trainees of the Employment – Certificate Programme have been recruited after their practical training. More than 1000 young promoters have been settled in many regions of the country as part of an operation self-employment. Lastly, in the area of health, in a bid to reduce infant mortality and to offer the very young a chance to make the best start in life, we have instituted free immunization campaigns with the help of our foreign partners.

But, all these efforts will be in vain if you, young Cameroonians, pupils, students, apprentices, young workers of urban and rural areas do not put into proper use the instruments of knowledge made available to you by the national community. It is your duty to study, to learn and even to be enterprising: in short, to take your destiny in your own hands. You are capable of doing so.

Those who are of voting age and who are full-fledged citizens have demonstrated it these past months through their responsible behaviour. Many of them have refused to give in to discouragement in the face of crisis and have engaged in the battle for life. Some by engaging in small trade in the informal sector while others have used their talents to launch income-generating projects. All in all, they have shown proof of their creativity and enterprising spirit. But is there a better example to give than that of our sportsmen and women?

I am referring of course to our football players who have qualified for the 1998 African Nations Cup and for the World Cup. By their qualification, our "Lions" have shown that they are among the world's best in their sports discipline. I also wish to mention the good performances of our athletes during the last Francophonie games in Madagascar and during the African championships.

Let me also underscore the courage of our compatriots who participated recently in the Mount Cameroon Race that was very appropriately dubbed the "Race of Hope".

Our sportsmen have therefore paved the way. You should follow their example. The public authorities will stand by you. In keeping with the commitments I made to you, we shall launch a national youth policy for a better co-ordination of efforts towards the socio-economic integration of the youth.

Thus, youth employment matters will be accorded special attention in a full-fledged Ministry in charge of employment. Similarly, the newly created Ministry in charge of Urban Affairs will follow up the specific situation of the youth in urban areas.

At the same time, a national Youth integration Fund will be created at the Ministry of Youth and Sports. This Fund is intended to promote entrepreneurial initiatives and to provide financial and material support to self-employment activities of the youth.

In the same light, a prize will be instituted to encourage creativity among young people aged up to 30 years. Lastly, in the area of culture, there are plans to organize as soon as possible, a biennial youth festivals.

My Young Countrymen,

In reality and you must have certainly noticed it – this new era for the youth has already begun. The National Assembly has been injected with young blood. So it is with the Government. Why should these young members of parliament and members of government not stand by you? They who, not long ago were amongst you?

Follow their example. Participate in public life. Make your contribution to the great task of democratization in your country. The day will come when you yourselves will hold public office.

You should also be involved in our economic recovery drive. Seize the opportunities that will be offered in the years ahead by economy recovery, the signs of which are already visible. Face these challenges with imagination, the intelligence and enthusiasm that characterize the youth. The future of our country, the bright future, depends on this. Build the Cameroon of tomorrow.

Happy Feast Day to all of you!

LONG LIVE THE CAMEROONIAN YOUTH!
LONG LIVE CAMEROON!

7.9: Address by the President of the Republic to the Youths of Cameroon on the Occasion of the 33rd National Youth Day, Yaounde, 10 February 1999

Theme: "Youth and Fight against Poverty"

My Young Fellow Cameroonians,

This 33rd Youth Day that you will be celebrating tomorrow is of special significance. It is indeed the last of this century-the last before the dawn of the Third Millennium. Whether you are 15, 20 or 25 years old, you who constitute the majority of our nation, the next century will be yours. It is a singular opportunity for you therefore to ponder together over the role you will play, the conditions under which you will, as you are already doing now, continue acquiring more knowledge, reflecting on your vocation, and make things easier for you. This lies essentially in your hands.

However, the State is there to make things easier for you. It is doing so through substantial efforts for your education, training and health. The considerable slice of the State budget allocated to education bears testimony to this. Last year I highlighted Government's contribution to the various levels of education and intended to make it more professionally oriented. I will not belabour the point. We will pursue our policy of making education accessible to the greater majority by expanding and modernizing it as our means permit.

However, the fear is that this may no longer be adequate. Indeed the world has experienced profound changes these past few decades especially within our continent. Twenty years ago, any young graduate was practically sure of having a job in the civil service, or semi-public or private sector. Unfortunately, this is no longer the case.

Obviously, the State will continue each year to recruit from among the best of you who will be responsible for lending it support in its endeavour to defend the general interest. Nevertheless, it has never stopped doing so. Dozens of judicial and legal officers and Registrars, as well as hundreds of teachers are being recruited. However, it will be necessary henceforth for some of our graduates to embark on activities that will boost the economic and social development of our country.

We can already observe that after many difficult years due to the crisis, there is a return to economic growth that has a positive impact on employment. This is a good omen for what will probably prevail in the decades ahead. The point is not being pessimistic or optimistic. It is being realistic; seeing the world as it is, or rather what is going to be and be prepared to face it.

Whether we like it or not, the next century will be one of globalization, that is, one of increased liberation and hence, of competiveness and rapid technological advances even if in Cameroon, the State will, of course, continue to play its role as a regulator and moderator.

Certainly, distinguished moral and religious authorities are already speaking out against the foreseeable excesses of a system that relegates such values as social progress to the background. It is possible that such an awakening of consciences might somehow attenuate the system, but basically, the key word will be competition.

In this light, what can a country like ours do?

Firstly, it must fully develop the most competitive sectors of its economy geared towards the international market by improving their productivity, the level of technology and product quality.

Secondly, it would be necessary to stimulate scientific research in such sectors. Lastly, it would be indispensable to foster the training of more qualified experts.

While more job opportunities may be expected from growth in these sectors, it should be borne in mind that increased productivity would probably limit their scope. It is necessary therefore, that our youth who are those primarily concerned should turn to new branches of activity where their enterprising spirit and creativity will be put to use.

Indeed our country is teeming with unexploited mines of activities that only need to e tapped and developed. Such is the case for instance of our agricultural potentialities like plantain cultivation or off-season fruits and vegetables which we could supply to countries of our sub-region and even export to countries of the North. This does not prevent us from developing our traditional cash crops for which we still have great expanses of farmland. The same applies to the growing services sector which still has significant prospects for expansion.

Lastly, such is the case for activities which in Cameroon, have not flourished as in other African countries where they constitute vibrant sectors of the economy generating foreign exchange and jobs. I am referring of course to tourism for which our country is particularly well endowed. The list is not at all exhaustive. Hence, there is no need for a defeatist attitude. On the contrary, I am certain that our youth, with their intellectual abilities, their creativity, dynamism and commitment to work are fully capable of facing the challenges of the great transition that lies ahead.

My Young Fellow Countrymen,

Now, I wish to briefly draw your attention to the ills besetting our society and which are likely to jeopardize your future.

Firstly, poverty, which has spread due to the crisis and has affected all age groups without distinction. The Government, with assistance from our foreign partners is launching a poverty alleviation campaign. However, it requires the participation of all, especially yours, in order to win this battle. I am asking you to join in the struggle so that tomorrow, economic competition does not change the values of solidarity characteristics of our traditional societies.

Secondly, I also wish to say a few words in relation to another by-product of the crisis: growing insecurity despite the laudable efforts of the Forces of Law and Order. It often involves youth who are lured into adventures that always end up badly most of the time. They must know that Justice will have no pity on them. I exhort them, before it is too late to return to the right path which they should not have deviated from in the first place.

My Young Countrymen,

As you can see, great tasks await you.

I know that you are very capable of tackling them.

I know that I can count on you.
You know that you can count on me.
Happy Feast Day to all of You!

LONG LIVE THE YOUTH OF CAMEROON!
LONG LIVE CAMEROON!

7.10: Address by the President of the Republic to the Youths of Cameroon on the Occasion of the 34th National Youth Day, Yaounde, 10 February 2000

Theme: "Youth and Moralization"

My Young Countrymen,

In my last message to the Nation a few weeks ago, I said that you the youth have a primary role to play in achieving the major tasks Cameroon will tackle in the year 2000.

I wish to specify my thought today by reviewing some of the major tasks of the 21st century which, as I underlined one year ago today, will basically be yours. At the moment our most pressing task, seem to me to be economic recovery which I think is on the right track. But, in the present context marked by stiff competition, nothing can be taken for granted. It is necessary therefore that we keep on fighting. It is necessary that you keep on fighting.

For this purpose, it would be necessary to be well prepared for the task. Training oriented towards economic development, whether scientific, technical commercial or other, will be great asset. In particular, the mastery of new technologies is an undeniable advantage. The State, by putting the focus on vocational training at all levels will continue to lend support to these orientations. While one may expect some improvement in the job situation because of economic growth, as can be seen already in few sectors, this unfortunately does not hold true for the general problems of youth unemployment which remains a major preoccupation.

I told you last year that the solution undoubtedly can be found in reviving sectors of activities where our competitiveness is sound, and in the promotion of new activities in the agricultural, industrial and service sectors, not to talk of tourism. In this respect, I have confidence in the enterprising spirit of Cameroonians and more especially of the youth of our country. Alongside the legitimate goal for individual success, you must know that through entrepreneurial initiative you equally perform a civic duty beneficial to our society. I take this opportunity to announce to you that in the course of this year, under the patronage of the Presidency of the Republic," Business Creation Forums" will be organized in the ten provincial capitals of our country. The idea is to contribute to the emergence of dynamic class of young entrepreneurs by providing them with information on the creation of businesses.

Africa Cup of Nations 2000, after performing in a manner commensurate with their reputation. I see this is not only as proof of their talent but also as a reward of their persevering efforts. I encourage them to keep it up. Lastly, Cameroonian youth of both sexes successfully took part in international forums.

And this list, I universities. It has resumed investments especially in Dschang, Ngaoundéré and Yaoundé II. Implementing instruments of the 1993 University Reforms have been signed. Various actions have been initiated aimed at improving the functioning of university institutions through the promotion of participatory management and constant dialogue. A special recruitment of 544 new teachers was authorized and has already resulted in effective assumption of duty by teachers in some schools. Furthermore, the State has pursued its policy of financial assistance to students both in Cameroon and abroad.

Lastly, I take this opportunity to announce the imminent holding of a meeting of the Council of Higher Education and Scientific and Technical Research during which guidelines for our universities and science sector systems in the years ahead may be formulated. On another score, I wish to point out, as this concerns particularly the youth, that considerable recruitment has been made in the Army, the Gendarmerie and the Police. There is also an area I which I would like you to be actively involved. I mean the raising of public and individual morality. Moreover, I do know that it is the theme of your feast day this year. You are starting life with the freshness of your convictions and the purity of your intentions, without having yet been influenced by the realities of life. I am therefore counting on you and on your enthusiasm not only that you behave in an honest and responsible manner but also as a good example in your schools, universities, professional circles and associations.

We are today witnessing a moral decay I our society, due principally to an unbridled quest for wealth, but also to falling moral standards. This is certainly not specific to Cameroon but that is no excuse for inaction. This is certainly not specific to Cameroon but that is no excuse for inaction. This moral decay is the cause of many ills in our society especially-acts of insecurity in which young delinquents are often involved.- the spread of pandemics, like Aids which threatens mostly the youth, etc.

My Young Countrymen,

If you want all the efforts which have been made in recent years to put our country back on the path of stability and progress to bear fruit, you should mobilize to make Cameroon a better place to live in, and one you will be proud of belonging to. You are the ones who are primarily concerned. It is your future which is at Stake. I know I can trust you.

Happy Feast Day!

Long live the Cameroonian Youth!

7.11: Address by the President of the Republic to the Youths of Cameroon on the Occasion of the 35ᵗʰ National Youth Day, Yaounde, 10 February 2001

Theme: "Youth and the Fight against AIDS"

My Young Fellow Countrymen,

Yaoundé has just lived an event that will remain a landmark in the history of our country. Several dozen Heads of State and top officials from African countries and France met in our capital to address the issue of globalization. We believe that this is a source of legitimate pride for us. However, today, I wish to address you on another aspect of that important event. Most of you who followed the debate probably found this an abstract topic that was far removed from your daily concerns. As a matter of fact, I do not think so.

Globalization, my young fellow countrymen, is shaping tomorrow's world, a world which will essentially be yours. It is of vital importance therefore, that you grasp what is awaiting you and how you will prepare for it. In a nutshell, the options are as follows:

Either we wait passively for the tide of globalization to reach us, thereby running the high risk of being submerged, or more precisely, of being cast ashore or marginalized. Or, we strive to anticipate the trend in order to easily join the mainstream of global economic integration which, alone, can secure us a place in the race for economic and social progress.

Of course, we have chosen the second option. Indeed, for several years now, our entire policy has been geared towards creating the best conditions for us and for you to board the globalization train.

Let's take the economy, if you permit, for example. Trade globalization means stiffer competition and, therefore greater competitiveness. In order to cope with these challenges, we have had to re-establish our major balances, reduce our deficits, curb inflation, boost our revenue and exports, and promote investment. That was the very essence of our efforts, the fruits of which have been recognized by international financial institutions and our major partners.

It goes without saying that were these measures not taken, the competition which we will have to face would have been too much for us. Today, the coast is clear for a new beginning.

My Fellow Countrymen,

The state will continue relentless to pursue its objective of adapting to the condition of the "new economy". But, you must also contribute your own quota. There are a number of ways of doing this. One of them is b y emulating many of your peers, who taking advantage of the return to economic growth, have set up their own small and medium sized enterprises and have succeeded. Several sectors of our economy have untapped potentials. A good well designed project will almost always find funding. The long to success is sometimes long and difficult, but the enterprising spirit you are famous for should enable most of you attain your goal.

In this respect, I wish to confirm that the "Forums for the Creation of Enterprises", placed under the patronage of the Presidency of the Republic which I mentioned last year, will actually be organized this year. Their aim is to make things easier for young Cameroonians who wish to set up their own businesses and who need information and advice for their projects.

Another way of acceding to the budding "global society" is through the mastery of information technologies. I know how fascinated you are by these technologies and I also know the difficulties you face to train in this area. These difficulties are of various sorts. They stem from insufficient telecommunications infrastructure, the high cost of equipment and inadequate training. This situation has led to a certain lag that might seriously hamper our entry into the digital age. The State is aware of this and well, for its part, strive to bridge this gap.

Special efforts will be made to develop the said infrastructure. As concerns equipment, tax exemptions will be granted during the next budget so as to reduce their cost. Lastly, there are plans with effect from the next school year if possible, to introduce and generalize computer literacy in our schools. In the long run, at least, one high school per province will have to be equipped with a computer room hooked up to the internet.

Without any hesitation, we have supported the initiative to organize the "Information Technology Exhibition". I urge all those who are interested to visit this important event currently taking place in Yaoundé. Simultaneously, and in the same venue, is a symposium on the creation of new businesses will be held as a prelude to the various provincial forums that I have already alluded to.

It goes without saying that the more general and technical knowledge you acquire, the more it will be easier for you to step into this new era. The public authorities are allocating substantial resources to ensure that you receive quality education accessible to all. You must certainly be aware that national education has the highest allocation in the state budget: one hundred and sixty-seven thousand million.

Hundreds of classrooms have been constructed for all levels of education. Free primary education is now a reality. Thousands of teachers have been recruited, absorbed or are undergoing training. Anglophone education now has official syllabuses. Higher education has not been left out of this extensive overwhelming exercise. Without going into detail, I would mention the construction or rehabilitation of numerous university facilities, the review of curricula, continuing efforts for scholarship holders and the signing of various cooperation agreements with foreign universities.

My young fellow Countrymen,

It is quite obvious that you will not take your rightful place in the world unless you abide by the code of conduct generally observed by the international community. It is for this reason that I urge you, once more, to be actively involved in the campaign we have launched to raise public and individual morality. I count on you in particular to put an end to deviant behaviour that tarnishes the image of our country and can discourage our potential partners.

I also appeal this time to your individual sense of responsibility, to help check the alarming spread of the AIDS Pandemic in our country. Besides the threat it poses to every individual – and we know that the youth are particularly vulnerable – AIDS constitute a major handicap for our Nation on account of the toll it could take on our active population.

Do not be surprised if, this time again I cite the example of our young footballers who proved their worth last year during the African Cup of Nations and the Sydney Olympic Games. We will do everything possible to offer those of you who have the will and the talent, the opportunity to follow in their footsteps, by rehabilitating existing sports facilities, providing new ones, expanding physical education and sporting activities and training high-level instructors.

As you can see, my young fellow countrymen, your role is already a decisive one and will be even more so in the years ahead, so that our country can become a more just and prosperous society.

Just look around you, and you will see many places where there are conflicts, civil wars, famine, and displaced persons.

Thank goodness, we do not have such misfortunes.

Therefore, seize the opportunity. Take your destiny in your hands with courage and determination.

HAPPY YOUTH DAY TO YOU ALL!

LONG LIVE THE CAMEROON YOUTH!
LONG LIVE CAMEROON!

7.12: Address by the President of the Republic to the Youths of Cameroon on the Occasion of the 36th National Youth Day, Yaounde, 10 February 2002

Theme: "Youth and Entrepreneurship"

My Young Fellow Countrymen,

By speaking to you each year on the occasion of the Youth Day, it has never escaped my mind that I am addressing an essential component of the nation.

Essential because, as I am fond of saying, you are the future of our country. Essential also because in terms of numbers, you constitute the majority of our people. It is normal therefore, that I call on you, on your sense of responsibility for, irrespective of your place in the society, you are in the main, concerned by the major problems confronting our country, the solutions of which will determine its evolution in the decades ahead.

Political problems first. I mean those that touch on the consolidation of our democratic system. All of you are citizens or will soon be. It is critical therefore that you be able at best to exercise your rights and fulfil your obligations in like manner. To this end, you must be acquainted with the functioning of our institutions, understand their purpose, prepare yourselves where necessary to take part in public life, by never forgetting that your commitment should not serve your personal ambition but the general interest. That is the nobility of politics.

Economic problems too. It is not only to ensure the ongoing revival of our economy but also to adapt it to the new order of liberalization and globalization. This means greater competition and competiveness, and therefore more effort and competence. It also requires more freedom to undertake and better collaboration between the state and the private sector. You will be the future actors in the "new economy". It is necessary to prepare yourselves well for it. In this regard, the success of the Business Development Forums organized throughout the country bears excellent promises.

Lastly are social problems. Our country, like most developing countries has been lagging behind considerably in this domain due to the economic crisis. We are doing everything to fill this gap by drawing from our own resources, or through international cooperation. In the education and health sectors for example, significant job opportunities at various levels will emerge in the years ahead. To grab them, you would have found not only your vocation, but also acquired the necessary skills.

This civic, intellectual and technical training will not only be complete unless it is coupled with the adherence to certain moral values. This is what I referred to last year on this same occasion as the "Code of Conduct" generally accepted in today's world. I am talking about respect of the law, the rules, agreements and one's word in public life and in society. This also holds true at school, in private life and more especially in family circles.

Our youth must have the noble ambition of restoring those values that have declined significantly over the years. Modern society in gestation is a society of freedom. We should be pleased about it. It is undoubtedly one of the major conquests of today's world. Freedom, of course does not rhyme with license, less still with anarchy. It raises the question of its use. In other words, the use of freedom involves conscience and responsibility.

I am sure you have understood me. You will only be free when you fell yourself fully responsible in all acts of your life, public or private. Responsibility is acquired only through an effort of inner reflection, nurtured it is true, by experience. But the sooner you achieve this, the sooner you will be able to play the role you are supposed to assume in our society. By definition, it is a personal effort that each of you must make in all conscience.

My Young Fellow Countrymen,

You are not and will not really be alone in this endeavour. The state that has the duty to protect its citizens, and in particular the youth, and to create conditions for their fulfilment, is doing and will continue to do its own part.

In the area of education, important instruments have been signed to organize schools and the Ministry of National Education. Their purpose is to improve on the quality of our educational system and to nationalize it.

Significant progress has been made in the area of infrastructure and equipment. New institutions have been especially in Technical Training Colleges. Furthermore, conventions were signed with a friendly country for the construction of primary schools in Yaoundé and in the South and west provinces. This infrastructure represents investments worth tens of thousands million francs. Huge credits were also allocated to the purchase of didactic material for public primary schools. On my part, I commissioned multimedia centres in Yaoundé in the Lycée Leclerc and the Bilingual High School. This effort will be gradually pursued and extended to all provincial capitals.

Regarding school aid, assistance was given to over twenty-seven thousand students. I wish to mention also that state subsidies to private institutions have been paid.

With regard to the number of teachers, it is worth mentioning that 1700 part-time primary school teachers have been absorbed in the public service while 170 contract teachers are in the process of being recruited. Furthermore, while awaiting the signing of special rules and regulations governing their corps, the allowances and other bonuses of teaching staff were raised.

Similar progress was made in higher education. With the law organizing higher education, we now have a modern and specific legal framework.

In the area of infrastructure, the public investment budget permitted the construction or rehabilitation of university buildings in Yaoundé I and Yaoundé II as well as in Ngaoundere and Douala. In order to cope with the increasing number of students, we are going to speed up the construction of new academic and social facilities in state universities. They will also be provided with computer equipment as part of the promotion of information technology decided upon by the Government.

Lastly, in view of the upcoming session of the Council of Higher Education and Scientific and Technical Research, we shall embark on the laying down of new orientation of higher education for the year ahead. We are encouraged by the responsible behaviour of our students who appreciate the true value of the sacrifices made for them by the nation, and who are clearly aware of the role in their building of tomorrow's Cameroon. I am happy to use this occasion to exhort them to continue in that direction.

There are also unfortunately, those of our children, very young once, who elude family supervision and don't attend school. These "street children" are more than one can imagine. They are first of all, victims whose rights are sometimes violated and who are subjected to all forms of exploitation. The Ministry of Social Affairs, supported by private initiatives is doing its best to ensure their protection to rehabilitate them and provide them adapted training.

But, it faces an obvious lack of means, unadapted existing structures and the lack of specific legislation. To enable these disadvantaged children to find their rightful place in society rather than increase the ranks of delinquents, which is already the case sometimes, the Government will have to make a significant effort to reverse this trend. But these efforts will be vain if the parents concerned don't assume their responsibilities vis-à-vis their offspring.

Moreover, in some regions of our country, the integration of the girl child in modern society continues to pose specific problems both in terms of education or access to professional life. While respecting traditions, actions are under way and will be pursued to facilitate the school attendance of girls and their training for gainful activities.

I would certainly not end without speaking about sports, which for our country is emblematic. This is why we will continue to support sporting activities more especially by rehabilitating existing facilities and creating new ones like the future sports complex in Yaoundé, in collaboration with a great friendly country.

When one talks of sports in Cameroon, it is obviously football. I wish to use this opportunity to heartily congratulate our national team, the Indomitable Lions on their performances during the African Cup of Nations in Mali. But their success should not make us forget those of our young compatriots who have excelled in other disciplines which also deserve to be developed.

Young Fellow Countrymen,

On several occasions, you have heard me refer to "responsibility". Responsibility in your studies. Responsibility in your social life. Responsibility in your public life. Responsibility in your future working life. That is, I believe, the keyword that should guide your behaviour. It will permit you as a person and as a citizen, to make the right choices. This indeed, is my wish for you and for our country.

HAPPY FEAST DAY!

LONG LIVE THE YOUTH!
LONG LIVE CAMEROON!

7.13: Address by the President of the Republic to the Youths of Cameroon on the Occasion of the 37th National Youth Day Yaounde, 11 February 2003

Theme: "Youth and the Culture of Peace"

Fellow Cameroonians,

The theme chosen for your feast day this year – YOUTH AND THE CULTURE OF PEACE - could not have been more appropriate. To associate the age when everything is possible to peace without which nothing is possible is a wonderful idea.

Wonderful and appropriate, indeed, because at this time when ominous clouds are gathering over the Middle East, when tensions are being revived in the Far East and when many domestic and cross-border conflicts are lingering in Africa, addressing the issue of peace is a burning obligation. It is not a matter of speaking about youthfulness to the youth but ensuring that the youth are on the right path. Peace alone can provide us all with the means to achieve Democracy and Development.

In the Security Council of the United Nations, within the Economic and Monetary Community of Central Africa and in the Economic Community of West African States, Cameroon is acting to preserve peace.

As a matter of principle, everyone is for peace. The international community after drawing lessons from the last two World Wars, adopted at San Francisco in

1945, a set of principles and rules to prevent the reoccurrence of such disasters. Compiled in the Charter of the United Nations, these rules and principles have as a fundamental goal (I quote) "to maintain international peace and security".

In fact, for more than fifty years a third world war has been averted, even if on occasion we have had the feeling of being on the edge of a precipice. However, this has not eliminated the risk of major conflicts because of the behaviour of States that have remained on the fringes of international law. This risk has been compounded very recently by the threat of terrorism which is all the more dangerous as it defies logic and morality.

The balance of power at the international level has unfortunately not been accompanied by the cessation of local conflicts that have continued to undermine the efforts of the Third World and of Africa in particular. Hence, we continue to live in a dangerous world. And we should obviously bear this in mind. And how does this concern the youth, you may ask?

Directly, first of all, because they are almost always on the frontline of war, and most unfortunately, fighting at times from a very tender age as "child combatants". Let us not also forget that the weak are the first victims of conflicts.

Secondly, and may be even worse, because it is the future of all youth that is at stake in this dramatic option between war and peace. Just look around you and see the damage caused by numerous ongoing conflicts, whatever their nature: massacres, destruction,, decline. War is a fatal spiral. A great thinker said: we make war when we want, we end it when we can.

It is better therefore to do everything to prevent it. That is the very essence of Cameroon's policy which, while scrupulously defending its interests, accords priority to solutions that conforms to international law. At the international level, we endorse the decisions of the United Nations in its efforts to resolve conflicts through negotiation and to use force only as a last resort.

Consequently, we resolutely stand on the side of peace, because we think that it alone can guarantee the development of our country and the social progress of our people. Development and progress of which you will, in the decades ahead, be the main actors whether you operate in the political, economic or social domain.

To this end, you must strive to be exemplary citizens. That is to say, by respecting the rules laid down by law and by participating in the running of institutions. In short, by displaying a sense of civic responsibility. But at the individual level too, by adopting responsible behaviour within the family and society, and by putting the general interest before personal ambition.

Your task would be all the easier as you would have acquired skills that expand your general knowledge and strengthen your sense of judgment. The public authorities are working hard to create conditions that are conducive to such progress.

For many years now, the State has been devoting a considerable share of its budget to the various types of education, with remarkable results.

In basic education, the enrolment ratio has risen from 79% to 99% thanks to free primary education instituted two years ago. The enrolment of this new wave of pupils has been ensured by the opening of over 200 government primary schools. Three thousand million CFA francs were allocated for the purchase of teaching aids, which were given in the form of a "minimum package".

Furthermore, access to education was increased through the opening of 61 government general secondary schools and the upgrading of some colleges into high schools, including five bilingual high schools. The multimedia centres established in Lycée Leclerc and in the Yaoundé Bilingual High School helped to bring computer literacy to several thousand students. This programme is being extended to schools in Douala, Bamenda and Garoua.

The partnership between the State and private education, recognized as being in the public interest, is the subject of a bill which will be tabled before the National Assembly. Six thousand million CFA francs have been included in the State budget as subsidies to private education.

An unprecedented effort is being made to build new classrooms with funds from the State budget and from bilateral and international cooperation. About 30,000 secondary school students will be granted scholarships while over 15,000 will receive school needs. Lastly, the process of absorbing part-time teachers will be pursued and will cover some 30,000 primary school teachers.

Aware of the need to give a vocational focus to education, to match training to employment, to prepare young people for the labour market and promote self-employment, we decided to create a Ministry of Technical Education and Vocational Training, which translates the Government's determination to open up new avenues to youth employment.

Various actions have already been undertaken in this direction: partnership between vocational training institutions and enterprises has been strengthened; access to information and communication technologies has helped to open up the external world and in particular the world of economics to the youth; and lastly new industrial and commercial technical colleges and technical high schools were opened to meet the growing demand for vocational training.

Other projects have been planned for the near future such as the rehabilitation of a number of technical schools, the building of some sixty workshops for various disciplines and the introduction of agricultural options into the curricular of four industrial and commercial technical colleges. These initiatives fall within the general framework of the technical education sector strategy being formulated.

At the level of higher education, the Government continued to implement its policy in a spirit of dialogue with lecturers and students. The implementation of the social infrastructure development programme continued in many State universities. Measures have also been taken to improve the working and living conditions of students and faculty, particularly through the payment of stipends and allowances as well as the provision of material support. In the same vein, their security will not be overlooked.

Initiatives taken to modernize and give a vocational focus to higher education resulted in access to information and communication technologies and recruitment, by competitive examination, of 4,000 young people into various higher education and vocational training institutions. Measures are under way to standardize the functioning of private institutions of higher learning. All these efforts will be pursued in the financial years ahead. They will be in keeping with the modernization and performance option in higher education.

Fellow compatriots,

As you can see, the national community is allocating considerable means to enable you to face the future under the best possible conditions. These sacrifices, made wholeheartedly, will best be rewarded by the good use you make of the facilities put at your disposal and by your success.

This, I daresay, is your side of the bargain. Government, for its part, will do all within its power to guarantee you stability and peace, without which our combined efforts will be in vain.

Happy feast day to you all,

Long live the Cameroonian youth,
Long live Cameroon.

7.14: Address by the President of the Republic to the Youths of Cameroon on the Occasion of the 38th National Youth Day, Yaounde, 10 February 2004

Theme: "Youth, Peace, Participation, and National Prosperity"

Dear young compatriots,

In my New Year message a few weeks ago, I told Cameroonians that this year will be a year of choices that will shape their future. Since you, my young compatriots, are those who are called upon to hold the future of our country in your hands, I deem it appropriate to dwell again on this issue and expound a little more on the subject.

After passing through difficult years due to the global economic crisis, the decline in prices of our basic commodities, the consequences of our currency devaluation, the sacrifices prescribed by successive adjustment programmes, we have been benefiting for some time now from more auspicious conditions that have permitted us to return to growth. Besides, the democratic institutions we have put in place have already proved their worth.

Hence, we will be able to build our common future on a sure foundation. Because, I am convinced that the time is right for a Cameroon nation that has great ambitions. And of course, you are called upon to be the key players in these vast construction sites of the nation. For this purpose, it is necessary therefore, that you get yourselves prepared to tackle them.

As a matter of priority, each one of you must strive according to your capability, to acquire knowledge at the highest possible level. Indeed, the new civilisation unfolding before us is driven by science and technology. Human societies that fail to understand this will be irremediably marginalized or left to lag behind. However, this does not imply that other disciplines will be relegated to the background, but that, more than ever before: they will have to integrate this new dimension within the scope of reflection. Besides, I observe that many eminent scientists were equally great thinkers and vice versa.

This need for knowledge explains the sustained efforts we have been making and are continuing to make so that our youth can have the best possible conditions for such knowledge acquisition. You must know that budget allocations of the relevant ministries responsible for education and training in the broadest sense of the word account for approximately 15% of the total State budget, with the Ministry of National Education alone having nearly 11%.

In order to secure the widest possible base for this "pyramid knowledge", we have put the main focus on those levels of education that can ensure equal opportunity. We should not blush at the results obtained this far because I think that almost all of the entire population of school-age can, in principle, attend school.

To this end, 173 new nursery schools, 369 primary

schools, and 87 secondary schools were opened, more than one million textbooks were distributed, the reform of the First School leaving Certificate successfully carried out, and the putting in place of computer learning programmes pursued. Concurrently, more than 1500 classrooms were constructed, hundreds of schools equipped with desks and teaching material including computers, and hygiene and sanitation works carried out, all of them funded from our own internal resources and through assistance from various donor agencies and friendly countries.

I dare not forget that the edifice of National Education rests on a competent, devoted, and respected corps of teachers. In the years ahead, we will have to increase the number of teachers as it still remains low. In the meantime however, we must address the problem of part-time teachers and finalise the special rules and regulations which govern the teaching corps.

With regard to Higher Education, measures have been taken in various areas to improve the academic environment of students, their living conditions and their entry into professional life. In practically all our universities, work has begun to strengthen academic and social infrastructure. Furthermore, the Information Technologies deployment programme in Higher-Education is being pursued and our students already have internet links in all our State universities.

Besides, measures have been taken to provide financial assistance to the tune of about 1,500 million CFA to some 10,000 students in Cameroon and abroad, and to strengthen their students associations. Paid holiday jobs were also made available to them in local councils and some government services.

Lastly, steps have been taken to facilitate the insertion of students in society and the creation of job opportunities. During this academic year, some 3,000 openings would be available to them in the Education and Public Health sectors after completing their training. This policy which aims to make education more professionally-oriented will continue to be monitored very specially.

In this respect, the ministry of technical and vocational education has already taken a number of initiatives. Hundreds of new teachers have been posted to technical education institutions. Here also, classrooms and workshops have been constructed or rehabilitated and equipped with teaching material and computers. This year will see the carrying out of a series of infrastructure projects, the introduction of vocational training programmes to rural areas and the expansion of institutional and in-house training modules as part of our partnership with the private sector.

In order to be able to step into this new civilisation in gestation where competition reigns supreme and the quest for profit is rampant, you will need not just to have "good mind", but to also abide by great moral principles in order not to lose your bearings in a world where at times, rules are vague and it is difficult for the law to prevail.

What I am referring to here is not just a mere sense of good citizenship which, indeed, is normally required of all of us, but, as I have had occasion to say recently, it is to adopt a "sense of community",   in other words, one that respects others and upholds the general interest. I count above all on you who belong to this new generation to steer our social relations towards that direction.

In particular, you must continue the difficult battle we are waging against corruption, that cankerworm that is gnawing deep into our society and is impeding our forward match to progress. In this regard, it is with satisfaction that I note the re-introduction of moral and civic education in our school curriculum.

With regard to AIDS control, you are principally concerned as you are also the most exposed. Government is doing all it can in the area of treatment,   prevention, and information but you must bear in mind that you hold the key to the problem. If, by your behaviour the pandemic stops spreading, the prevalence rate will drop and, because of breakthroughs in research and easier access to the most effective therapies, the pandemic will roll bock. I am requesting you to be fully involved in this fight because it is not just your own future that is at stake, it is also that of the entire nation.

I also wish to draw your attention to a problem which we probably became conscious of too belatedly. I am referring to respect for the environment. Obviously, we have taken measures but quite some damage has already been done to our forests, to our coasts, to the urbanisation in our towns, and to the beauty of our scenery. Of course, you are not to be held responsible for this but inasmuch as the consequences will continue to linger on for decades, I think it is important to alert you on the subject. Respect for the environment begins with little gestures in our daily lives such as refuse disposal in the appropriate bins, and ends up the scale with the control of industrial pollution.

Basically, what is it all about? It is about protecting our natural environment as much as possible so that we can bequeath to future generations a world that is fit to live in without however jeopardising our development. The sustainable development policy we are striving to implement should permit us to win this bet I urge you to be active and convinced stakeholders in this fight.

Well armed morally and intellectually to take your place in tomorrow's Cameroon, you must not also neglect your physical fitness. The Latin saying "a healthy mind in a healthy body" still holds true today. Sport, since this is what we are talking about, remains one of the areas in which we excel and constitutes one of our best "showcases" abroad. As ample proof, we have several of our countrymen heading various pan African sports organisations.

International competitions in various disciplines are they team sports like football for example, or individual, have proved that our country's athletes can reach the greatest heights. Cameroon, I am certain, is a nursery of sports talents that is far from being exhausted. It is up to you to prove it and prepare yourselves to take the relay baton from the Indomitable Lions and from other athletes who will be representing us at the upcoming Olympic Games in Athens, Greece.

I told you at the beginning that as our major balances have been restored we will now embark on increasing our economic performance. Alongside the traditional sectors of our economy that still have the capacity for expansion we intend to launch a number of major agricultural and industrial projects we could not carry out because of the crisis. The global economic recovery we are witnessing in Asia, America and in an expanding Europe offers us bright prospects that we must grasp. Most of these projects will have multiplier effects at various levels: farmers, small-and-medium-sized enterprises, and the tertiary sector. Facilitated by the development of our infrastructure, this dynamic policy which can only be envisaged within the context of a close partnership between the public and private sectors is probably the only one that can bring a lasting solution to the problem of unemployment, and more especially, to that of youth employment which remains preoccupying. Obviously, this scenario can be conceived only within a context of political and social stability. For many of you who will be exercising your right to vote for the first time, this year will give you the real opportunity to demonstrate your civic responsibility and, through the choice you make, the vision you have of our country's future. In all freedom, you are called upon to thoroughly reflect on this and weigh the importance of the stakes as always, I trust the common sense and sound judgment of Cameroonians in general and of the Youth in particular, in making the right decisions.

Lastly, I wish to say a word about your role in strengthening the community we form with other countries of the Central African Region. Gradually, the links we have forged within the region are growing stronger and many issues of common interest are raised each passing day. Some may find that the rapprochement between us is moving at a rather slow pace, but we must reckon with all sorts of hurdles that must be scaled on the road to integration. Indeed, until now this process has remained an affair between States. Undoubtedly, there is a need for our people especially the youth to be closely involved in this endeavour.

Because of its geographic location, our country can, through its youth make a decisive contribution to the ongoing process. I urge the youth therefore to increase contacts with their peers in countries of our sub-region so that, in the decades ahead, our community can become not only a successful entity of economic solidarity, but also one of real fraternity between peoples bound together in all aspects.

My young compatriots,

As you can see, it is not the challenges that are lacking. I know that you can tackle them. To this end you will need a great deal of perseverance and creativity. You can do it, I am sure. On my part, remember that you can count on me.

Happy Feast day.

Long live the Cameroonian youth
Long live Cameroon!"

7.15: Address by the President of the Republic to the Youths of Cameroon on the Occasion of the 39th National Youth Day, Yaounde, 10 February 2005

Theme: "Youth and Mastery of New Challenges"

As you know, I have placed my current seven-year term of office under the banner of *"**Greater Achievements**"* for Cameroon. I believe that I need not dwell on the details of this great plan which I have explained on several occasions lately.

Conversely, it may be necessary for me to tell you why I deemed it appropriate to put forward this action programme which definitely represents a long-term commitment for our country. Hence, you are particularly concerned.

Allow me by the way, to recall that you were the first to be informed about my intentions. Indeed, on this same occasion last year, I told you: *"the time is right for a Cameroon of Greater Achievements"* And I added: *"of course, you are called upon to be the key players in these major national projects"*. Obviously, my opinion has not changed.

It is clear that in the constantly changing world of today, there is a need to anticipate change or else run the risk of being marginalized. That is why we must, I insist, set high and long-term goals.

When, in the coming decades, you will take over, it will be your responsibility to carry on the work being done by those currently in charge. We will therefore need more teachers, engineers, jurists, physicians, technicians, researchers etc. to continue. This accounts for the substantial efforts being made by the State to support and develop at the different levels of education which absorb approximately 15 % of our budgetary resources. This sacrifice being made by the nation requires that you should not only work seriously, but also and above all, succeed for yourself and for your country.

It goes without saying that the government will continue to build primary, secondary .and high schools, and to open Universities. As in the past, the government will facilitate access to school for the most needy and grant scholarships to the most deserving. It will strive to improve the equipment of schools and gradually provide them with the facilities for initiation to new information and communication technologies. Emphasis will, where necessary, be placed on professionalization and socio-professional integration.

For these efforts to fully pay off, we will need many trained teachers who can cope with these new tasks. The reflection which, on my instructions, the government will be conducting should enlighten us on the way forward. I attach much importance to this, for a competent and respected teaching corps is key to a society of equal opportunity and progress.

You must have noticed that the structure of the government has been tailored to its new tasks. You now have **"your"** Ministry of Youth Affairs which will be able to devote itself, on a full-time basis, to problems concerning you. It is your right to expect this ministry, apart from its routine management duties, to open avenues for reflection and action on the future of persons who account for no less than 50% of our population. I need not underscore the strategic dimension of this task.

Actually, it is not one but two ministries that will henceforth take care of you since the activities of the Ministry of Sports and Physical Education mainly target the youth. This Ministry has a double mission not only to explore ways and means of keeping our youth physically fit but also to enable our sports men and women to compete in international events as has often been the case in the past.

Accordingly, we hope that the Indomitable Lions will regain their place among the elite of world football, while in athletics, Cameroon can produce more champions like Françoise Mbango, the gold medallist at the last Olympic Games. Obviously such exploits contribute to boost our country's image abroad, an objective we can equally strive for.

However, I cannot overlook the fact that for most of you – graduates and students alike – a job now or in the future, is the main concern. But government action, whether relating to the professionalization of teaching, to vocational training, to casual jobs in the administration or in conjunction with the private sector or to support from the National Employment Fund, I believe, is certainly useful but cannot, alone, solve the problem of unemployment, particularly among the youth.

Today, the obvious answer lies in boosting growth to achieve economic revival. That precisely is one of the main tasks of the new government. Indeed, as I have often said, one of our Greater Achievements would be the launching of major agricultural, industrial and tourism projects; they would constitute a true mine for jobs and provide an opportunity for more enterprising youths to set up their own undertakings, small or medium.

If these projects were carried out successfully, as I hope, we would witness a blossoming of activities which would mainly benefit you the youth.

My dear young compatriots, As a result of rapid advances in science and technology, events are unfolding faster than ever. You who are not prisoners of ideas of the past, you who are free of complexes and unbiased, you who are open to the innovations of the modern society in gestation, are better placed to grasp the significance of the changes taking place before you.

I count on you to be part of these changes and thereby .contribute to the realization of our Greater Achievements.

Happy Youth Day!

Long Live the Youth of Cameroon!
Long Live Cameroon

7.16: Address by the President of the Republic to the Youths of Cameroon on the Occasion of the 40th National Youth Day, Yaounde, 10 February 2006

Theme: "Youth, Moral Rectitude, and National Development"

"My dear young compatriots,

We are celebrating the 40th National Youth Day this year.

This means that almost two generations have gone by since the first celebration and that people who were twenty years old at the time have now reached the age of maturity.

This confirms, if you will, the fact that youth is a transitional period and not at all a parenthesis in life, in the etymological sense of the word, which "sets the youth apart" in society.

On the contrary, I believe that youth is an important phase in life, during which the broad strokes of one's destiny are shaped. It is a period during which the moral principles one is imbued with guarantee harmonious integration into society, a period during which the sense of responsibility which is nurtured shapes the citizen of tomorrow, a period during which the knowledge acquired facilitates access to a professional career.

In short, it is a period when the woman or the man that you will become moulds her or his future. It is therefore necessary to make good choices. But you may ask me how this is possible, when the hardships of life cause us to prioritize the satisfaction of day-to-day needs, when success in society fails to match merit, when upon graduation from school or university, there are no jobs in sight?

These objections are relevant, but I will attempt an answer. We are not living in an ideal society in Cameroon, which is no worse than any other place. For my part, I have on many occasions deplored our weaknesses and dysfunctions. But this should not discourage us in any way. Rather, we should harness more energy to overcome these ills and improve our performances.

I am counting a lot on you, dear young compatriots, to rally round me in this task. Because I know that you wish, as I do, to build a society in which each person will find their rightful place, according to their effort and their merit. Obviously, we need to make greater efforts to achieve this goal.

I am well aware of the fact that, at the moment, your main concerns are education and employment. For my part, I am making sure that government provides, at the various levels of education, the best possible working conditions, of course, taking into account the means available. The budgetary appropriations for the ministries in charge of education represent close to 20% of the overall State budget, which, I believe, is considerable.

For the youth, especially those in rural areas who do not have access to the formal education system, the National Literacy Programme aims to provide them with basic knowledge indispensable for the exercise of their citizenship. Several hundreds of new literacy centres will be opened in the coming months.

With regard to higher education, the problems are more complex. The exponential growth in the number of students in recent years, while our financial resources have remained stagnant, has highlighted the glaring inadequacy of our university infrastructure. In this regard, some claims concerning working and lodging conditions were not unfounded. The most pressing demands have however already been met. This rehabilitation effort will be pursued.

However, the problem is more general. It entails reviewing what can be referred to as "university governance". The university of today can no longer be what it used to be forty years back. I believe that the guidelines that were defined recently for our rectors are a step in the right direction. The goal of autonomy which was set, though far-fetched, may however be met if the parties concerned show proof of responsibility and a spirit of conciliation. Such is the price for the modernization of our university system.

Your generation is even more concerned with the issue of employment or future employment. Too many of our young people are unable to enter the job market, even when they are holders of recognized certificates. Doubtless therefore to find some of them lose courage, seek refuge in the informal sector or, worse still, drift into delinquency.

The State is however not insensitive to their plight. Education is being professionalized. The Ministry of Employment and Vocational Training is drawing lessons from labour market trends. The National Employment Fund, with government subsidies, regularly organizes training courses and facilitates access to the professional milieu. For its part, the Ministry of Small-and Medium-Size Enterprises, Social Economy and Handicrafts makes contributions in sectors where self-employment can be developed.

The Ministry of Youth Affairs has just launched a rural youth support programme. This initiative made it possible to provide a trade to hundreds of youths in two provinces in 2005. There are plans to extend it to the rest of the country. Lastly, the National Forum on Employment held recently opened up new avenues for brainstorming that make it possible to better grasp the various aspects of the problem in the years ahead.

These efforts, which I have just mentioned, were not in vain. The results obtained are by no means insignificant, but it is obvious that we could not expect them to provide a solution to the overall problem of employment in Cameroon, particularly that of the youth.

As I told you last year, the answer lies in economic revival through the stimulation of growth. That is still true. But let me also say that the prospects seem brighter today than they were a year ago. We have a new economic and financial programme which should, save for the unforeseen, enable us to reach the completion point of the HIPC Initiative. Moreover, some of our major energy, industrial and agricultural projects are on the right track. Apart from their expected ripple effect on other sectors of the economy, it is reasonable to believe that, in the medium term, they will generate significant job opportunities.

I noticed that despite the difficult conditions we are experiencing, some young entrepreneurs of our country are not throwing in the towel and are putting in a lot of efforts into development projects or into launching businesses. I want to cite the "best business plans" of the Junior Chamber International of Cameroon, which were recently rewarded, and which stand out as the best examples of what an enterprising spirit can produce.

Your elders were spurred on by the desire to build a State and forge a Nation. You have an equally lofty task since you have to pursue the modernization of our country so that it can emerge from under-development. To achieve this goal, you will need to define a system of values whereby the sense of duty, the spirit of dialogue, the general interest, and commitment to solidarity will be guarantors of our national unity. This really means, let us not mince words, inventing a new form of patriotism for Cameroon.

Various instruments are currently under study which would provide a framework for such discussion. They concern particularly the Youth Plan Strategy Committee which will soon be set up. More concretely, the National Civic Service for Participation in Development, which I intend to re-launch, will help strengthen the civic education of the youth and increase their chances of social integration.

My dear young compatriots,

The society of freedom and progress that we are trying to build implies common attachment to the democratic institutions which we are putting in place and respect for human beings as regards their most fundamental and most sacred rights. For, it should be borne in mind, human beings are the cornerstone of that society. It is, unquestionably, a difficult and exacting task because of our ethnic, social and cultural diversities which require the cooperation of each and everyone in strengthening social peace and national unity.

It is therefore intolerable for anyone, under cover of an unverified rumour, to take the liberty, as was recently the case, of speculating about the vices and virtues of other persons, thus perhaps unconsciously invading their privacy and damaging their reputation.

Writing and communicating are, of course, a way of expressing our freedom. But freedom knows limits imposed by respect for privacy and law and order. I am therefore appealing to the spirit of responsibility and to the wisdom of communicators and journalists for them to respect the rules of ethics of their noble profession and henceforth take into consideration the principles of propriety inherent in all civilized societies.

My dear Young compatriots,

I know your difficulties. I share your worries but also your hopes. I urge you not to be discouraged, not to give up, not to resign. This is also the advice that I will give to our Indomitable Lions who, after a very brilliant track record in the first round of the African Cup of Nations, bowed out, in the quarter finals, without falling from grace.

I strongly believe that your future is full of promise. I have the conviction that together we can give it substance.

Happy Youth Day!

Long Live the Youth of Cameroon!
Long Live Cameroon!"

7.17: Address by the President of the Republic to the Youths of Cameroon on the Occasion of the 41st National Youth Day, Yaounde, 10 February 2007

Theme: "Youth Citizenship and the Fight against Social Ills"

My dear young compatriots,

I am pleased to address you this evening, as it is the case each year, on the occasion of the Youth Day. I, of course, share your joy in the various events you are organizing. But, above all, I want to underscore that you have pride of place in the nation and to restate my concern for you. For, as I have often said, the future of a country lies with its youth. You are the future of Cameroon. You must be keen in preparing to build the Cameroon of tomorrow.

As you are aware, my ambition in this respect is to modernize our country and, at the same time, to roll back poverty which is still widespread in our society. In conjunction with the World Bank and the IMF, the Government has, to that end, devised strategies which it is gradually putting in place.

However, let us face it, it will be a long haul spanning many years. And here, dear young compatriots, is where you come on stage. For, it is crystal clear that while your elders are laying the foundation of our new society, you will have the daunting, yet lofty, task of pursuing the construction of the edifice.

I can safely say that the circumstances surrounding the launching of this major project seem to be more favourable than they were a few years ago. Indeed, with the attainment of the completion point of the HIPC initiative, we will have relatively substantial financial resources to invest in the social sectors, notably in education and infrastructure, which are areas that concern you specifically.

You should therefore brace yourselves to become the actors of what would be Act Two of the New Deal in our country. That of the emergence of its economy after the irreversible institution of democracy. To that end, we will continue to extend our educational system to ensure access to all our children and to all our youth. In so doing, we will be giving equal opportunity its true meaning.

With respect to basic education, we will build even more schools with our own resources or with the assistance of our bilateral partners. Having recruited, on a contractual basis, thousands of part-time school teachers, we will recruit more teachers to ensure appropriate and quality pedagogic guidance.

Concerning secondary education, we will complete the school map by opening new schools equipped with teaching aids, technical facilities as well as information technology and communication tools.

As concerns higher education that is responsible for the training of future senior officers of the nation, I would like to point out the importance of the changes under way through new university governance.

Various actions are envisaged or ongoing as part of a professionalization and diversification programme. In fulfilment of the commitment I made, an Advanced Teachers' Training College will be created in Maroua. Those of Yaoundé and Bambili, as well as the Douala Advanced Technical Teachers' Training College, will be rehabilitated. The technology branch will be restructured. In this regard, the National Advanced School of Food Technology in Ngaoundere will be rehabilitated. Medical studies will not been left out. The Faculty of Medicine and Biomedical Sciences of the University of Yaoundé I will be revamped. A Faculty of Medicine and Pharmaceutical Sciences and a Faculty of Industrial Engineering have been opened in Douala while a Department of Medicine within the Faculty of Health Sciences has been opened in Buea.

Other programmes seek to improve the quality of teaching through the study of the Bachelor-Masters-Doctorate system and the popularization of ICTs in all higher education institutions. Lastly, various actions are planned in the areas of cooperation, regionalization, research and introduction of control and assessment instruments. In a few years, the image of our higher education should be completely changed. Furthermore, measures will be taken or pursued to improve the plight and working conditions of higher education teachers who, in any case, have always received my attention.

A remarkable effort is also under way to improve the living conditions of students through the building of new infrastructure, lecture halls and halls of residence. I must admit that there are chronic deficiencies in this area. However, we now have the means to start remedying this situation.

Nonetheless, while I can understand that some claims made by our university students are legitimate and justified, I cannot tolerate that they should result in violence against persons or in the destruction of public property. In other words, if our youth, our university students in particular, have any complaints, the appropriate authorities are always willing to entertain them, so long as they are legitimate. I count on the good understanding and judgment of the vast majority of students in our country.

Generally speaking, the importance the State accords to the education of our youth is reflected in budget allocations of the relevant ministries.

Normally, certificates awarded to our primary school, college, high school and university graduates should enable our youth to find jobs. Unfortunately, it must be acknowledged that such is not always the case.

According to available statistics, the unemployment rate among the youth is approximately 13%. However, it is said to be much higher in urban centres like Yaoundé and Douala. These figures clearly reflect the scope and gravity of the problem.

The government addressed the issue by mobilizing the various departments responsible for youth employment. The Ministry of Youth Affairs is preparing a national youth employment action plan based on lessons drawn from the Employment Forum. A National Youth Council will define the areas for their involvement in the development of our country with a view to reducing poverty.

For its part, the Ministry of Employment and Vocational Training has embarked on what it has dubbed a veritable "crusade" against youth unemployment. It seeks, within that context, to participate in the professionalization of education, to foster youth entrepreneurship and to promote partnerships between schools and universities and enterprises. In 2006, thanks to a special appropriation, the National Employment Fund launched several hundred micro-projects primarily targeting the youth.

The Ministry of Small- and Medium-sized Enterprises, Social Economy and Handicrafts intervened in our ten provinces within the framework of the Integrated Informal Sector Stakeholder Support Project. Thousands of young people thus entered the world of work through self-employment initiatives. These initiatives, though useful and commendable, cannot help resolve the general problem of unemployment in Cameroon, and particularly among the youth. The one and only solution to this issue – I will keep repeating – is the revival of growth. Growth which will stimulate the economy, and consequently, create jobs.

All our efforts are currently geared toward this goal. As I said earlier on, the attainment of the completion point should make things easier for us by giving us room to invest in productive sectors. The ongoing settlement of the internal debt should also provide the national economic operators with funds to develop their activities.

I am however counting mostly on our major energy and industrial projects, as well as on the revitalization of our agriculture, to bring about this change in our economy, whose necessity I have often emphasized.

Dear young compatriots,

I told you last year, on this same occasion, that I was counting on you to invent a "new form of patriotism", based on commitment to solidarity and attachment to the general interest. I am renewing this appeal to you, as I believe that we can achieve the "New Deal" which I am proposing only through a radical change in behaviour. I expect you to be pioneers of this change.

This is therefore not the time to give up. I am indeed convinced that the conditions are now met for us to look to the future with confidence. This future will mostly be yours; therefore, I entreat you to help me give it a chance through your work, through your commitment, through your enthusiasm and, once again, through your patriotism.

Happy Youth Day!

Long live the youth of Cameroon!
Long live Cameroon!

7.18: Address by the President of the Republic to the Youths of Cameroon on the Occasion of the 42nd National Youth Day, Yaounde, 10 February 2008

Theme: "Youth, Patriotism, and Participation in Development"

"My dear young compatriots,

In the recent past, I have, on several occasions, urged Cameroonians to take cognizance of the important changes that are affecting the world around us.

In the face of this changing and complex situation, it is very difficult to say what tomorrow's world will be. We must therefore consolidate and develop our achievements, by making the best of the peace and stability that our country enjoys.

This affords me the opportunity to deplore the recent external attacks on Chad, a brotherly and friendly country. In agreement with the international community, I hereby wish to express to our Chadian brothers our solidarity and our strong condemnation of any attempt to destabilize a legitimate government through the use of force.

My dear young compatriots,

In view of the uncertainties of the future, you should gear up to face, under the best conditions, the new global landscape marked by competition.

To my mind, there is only one real solution to the problem I have mentioned: acquiring through education, the highest possible qualification.

It all begins at the primary school level where the basic concepts are taught. Its importance cannot be overemphasized. That is why, a few years back, we decreed free primary education in order to give equal opportunity its true meaning. We will therefore continue to build new schools and recruit new teachers, as we promised. Bear in mind that basic education has the fourth highest budget of the State.

Our effort has even been more pronounced in secondary education which has the highest budget of the State. At this level where students start deciding in what fields to pursue their studies, it is important for them to have access to modern teaching aids, appropriate technical premises and information and communication technologies, which are all indispensable for their initial steps towards professionalization.

Like last year, I will dwell a little more on higher education, firstly, because the students are more immediately concerned by adaptation to the new global dispensation mentioned above and secondly, because a major reform of our University system is under way.

I will first of all recall the problems it must deal with, namely an excessive student population (approximately 140 000), weak intake capacity, high unemployment of graduates, lack of interaction with the socio-professional world and insufficient opportunities for professionalization.

To cope with these problems, there is a need to develop a support programme for the technological and professional component of higher education. This programme will seek to enhance the capacity of the fields of study concerned to support the country's socio-economic development, notably in the areas of health, engineering and education.

To give you an idea of the expected outcomes at the end of the first phase of the programme (2007-2012), it is envisaged that the number of physicians trained will increase from 85 to 450 per year, pharmacists from 0 to 125, dental surgeons from 0 to 125, and health technicians from 140 to 200.

- For the technological field of study, the number of engineers will increase from 500 to 1 000 per year.
- For the teaching field, the flow of graduates will increase from 2 500 to 3260 per year.

Furthermore, last October, we launched the Bachelor's-Master's-Doctorate system, with emphasis on the professionalization of courses. The objective is that each student should have a job that matches his or her qualification. Similarly and in accordance with the commitments made, several new faculties and fields of study were opened at the start of the 2007 academic year in the Universities of Douala, Ngaoundéré, Yaoundé 1, Buea and Dschang.

In 2008, there are plans to create an academic free zone for training high-level technologists as well as two virtual universities, one of which will be sub-regional. Also in the course of this year, the construction of the Maroua Advanced Teacher Training College should start while the medical and biomedical fields of study will be introduced in Dschang and Ngaoundéré Universities.

Under the aforementioned programme, the number of academic and social facilities will grow in the form of new structures in Buea, Douala and Bamenda, and rehabilitation of existing institutions in Yaoundé 1, Dschang and Ngaoundéré Universities. Besides, offices and university halls of residence will be built in different places.

As you can see, we have not remained inactive. The best way of preparing you to enter the civilization of the 21st century and to meet its challenges is unquestionably to train generations of high-level intellectuals and scientists, who believe in the culture of excellence.

That is precisely what we are trying to do.

It goes without saying that the upgrading of our entire system of education will fully bear fruit only in a few years. In the meantime, the Government must, through various actions, supervise our youth, in order to guide them in their choices, prepare them for proper integration into working and social life, protect them from going astray and strengthen their moral and civic education.

To do so, there was a need to develop a veritable national youth policy aimed at encouraging greater involvement of the youth in production channels, promoting indispensable values of a democratic and interdependent society and defending our cultural identity. This is as good as done with the Youth Plan which will be finalized in the course of the year.

The more pressing issue is without doubt involving our youth in the development of our country. To this end, it was deemed necessary to reorganize our associations and put in place a National Youth Council which will be operational in a few months. As the representative of the youth of our 10 provinces, it will supervise the functioning of associations and youth and mass education movements involved in development actions.

I also want to underscore the role of the National Civic Service for Participation in Development which is to foster the moral rearmament and social and vocational integration of youth. The law instituting the civic service, which was passed in 2007, will be implemented in 2008. Lastly, the organization of holiday camps, a strong socialization factor, will be pursued in the coming years.

But the most nagging problem remains that of access by youth to employment and self-employment. The Ministry of Youth Affairs has addressed this problem in collaboration with the Ministry of Employment and Vocational Training and the Ministry of Small- and Medium-Sized Enterprises, Social Economy and Handicrafts. Two important projects were launched last November:

The Rural and Urban Youth Support Programme whose objective is to promote the socioeconomic integration of young people who are not attending school or who have dropped out of school;

The project for the socioeconomic integration of youth through the setting up of micro-enterprises for the manufacture of sport equipment. Both projects immediately aroused keen interest. Several thousands of youth, especially in Yaoundé and Douala, registered to participate in the projects. It is thus estimated that, in the medium term, hundreds of micro-enterprises could be created.

In general, I want to underline the efforts being made to establish a partnership between public services and the private sector, a partnership centred on the promotion of employment and placement opportunities for youth. In this regard, a position of Vice Rector in charge of Relations with enterprises was added to the internal structure of State Universities. In the same spirit, a National Youth Employment Plan is being prepared. It seeks to define a strategy to promote the employment of young people specifically. At the same time, the National Youth Integration Fund should go operational from this year. Its role is to make available to young people credit to develop their micro-enterprises. Finally, the imminent launching of major projects in the energy and mining sectors will contribute to the creation of many jobs.

Dear young compatriots,

As you can see, the Nation is leaving no stone unturned to provide you with the best conditions to prepare yourselves for an uncertain world. It is doing so without hesitating, because you are its children and you embody its future and its hopes.

The Nation also expects you to make good use of the facilities that it is putting at your disposal. It has confidence in you. It has no doubts that, by dint of your conscientiousness and hard work, tomorrow you will be eminent professors, doctors and engineers, servants of the State, whom we need. Whatever the sector in which you will be carrying on your activity, be it agriculture, industry, services, civil service, etc., our country counts on your commitment in the service of its development.

In fact, the great ambitions that we all have for Cameroon would not be achieved without the contribution and youthful enthusiasm of each of you.

At this juncture, I wish to say how much the Cameroonian people appreciate the Indomitable Lions for reaching the finals of the 26th Africa Cup of Nations. Though they have not won it this time, they nevertheless put up a creditable performance, because we must always take into account the "glorious uncertainty of sport". It goes without saying that they still have our esteem and our confidence. Anyway, the qualities that they have displayed unquestionably assure them a choice place among the elite of world football.

Happy Youth Day!

Long live the Cameroonian Youth!
Long live Cameroon! "

7.19: Address by the President of the Republic to the Youths of Cameroon on the Occasion of the 43rd National Youth Day, Yaounde, 10 February 2009

Theme: "Youth and the Values to Acquire and Develop from State Emblems and Symbols"

My Dear Young Compatriots,

Last year at the same time, I urged you to wake up to the fundamental changes taking place in the world, changes which will shape the 21st century, and I encouraged you to prepare yourselves for them, in order to seize the opportunities that were bound to arise. I however added that the complexity of the phenomenon made it difficult to analyze its trend and predict its effects. I did not realize how right I was. In fact, a few months later, the crisis rocked the global financial system and soon after affected the real economy all over the world.

As I pointed out recently, although we are affected only moderately, it is obvious that we will not be completely spared. Should we for this reason scale down our development objectives and particularly those concerning our youth?

I do not believe so. Indeed, I think that we should transcend the crisis and prepare ourselves for the recovery which will inevitably follow. For you, dear young compatriots, there is no other way out, I repeat, than to acquire the best possible qualification in order to compete.

To meet such demand for education, the State pursued and accelerated the reform of our educational system.

Regarding basic education, the resources made available to the ministry have increased significantly. The latter is ranked fourth in terms of budgetary allocations. It can also be noticed that enrolment rates in nursery and primary schools are rising sharply thanks notably to free education. Also, 5 525 new teachers were recruited, raising the number of teachers on contract to nearly 25 000. Some 1 458 new classrooms were built during the 2008 financial year.

Pedagogically, the quality of education has been enhanced through, among others, the development of information and communication technology programmes. These efforts have resulted in an increase in the rate of success in graduation examination to about 80% while the school repeater rate has dropped significantly.

It should also be underscored that private education reform has been completed. It is therefore hoped that more opportunities will henceforth be open to promoters of this sector of education.

Concerning secondary education, the remarkable effort already made was pursued. Let us recall that with CFAF 204 billion, this sector of education has the highest State budget allocation.

One of the priorities in this sector was to expand the school map by setting up 155 new schools in all regions, building many classrooms and transforming 46 existing schools in order to increase the number of technical and bilingual high schools.

To improve the educational service quality, 2 000 new teachers from Advanced Teacher Training Colleges were recruited. Ten thousand other teachers benefited from continuing training programmes and 4 000 were inspected. Multimedia resource centres were installed in six new schools while five others voluntarily experimented with the teaching of national languages and cultures.

At the same time, initiatives were taken to develop partnerships with the private sector. Thus, more than 500 teachers were able to undergo internship in enterprises and nearly 500 private schools received subsidies amounting to about CFAF one billion. It should be noted that, in general, results in official examinations are improving. For this year, plans have been made to implement a vast construction and rehabilitation programme particularly in the Bakassi area. Several thousands of teachers and cadres will also be recruited.

Higher education for its part pursued its great transformation methodically. Let me give you a few examples. At the academic level, as planned, lectures effectively started at the Advanced Teacher Training College of the University of Maroua as well as in the faculties of medicine, pharmacy and bio-medical sciences of the Universities of Dschang and Ngaoundere. Furthermore, studies are under way to open the Higher Institute of the Sahel in the Far North Region.

Also noteworthy is the opening of the technology centre of the National Advanced Polytechnic School of Yaoundé I University to provide students from our various universities with professional training in business creation and management. A free trade zone has been launched in the same school. Similarly, the university authorities pursued the consolidation of the Bachelor's-Master's-Doctorate system.

It is also important to mention the installation of satellite equipment and servers of two virtual universities at Yaoundé 1, one national and the other sub-regional. Prior to that, the activities of the Information Technology University Centre had been launched.

It should also be pointed out that during the year just ended, 16 private higher education institutions were opened, bringing to 73, the number of institutions in this category operating in Cameroon. Very soon, the Fine Arts Institutes will be opened in the Universities of Douala and Dschang and the Institute of Fisheries Sciences in the economic capital.

Regarding infrastructure, it would be tedious to list the numerous facilities that have been completed or under construction in our universities. These include administrative buildings, laboratories, libraries, amphitheatres, lecture halls.

Similarly, important measures have been taken to improve the living conditions of students. Two University halls of residence are nearing completion at Yaoundé 1. Sports complexes are under construction in Douala and Yaoundé II as well as University restaurants in several universities.

Within the framework of university corporate governance, an agreement was recently signed with a local insurance company. Over a thousand lecturers and their families are already covered by this health insurance, which includes evacuation abroad where necessary.

Lastly, several appointments were recently made at the helm of some universities to consolidate the new university governance. This groundwork in the general domain of education which seeks to ensure equal opportunity for our youth and train various levels of cadre for our country must not make us forget that it is also our duty to prepare them for working and social life and to provide them with moral and civic education as well.

To that end, we need a veritable national youth policy that defines programmes to enable youth to acquire patriotic and democratic values and enter the production system. The Youth Plan on which there was extensive consultation in 2008 is in line with these objectives. It is now finalized and should be implemented once approved by the government.

Mention should also be made of the National Action Plan for Youth Employment which outlines actions to be undertaken to promote youth employment specifically. Prepared in collaboration with the Ministry of Employment, it will require financing of about CFA F 165 billion. Its implementation should start during the 2009 fiscal year.

Concerning precisely the socio-economic integration of the youth, several major actions were undertaken last year. The rural and urban youth support programme, which is intended mostly for youth who are not attending or who have dropped out of school, helped to train over a thousand of them in 17 branches of activity, provided a good number with gainful employment and financed several hundreds of micro-businesses and junior enterprises. In the long term, these projects should generate thousands of direct or indirect jobs. Similarly, the youth socio-economic integration through the manufacture of sport equipment project has enabled the creation of 16 cooperatives for the production of this type of equipment.

Strategically, it was deemed necessary to study mechanisms likely to mobilize our youth for the development of our country. In this light, the organic instruments of the National Youth Council have been prepared. They should enable the putting in place of this body during the year.

Similarly, the instruments to set up and organize the National civic service for participation in Development have been finalized. I attach the utmost importance to this structure which seeks the moral rearmament and social integration of youth. I want to hope that it will see the light of day as soon as possible.

To improve youth guidance for its full participation in development activities, collective brainstorming was undertaken on the role that could be played by associations. In this spirit, there are plans to put in place in 2009, the National Youth and Mass Education

Committee which will be responsible for coordinating activities in these two domains.

Extra-curricular training has not been sidelined. The implementation of the programme to construct Multi-purpose Youth Promotion Centres is ongoing. Such centres offer the youth leisure and social integration activities and prepare them to enter working life. The Government's intention is to provide a centre in each administrative unit. There are plans to build thirty of them over the next three years.

My dear young compatriots,

As you can see, the State is making an enormous effort for the youth, be it in the domain of education in the broadest sense or socio- professional integration. The figures are there to testify. It devotes nearly one-fifth of the national budget to youth-oriented activities in all sectors. That is necessary. That is normal.

It would only be normal also that in return for the sacrifices thus made by the Nation, you should be strongly committed to the development of our country. Beyond your personal ambitions, which by the way are legitimate, you should be asking yourselves what you can do for your country. In this respect, the knowledge and skills you have acquired will be significant contributions to the implementation of strategic projects that will secure Cameroon's future.

I want to believe that every one of you will make a point of contributing to the success of this great national endeavour.

Happy Youth Day to all!

Long live Cameroonian Youth!
Long live Cameroon!

Epilogue

The Youth and African Renaissance:
New Challenges for a Changing Continent

The proclamation of 2008 by the African Union as the African Youth Year rekindled interest in the potentials and untapped energy in the continent's young population as agents of development. In effect, Africa's political liberation is largely owed to its youths and youth organizations. The independence generation of African leaders were in their twenties and thirties.

In spite of their active participation in the early liberation struggle, youth governance in Africa has been slow largely because of the absence of an aggregated continental framework policy.

Prior to the creation of the OAU, the Pan African Youth Movement (PYM) was created in Conakry in 1962 to coordinate youth activities in the continent notably by organising youth festivals, leadership training seminars, and voluntary services. With headquarters in Algiers, where it published its *PYM News*, the organization soon became a victim of the Cold War politics in Africa as it congresses were increasingly branded with suspicion as socialist propaganda fora.

The necessity for a Pan-African forum to coordinate youth activities was highlighted in the inaugural meeting of the OAU in Addis Ababa in 1963 which recommended the creation among other things, of an African Youth Organization and an African Scouts Union alongside the ECOSOC and the African Trade Union to coordinate the continent's mass movements.

In spite of this high note, the emergence of a dynamic youth policy within the OAU between 1963 and 1995 was slow. In effect, youth activities were relegated to three organizations with observer status: the Pan African Youth Movement in Algiers, the All African Students Union (AASU) created in Accra in 1972, and the Pan Africa Youth Organization in Kampala. These organizations participated in the World Youth Festivals as well as organized continent-wide youth activities such as the Pan African Youth Festivals in Tunis in 1973 and 1993, the Pan African Youth Festival in Tripoli, and the Pan African Festival of Youth and Sports in Algiers in 1978.

Youth governance within the OAU however entered a new era between 1995 and 2002 when it was transformed to the AU. Three issues helped in the growth of this trend. First in 1995, the African Youth Network (RAJ-AYN) was created within the UNECA to unite National Youth Councils and NGOs. Second, in June 1995, the OAU Council of Ministers adopted two resolutions on youth governance: Resolution CM/Res 1607 (LXII) on the Scouting Movement in Africa, in which it called on Member States to support national scouting structures; and Resolution 1608 (LXIII) on the role of the Olympic Ideal in building a peaceful world in which Member States were invited to send representations of Ministers of Youth and Sports at the 50th Session of the UN General Assembly in New York in November 1995. The year 1995 was also a watershed in global youth governance which prompted the participation of African delegations in world youth events in Cairo, Vienna, Copenhagen, and New York, leading to the adoption of the WPAY.

It is against this backdrop that the OAU organized the First African Conference on Youth and Development in Addis Ababa in March 1996 on the theme "African Youth in the 1990s and Beyond: Peace, Participation, and Development". The OAU's efforts were again complemented by those of the ECA which in turn organized an African Youth Forum in April 1996.

The Yaoundé OAU Summit of July 1996 however gave a clear impetus to the quest for a continental youth policy. In its Resolution CM/Res 1667 (LXIV) on the Follow-Up of the First Pan African Conference on Youth and Development, the African leaders expressed their deep concern for the:

> " current situation and plight of the Youth in Africa with regard to health, education, employment, drug, and crime as well as the role of the Youth in environmental protection, peace, security, democratization process and socio-economic, political and cultural development of the continent".

The Council recommended greater partnership in addressing the continent's youth crisis, the establishment of a Youth Fund, the convening of a Youth Conference on a biannual basis, a Youth Forum during which Creativity Awards will be given to distinguished African Youths, and the convening of the 8th Congress of the Pan African Movement.[21]

Between 1996 and 2002, the issue of creating a continent-wide youth policy and mechanism surfaced in the debates of transforming the OAU to the AU. Within the civil society, the African Program of the Social Science Research Council (SSRC) launched the African Youth and Globalization Programme in collaboration with CODESRIA's Leadership Institute in March 2001. Within five years, the programme had granted fellowships to over 50 African Youth Leaders based on themes like "Youth Violence, Activism, and Citizenship" in 2001-2002; "African Youth, Civil Society, and NGO Sector" in 2003-2004; and "Youth, HIV-AIDS, and Social Transformation" in 2003-2004. In March 2004, the issue of Youth and HIV-AIDS preoccupied African policy-makers that a Pan-African Youth Forum was organized in Dakar on "AIDS: A matter of Education".

Apart from crafting a continental policy, youth governance also played a vital role in the AU's institutional development. Henceforth, the new organization was embedded with new mechanisms like the African Youth Forum with a Youth Festival, an African Young Volunteers Corps, a Young Professionals Programme at the African Union Commission, and a Pan African Youth Parliament. Other mechanisms include the Conference of Students from Africa and the Diaspora as well as an African Inter-Generational Dialogue. As part of this transformation, the AU organized a NEPAD Youth Summit under the theme "Building a Social

---

21. The OAU Resolution specifically recommended partnership in youth governance with UNICEF, ILO, UNFPA, FAO, UNEP, UNDCP, WHO, UNESCO, ICRC, UNECA, Scouts Movement, and other organizations

Movement for NEPAD in Africa" in November-December 2003 in Maputo. Moreover, during its 2003 Congress in Windhoek, Namibia, the Pan African Youth Movement was equally transformed into the Pan African Youth Union (PAYU), which held its 2nd Congress in Brazzaville in July-August 2008.

With regard to youth employment in Africa, African countries organized an International Conference on Youth Employment in Egypt in September 2002. This was followed by another conference in Nairobi in June 2004 on strategies for creating urban youth employment in the continent, while in September 2004, the issue of Youth Employment was also adequately addressed during the AU Extraordinary Summit on Employment and Poverty Reduction in Africa in Ouagadougou leading to an African Common Position arrived which was submitted in the Tripartite Meeting on Youth Employment: "The Way Forward" held in Geneva in October 2004.

But the most important issue at the time was on youth governance, especially youth leadership. In June 2004, a Pan-African Youth Leadership Summit was organized in Dakar. Moreover, during the ADF-V 2004, there was a Declaration on Youth and Governance in Africa, which also decided that the theme for the next Forum be focused on Youth and the Leadership Problem in Africa. This issue of leadership further led to the second Pan African Leadership Summit in Morocco in August 2005.

In 2005, Pan-African initiatives on youth governance included the African Youth and Adolescent Network (AFRIYAN) launched by the UNFPA with branches in 40 countries, the Southern African Sub-Regional Conference on Youth Employment held in Harare in October 2005, and the first African Youth Forum in November 2005 against the backdrop of the 23rd France-Africa Summit of Heads of States and Government held in Bamako Mali in December 2005 under the theme "The Youth Problem in Africa". Among other things, the November 2005 Bamako Declaration addressed the urgent need for a continental youth policy within the frame of the African Union arguing that:

> The Forum of African Youth argues for the bringing about of good governance through existing institutional mechanisms such as the African Union and sub-regional organizations...
> We speak to the conscience of the young people you once were. We say, quite simply, that we do not have an infinite amount of time left to us. We are under an urgent, imperative obligation to move forward. If policymakers fail to attend to young people, the winds of change in the democratic arena will lead young people to attend to policymakers in order to give meaning to their commitments.[22]

---

22. See Bamako Declaration of the First African Youth Forum, France-Africa Summit, November 2005

But the Bamako Declaration also became a basis for an African Inter-generational Dialogue as on 9 December 2005, the Heads of State produced a set of leadership commitments to the African Youth, which among other things stated that:

> Our generation has seen Africa win its independence. Some among us contributed to that process. Today, faced with the numberless obstacles that block the way forward for young States, it is our ambition to build a new Africa that will fully achieve the Millennium Development Goals. This Africa is on the move and, to quicken its step, we need you.[23]

The Bamako Declaration and Commitments gave the necessary impetus to a continental youth policy, especially as its architect, Professor Alpha Omar Konare, the former Malian President and one time Minister of Youth and Sports, had a proper understanding of youth problems in the continent. Since his assumption of office as Chairperson of the AU Commission in 2004, he had capitalized on a forward-looking pan-African youth policy to mark his entry in Addis Ababa.

The year 2006 in many ways marked the turning-point in the development of youth governance in Africa. In January of that year, a meeting of African experts was organized by the AU in Addis Ababa to examine the zero draft of the African Youth Charter and the draft Pan African Youth Federation with a Parliament, Executive, Congress, and Secretariat. However, this proposal was not accepted and the Youth called for the revitalization of the Pan African Youth Union. In May 2006, the first ever Conference of African Ministers for Youth Affairs was organized by the AU Commission in Addis Ababa to examine the African Youth Charter, the strategy for its popularization, the establishment of a Ministerial Bureau of Youth Ministers. The Conference was preceded by the African Youth Forum and an Experts' Meeting, where the Charter was discussed, adopted and submitted to the Ministers who in turn adopted it and submitted it to the Assembly of Heads of State in Banjul in July 2006 where it was adopted as another Banjul Charter.

In November 2006, the ECA organized the fifth African Development Forum (ADF-V) on "Youth and Leadership in the 21st Century" in Addis Ababa resulting in the Consensus Statement on Youth Participation and Empowerment. Other regional youth governance initiatives were organized in the continent such as that on the capacity building workshop on Youth Development in Africa in Addis Ababa in June 2006, and the international conference on the participation of youth as partners in peace and development in post conflict countries in November 2006 in Windhoek.

In January 2007, the ADF-V Consensus Statement was presented to the African Leaders in their Summit in Addis Ababa, which decided to celebrate the African Youth Day in 2007 under the theme "Youth-Adult Partnership for Sustainable Development". This was followed by a number of initiatives on youth governance

---

23. Ibid

organized by the African Union Commission such as the Pan-African Youth Leadership Forum was organized in Accra of June 2007 followed by the African Youth Forum in Ouagadougou of September 2007 on the theme "Young People and Dialogue among Civilizations, Cultures, and Peoples".

Another one-day Pan-African Regional Development Seminar on Youth and Leadership was organized in October 2007 in Limbe, Cameroon, while in December 2007, an ICT Youth Empowerment Workshop was organized by the AU Commission in Addis Ababa.

The year 2008 was of important significance in the development of a continental youth policy as it was declared the Year of the African Youth (YAY) aimed among other things to sensitive the continent on the need to produce:

A new generation of African youth that would restore hope, build Peace, Social Justice and accelerate socioeconomic development in Africa through a reinforced capacity in Science and Technology, governance, entrepreneurship, volunteerism and a full respect of Human Rights, Democracy and natural resources preservation.[24]

In February 2008, the Second Conference of AU Ministers of Youth (COMY 11) took place in Addis Ababa, which among other things adopted 1st November as the African Youth Day to be celebrated annually to sensitize the population on African Youth development issues as well as creating awareness and mobilizing support on the AU Commission's initiatives like the African Youth Charter, the African Youth Anthem, the second edition of the African Youth Initiative and Creativity Award, the Year of the African Youth, the African Youth Network, and the African Youth Associations. The theme for the 2008 African Youth Day was "Positive African Values, Peace, and Solidarity". As part of the celebrations, the second Pan-African Leadership Forum (PAYLF II) was organized in June 2008 in Sharm El Sheik under the theme "New Generation of Leaders: Young People making change in Africa".

At the end of the Year of African Youth, the Executive Committee of the African Union met in January 2009 to examine the impact of the year's activities, and agreed that one day was not enough to generate the necessary policy actions. Consequently, the African Ministers proclaimed a Decade on Youth Decade in Africa covering 2009-2019 based on a 10-year Plan of Action for Youth Development. The priority areas of this decade include education, employment, health, safe spaces for recreation and leisure, participation in policy-making processes at national, regional, and continental levels.[25]

---

24. See African Union Draft Concept Paper on the Year of the African Youth, AU Commission, Addis Ababa 2007

25. See Decision EX CL.DEC (XV) 468 of January 2009

Youth matters have also been integrated in Africa's strategic partnerships as witnessed in the First China-Africa Youth Festival in August 2004, the Euro-African Youth Summit in Lisbon in December 2007, and the Afro-Arab Youth Festival, the second of which took place in Kampala in March 2008. In January 2007, a German-African Youth Forum was organized in Accra under the theme "Two Generations, One Future", resulting in the Accra Declaration which recommended the establishment of a "Youth Conference in advance of every Africa-related Conference of Heads of State to feed youth opinion into the proceedings".

In Cameroon, a one-day seminar on "European Union-African Union Strategy. A Youth Perspective" was organized at the Institute of International Relations of Cameroon, IRIC, on 13 June 2007, bringing together Pan-African youth organizations like the Cameroon Youth and Students Forum for Peace (CAMYOSFOP), the Cameroon Association for the Protection and Education of the Child (CAPEC), the Association Jeunesse Verte du Cameroun (AJVC), and the African Youth Forum for Peace (AYFP).

Finally, youth governance in Africa has also been through the organization regional youth festivals like the Southern African Youth Festival of August 2006 in Harare, and the Horn of Africa Youth Festival. In 1999, the African Renaissance Festival was launched in Kwazulu Natal with the African Renaissance Pioneers Conference.

Select Bibliography

Ahidjo, Ahmadou: *The Political Philosophy of Ahmadou Ahidjo.* Imprimerie Nationale, Yaoundé, 1967

————— : *National Development in Unity and Justice.* Editions Présence Africaine Paris, 1969

————— : *Anthologie des Discours, 1957-1979, 4 Vols.* Les Nouvelles Editions Africaines, Yaoundé, 1980

Biya, Paul: *Communal Liberalism,* MacMillan, London, 1986

—————: *Anthology of Speeches and Interviews of the President of Cameroon, 1982-2002. Vol and 2.* SOPECAM, Yaoundé, December 2002

Ejede Ejede, F: *Importance of the Youth Week Activities in Buea Town Populace.* INJS Memoire, June 1984

Ewumbue-Monono, Churchill: *Men of Courage.* CEREDDA, Buea, 2005

—————: *The Youth and Political Empowerment in Cameroon.* Unpublished

Fokwang, Jude: "Origins of the National Youth Day in Cameroon". *The Post,* February 2009

Genandze, Bobuin John: *Public Discourse, Governance, and Prospects for the Nation State Project in Cameroon.* CODESRIA, Yaoundé, December 2008

Mac-Ikemenjima, Dabesaki: *The Long Road to Banjul and Beyond: Process of the African Youth Charter and the Role of Youth in its Popularization and Ratification.* Addis Ababa, November 2006

Mbile, N.N: *Cameroon Political Story. Memories of an Authentic Eye Witness.* Presbook, Limbe, 1999

Ngoh, Julius Victor: *Constitutional Development in Southern Cameroons. 1946-1960,* Victoria, 1988

Soh, Pius, B: Dr. *John Ngu Foncha. The Cameroonian Statesman. A Biography.* CSSR. Bamenda, 1999

Ubi, Efem N: *African Youth Charter: Prospects for Development of the African Youth.* Dakar, October 2007

Annexes

Annex 1

List of Heads of the Ministerial Departments for Youth Affair: 1959-2009

1. Simon SONGUE (18 June 1959);
2. Gabriel NDIBO MBARSOLA (16 May 1960);
3. William ETEKI MBOUMOUA (20 June 1960);
4. VROUMSIA TCHINAYE (1963);
5. Ibrahim MBOMBO NJOYA (June 1964);
6. Zachée MONGO SO'O (25 May 1965);
7. Michel NJENSI (1st Minister of Youth and Sports 12 June 1970);
8. François Xavier NGOUBEYOU (9 March 1971);
9. Félix TONYE MBOG (3 June 1972)
10. René ZE NGUELE (8 November 1979);
11. André NGONGANG OUANDJI (17 July 1980);
12. Ibrahim MBOMBO NJOYA (18 June 1983);
13. Dr. FOFIE TAPYDJI (21 November 1986);
14. Ibrahim MBOMBO NJOYA (7 September 1990);
15. Theodore LANDO (9 April 1992);
16. Bernard MASSOUA II (27 November 1992);
17. Pr. Joseph Marie BIPOUNWOUM (21 July 1994);
18. Samuel MAKON WEHIONG (19 September 1996);
19. Pr. Joseph OWONA (7 December 1997);
20. Dr. BIDOUNG MKPATT (18 March 2000);
21. Siegfried David ETAME MASSOMA (27 April 2004).

Annex 2

List of themes for Youth Day Celebrations, 1967-2009

1967: Youth and Awareness
1968: Youth and Responsibility
1969: The Youth, Seeds and Actors for National Unity
1970: Responsibility and Participation in the Face of the Requirement of Nation-Building
1971: Youth and Development
1972: Youth Permanent Tool for Dialogue and Multiplying Factor
1973: Human Investment
1974: Youth and the Dignity of Manual Work
1975: Unity among the Youths of the Cameroon National Union
1976: Youth and the Green Revolution
1977: Culture and National Unity
1978: Participation of the Youths in the Green Revolution
1979: Commitment of the Youths to the National Political Life
1980: Commitment of the Youths to the National Political Life
1981: Civic Responsibility and Discipline
1982: Youth and the Mastery of Development
1983: Rigour and Moralization of the Cameroonian Society
1984: Youth and Rigour at Work
1985: Participation, Development, Peace
1986: Youth, Peace and Development
1987: What Youth for the New Deal?
1988: The Youth Facing their Responsibilities
1989: Youth and National Solidarity
1990: Sport, Faith, and Hope
1991: Freedom, Democracy and Discipline
1992: Patriotism, Responsibility and Commitment
1993: Youth, Peace, Unity and Future of Cameroon
1994: Sport, Youth and National Integration
1995: Youth and the Mastery of the Democratic Process
1996: Youth, National Unity, African Unity

1997:   Youth and Solidarity
1998:   Youth, Creativity and Economic Recovery
1999:   Youth and Fight against Poverty
2000:   Youth and Moralization
2001:   Youth and Fight against AIDS
2002:   Youth and Entrepreneurship
2003:   Youth and the Culture of Peace
2004:   Youth, Peace, Participation and National Prosperity
2005:   Youth and Mastery of New Challenges
2006:   Youth, Moral Rectitude and National Development
2007:   Youth Citizenship and Fight against Social Ills
2008:   Youth, Patriotism and Participation in Development
2009:   Youth and the Values to Acquire and Develop from State Emblems and Symbols

Annex 3

Declaration by the Forum of the Youth in Africa and the Diaspora, Bamako, 9 November 2005

If the policymakers fail to attend to young people…

We, the youth of Africa and the Diaspora, meeting in Bamako on 8-9 November 2005 at the first African Youth Forum, as a prelude to the Africa-France Summit of Heads of State and Government, aware of our place and responsibility in Africa's present and future, thank the leaders of Africa and France who have invited us to attend this Summit.

Going beyond concerns, with sentiment and folklore, we declare and we emphasize that Africa is suffering in its young people. Youth is the flagship of any civilized people, and youth in Africa is generally absent from decision-making and debate on the major issues of development. Reference is made to young people only when the question is one of riot, fire-setting, armed conflict, drug abuse, unemployment, paedophilia, AIDS, and so on and so forth.

Our political aspirations and the expression of our desires have long been muzzled. But we have despite all this made our mark as crucial contributors to the process of social and political change on our continent. In saying this we have in mind the African youth of past eras, those young people who fought for the liberation of Africa and also those who continue to fight for its development.

We call on the young adults you once were, you who preside today over the destinies of our countries and who forget all too often that you once dreamed when you were twenty, dreamed like Lumumba, Modibo Kéïta, Nkrumah, Nasser, Bourguiba, Négus Haïlé Sélassié, Amilcar Cabral, Agostinho Neto, Houphouet Boigny, Léoplod Sédar Senghor, Nelson Mandela, Cheick Modibo Diarra and so many others.

As we do today, you fought against injustice. As we do today, you dreamed of a better role for our countries on the global stage. And today we come to you as responsible citizens to claim our place on this rostrum, to speak forthrightly to Africa and to France.

Beyond the august authorities present here we are addressing the entire world - for borders, countries and nationalities fade into insignificance at a time when the new information and communication technologies, against the backdrop of globalization, are helping to build a new global citizenship. Going beyond what has been said above, we the young people of today, are at the centre of many struggles and hold high hopes for our future.

We, the youth of Africa, have a clear vision of the model of citizenship we need in our countries to bring our continent out of its impasse. We are innovating by creating everywhere in Africa hundreds of thousands of associations, NGOs, cooperatives and enterprises. We have invented new avenues for development, taking into account our needs and concerns and those of our populations.

Through rap and slam and every other possible mode of expression, we convey our vision of a more demanding African society, denounce pseudo-models of development and call for more ethical and innovative governance leading our States.

Time is short. And Africa can no longer afford either political excess and error or poor governance. The as-yet untapped creativity and energies of our generation and generations to come constitute an asset that must not be compromised. We do not want more declarations, or yet more action plans, what we want are structured and operational policies adopted by States with a view to effective improvement of the living conditions of African youth.

What we demand is the definition of clear and operational development policies based around youth and focused on the following areas:

With regard to youth training and employment, we wish to see the following:

- the reinforcement of national programmes for the promotion of employment,
- the implementation of appropriate measures to support rural production involving young people,
- an expansion of the resources for vocational training and apprenticeships,
- the ratification and application of international conventions in the field of employment and training for young people,
- inclusion in the various training and employment promotion programmes of the specific needs of young people in difficulty and those of the handicapped and school enrolment of young girls.

With regard to the major environmental and public health issues, we suggest the following:

Heads of State should give a personal commitment to the combat against HIV/AIDS; the application, monitoring and evaluation of the major communications programmes aimed at changes in personal behaviour; the development and reinforcement of local advice and assistance services for the promotion of sexual and reproductive health; free, universal access to antiretroviral drugs for those living with HIV/AIDS and free access to condoms for all; liberalization of licenses for the manufacture of essential drugs against HIV/AIDS.

With regard to socio-political and economic integration, we suggest the following:

- the implementation of legal provisions to ensure the representation of young people in all decision-making bodies at local, national and international levels;
- the reinforcement of mechanisms for the monitoring and assistance of initiatives taken by young people at local, national and sub-regional levels;
- giving young members of the rural population a start in life through access to land;
- specific measures in favour of vulnerable population groups;

- a relaxation of the conditions governing the access by young people to national and international financing;
- the creation and strengthening of National Youth Councils;
- the setting up of Youth Observatories;
- an increase in the numbers of regional and national creativity fairs both Africa-wide and within each country;
- the setting up of a Council of the Youth of Africa and the Diaspora.

With regard to migration, we wish to see the following:

- an increase in the numbers of cultural exchange and co-development programmes to ensure better understanding of migration as a factor for development,
- the promotion of locally-available training programmes and youth projects to reduce the North/South imbalance,
- the raising of the awareness of young people to the laws of host countries and the effective application of international agreements and conventions on immigration,
- the development of infrastructures, opportunities and mechanisms at rural level to attract young Africans back into the countryside,
- the adding of value to national and African human resources to halt the "brain drain" phenomenon,
- the implementation of the NEPAD peer review mechanism to facilitate good governance.

Many processes of change are now under way: sociological, political and economic. As Heads of State, you must note their existence, interpret them and set in train the appropriate reforms.

We, the youth of Africa, are eager to learn and impatient to act. We, the youth of Africa, are the bearers of a culture of peace, friendship and transnationality. We shall fight with your support to put an end to child soldiers, genocide and fratricidal conflict in the day-to-day life in Africa.

And to conclude, the Forum of African Youth argues for the bringing about of good governance through existing institutional mechanisms such as the African Union and sub-regional organizations. Good governance will make it possible, last but not least, to meet the commitments given to the achievement of the Millennium Development Goals, without which our efforts will not lead to the desired results.

We submit the above proposals, solemnly and with respect, to the parents that you are. We speak to the conscience of the young people you once were. We say, quite simply, that we do not have an infinite amount of time left to us. We are under an urgent, imperative obligation to move forward. If policymakers fail to attend to young people, the winds of change in the democratic arena will lead young people to attend to policymakers in order to give meaning to their commitments.

Annex 4

Commitments by the Franco-African Leader to the Youths of Africa and the Diaspora. Bamako, 4 December 2005

Dear Youth of Africa and of the African Diaspora, Dear Marie TAMOIFO NKOM,

You spoke to us this morning in the name of the youth of Africa. We have heard you. We welcome the energy, the commitment, and the ambition of the young on whose behalf you are speaking. They have told us about their hopes, their ambitions, all that makes them indignant, and about their rejection of what is allegedly inevitable. About their determination also to take their fate into their own hands, the fate of a youth as viewed in relation to history and to the memories of the struggles of previous generations. A youth that stands ready to make the 21st century the century of African renaissance.

This ideal is shared by us all, Heads of State and Government of Africa and France. Aware of the difficulties to be overcome by Africa, but trusting in its future, we will assume all the responsibilities entrusted to us by our peoples. We know you will assume yours by asserting yourselves as responsible citizens determined to put your lifeblood in the service of the African continent, a continent you are strengthening with all the vigour and dynamism of young people in their twenties.

The world's outlook on what Africa does and represents is changing, together with Africa's outlook on itself. Africa, you say, is eager to learn, but there is also a great deal for the world to learn from Africa. About what gives African cultures their inherent strength, namely deep-rootedness in a land that harks back to the origins of civilization, the sense of sharing, pragmatism and flexibility born of confrontation with a difficult environment, dialogue with the expanse of the African skies which makes higher abstractions part and parcel of everyday life.

Whether from Africa or the Diaspora, be proud of being Africans. Today, now that the information society is coming into its own, African creativity is spreading worldwide. This is shown by all the writers, film directors, artists, painters, sculptors, sportspersons, architects, and scientists who stand for African excellence everywhere.

For you yourselves, drawing strength from your roots, are opening up to the world and breathing the wind from the open sea. Information technology is giving you an additional means to embody this aspiration to the universal, to give it tangible, concrete expression. Thanks to them, today, you are citizens of the world, fully informed about the time you live in and determined to put your stamp on it.

We are committed to developing information technology and making it available to enable you to make your voice heard loud and clear throughout the continent and to assert your presence, your entrepreneurship and your creative capacities. You consider this a priority. For us, it is a duty. You are all the guardians of part of the soul of your continent, of part of its future, which will not be built without you. It is up to each of you to imagine this future and bring it to life.

And it is for us to put in place the conditions for you to succeed in this, before all else, by meeting vital requirements.

By working for peace, the prerequisite of all fulfilment, in order to end for good the intolerable conflicts in which Africa is tearing itself apart and in which its most vulnerable children are always the first victims. This is a priority for the African Union, who has established the Peace and Security Council, and for its partners, France foremost among them and mobilized alongside the UN in peacekeeping operations and training actions, always at the request of the African themselves.

By waging a daily, difficult and often frustrating battle to provide everyone with basic health care and knowledge. Health, as it is unacceptable for the youth of Africa to live under the constant threat of scourges such as AIDS, tuberculosis, malaria and waterborne diseases while solutions exist. We are redoubling efforts to implement effective systems for prevention, for developing health networks and providing access to drugs, and for research on neglected diseases. Education, which conditions the capacity to bring about a fairer society. Primary education to enable all children, girls and boys alike, to gain essential knowledge. Secondary education and vocational training to enable everyone to gain employment. Higher education, for Africa - where there are so many brilliant scientists - to play its full role in the knowledge economy.

By giving Africa the basic tools it lacks: we have decided to accelerate the realization of major regional and pan-African infrastructure projects to enable regional opening up and the improved movement of persons and goods. Roads, ports, airports, railways, sanitation networks, sustainable energy policies and information highways will help accelerate development and generate sustainable jobs in Africa. The resources exist and are commensurate with the immense wealth created by globalization. International institutions and governments will have to support this comprehensive investment effort. We are not just speaking fine words: our action is concrete and it will be possible to assess its results.

By working to ensure that all young people - young urbans and young rurals alike - find their rightful place in society and receive the right salary for their work, that all in Africa eat their fill, and to enable Africa to develop its agriculture. Africa's agricultural dimension must be reaffirmed, supported and defended in all international forums. This is what we are fighting for at the WTO.

By being the bearers of the continent's future into the far distance, because our choices affect future generations. We are, all of us, runners in a relay. The planet will be what you will make of it. In Africa, more than elsewhere, the danger is imminent: desertification, soil erosion, deforestation, shortages of fresh water, the accelerating disappearance of unique animal and plant species, life itself is under threat. We call upon you, the young people of Africa, to mobilize your energies to ensure that your continent remains the ecological jewel in the world's crown, to ensure that its natural resources are placed at the service of sustainable development, as a source of employment and new skills. That is a collective adventure on the same scale as your ambitions.

You are correct - the development of Africa depends on Africans in the first place. They are best able to define the ambitions and terms for development. By creating the African Union, by organizing around NEPAD, Africa has drawn itself a road map. You, the young people of Africa, you must make this commitment your own. Because it is Africa's role in the world that is at stake. It is your capacity to live in freedom and peace, to take part in the great adventure of our time: the humanization of globalization.

As you know, African leaders are proving highly ingenious in seeking to provide the continent's younger generations with the means to achieve true political fulfilment that should be vigorously supported.

To take control of one's own destiny, however, does not mean being left to fend for oneself. The handicaps bequeathed by history, climate and inappropriate rules of trade make it an obligation for the international community to assist Africa. It is a matter of the future of the continent as well as the future of the world. Such is the conviction first and foremost of France, with which many African countries maintain cultural, economic and personal ties. Serving peace and development, France is engaged at their side in a relationship of equality founded on respect and independence. France calls upon the international community to mobilize to find innovative sources of funding that will assure for the continent the stable revenues it continues to lack. In partnership with Africa, France is working to reform, for greater fairness, the rules of international trade; to assign priority to concrete action in favour of those countries that agree to make major sacrifices to give hope of a better life to their young people. According to a timetable followed by France, between 2002 and 2012 the level of its official development assistance will have more than doubled, reaching 0.7% of its GDP. France calls upon the European Union to do the same between now and 2015 and argues in favour of a special relationship between Africa and Europe.

We have mentioned the capital importance of study grants and visas. France will continue to welcome African students to its soil, seeking to ensure that the skills of young graduates can benefit their countries of origin to the full. France will facilitate travelling by all company managers, creative artists and researchers, who all need to be able to participate without restriction in international exchanges. France will support the strategy of co-development, a powerful tool for giving leverage to the contribution made to their countries of origin by the Africans of France and of the Diaspora.

Dear Youth of Africa and of the African Diaspora and Dear Marie Tamoifo Nkom,

It is no accident if today the voice of Africa is embodied in a young woman. It will also be the responsibility of your generation to commit itself to ensuring that the rights of women, African mothers and daughters, both their political rights and their rights to health and security, are fully recognized and protected everywhere on the continent. Freed of the restrictions by which they are so often burdened, they will able to play an even greater part in the continent's development.

We salute you all, the young women and men who are the bearers of Africa's highest hopes: your message is one of eloquence, justice and lucidity. By responding to our call, you have made a dramatic entry into the public arena to remind us of the universal principles: the demand for democracy, human rights, and the consolidation of the rule of law. Those are the principles that the African Union has decided to make the core of its action. We are aware of the road that remains to be travelled before they can take root everywhere. But increasingly numerous experiments throughout the continent show that they meet an aspiration that is general and that they will continue to spread, quite simply because they express the irrepressible aspiration of human beings to dignity and respect.

Dear Youth of Africa and of the African Diaspora, Dear Marie TAMOIFO NKOM,

Our generation has seen Africa win its independence. Some among us contributed to that process. Today, faced with the numberless obstacles that block the way forward for young States, it is our ambition to build a new Africa that will fully achieve the Millennium Development Goals. This Africa is on the move and, to quicken its step, we need you. We approve your proposal for an "African and Diaspora Youth Council" that will meet as a prelude to our summits. It will be voice of an Africa that has made its own Mahatma GANDHI's exhortation: "Be the change you want to see in the world".

Amadou TOUMANI TOURÉ, President of the Republic of Mali.

Jacques CHIRAC, President of the French Republic.

www.ingramcontent.com/pod-product-compliance
Lightning Source LLC
Chambersburg PA
CBHW021816270326
41932CB00007B/215